QUOTABLE BUSINESS

Other Books by Louis E. Boone

CEO: Who Gets to the Top in America
(with C. Patrick Fleenor and David L. Kurtz)

Contemporary Business
(with David L. Kurtz)

Contemporary Marketing
(with David L. Kurtz)

The Great Writings in Management
(with Donald D. Bowen)

Management
(with David L. Kurtz)

Personal Financial Management
(with David L. Kurtz)

QUOTABLE BUSINESS

Over 2,500 Funny, Irreverent, and Insightful Quotations About Corporate Life

Louis E. Boone

Random House   NEW YORK

Grateful acknowledgment is made to Villard Books, a division of Random House, Inc., for permission to reprint an excerpt from *All I Really Need to Know I Learned in Kindergarten* by Robert Fulghum. Copyright © 1986, 1988 by Robert Fulghum. Reprinted by permission of Villard Books, a division of Random House, Inc.

Library of Congress Cataloging-in-Publication Data
Boone, Louis E.
    Quotable business : over 2,500 funny, irreverent, and insightful quotations about corporate life / Louis E. Boone.
        p.   cm.
    Includes indexes.
    ISBN 0-679-74080-5
    1. Business—Quotations, maxims, etc.   2. Management—Quotations, maxims, etc.   I. Title.
PN6084.B87B66   1992
082—dc20   92-10190
                                                                            CIP

Manufactured in the United States of America

6 5 4 3 2

To David L. Kurtz
longtime coauthor and longer-time friend

Contents

vii

viii   *Contents*

Preface

A government that robs Peter to pay Paul can always count on the support of Paul.

> *George Bernard Shaw (1856–1950)*
> *British playwright and social reformer*

Diplomacy is the art of saying "Nice Doggie" until you can find a rock.

> *Will Rogers (1879–1935)*
> *American author and humorist*

To qualify for inclusion in *Quotable Business*, a quotation must pass at least two of three tests. A great quotation will pass all three tests; an acceptable quotation must earn an affirmative response to Test 3 and at least one of the first two tests:

Test 1: "That's funny!"
Test 2: "That's profound."
Test 3: "That's relevant to organizations, their people, and their dreams."

The Shaw and Rogers quotations meet at least two of these three tests. They are but two of the more than twenty-five hundred quotations that qualified for inclusion in this book.

ORIGINS

During the past two decades, I have been fortunate enough to coauthor not one but two books that sold over a million copies. This accomplishment is even more remarkable because the two books were not about dogs, sex, or weight loss; nor were they techno-thrillers. Far from it. The million-sellers were produced in the stuffy world of college texts.

What went right? After all, text sales are usually measured in thousands, not tens of thousands, not hundred thousands, and almost never in millions. And no author in recent memory has ever produced million-sellers in two different fields.

A quick perusal reveals that these are no ordinary texts. The books are filled with stories, illustrations, quotations, and anecdotes, all illustrating the application of business and management concepts. While the conceptual materials are rigorous enough to satisfy the most demanding scholar, the never-ending series of humorous examples, the wry quotations, and the stories of inept—and brilliant—execution of business strategies rarely fail to pique student interest, aid in exam preparation ("I remember the example of . . ."), and motivate them to continue their academic studies. This heretofore novel style of breathing humanity into the world of business education has been imitated in dozens of succeeding books, ushering in a new era in business education. B-school graduates of the 1960s and 1970s never fail to be astounded by the readability and interest-generating style of the business texts of the 1990s.

During the past two decades, I have delivered thousands of speeches to audiences as varied as high school students, garden clubs, and top-level executives. I have studied speechwriting and delivery extensively. I have made great speeches and terrible speeches, but through years of practice, analysis, and experimentation, I have learned much about speeches.

The basics of an effective speech—preparation, knowing your audience, practice, even understanding what to do with your hands—are fundamental topics of books such as entertainer Steve Allen's *How to Make a Speech* (McGraw-Hill, 1986) and are honed through practice by participants in such organizations as Toastmasters International and International Training in Communication. Among my most important discoveries was the impact of humor—and the danger of telling jokes. Since few speakers are true comedians, resorting to a series of jokes, particularly jokes not relevant to the speech, is asking for trouble. At the same time, humor frequently is the ingredient that separates good speeches from mediocre ones.

> Once you get people laughing, they're listening, and you can tell them almost anything.
> *Herbert Gardner (1872–1955)*
> *American author*

The trick, then, is how to insert humor in the speech without resorting to memorizing a joke from some comedy routine. I've accomplished this through a liberal sprinkling of relevant anecdotes and quotations in both my speeches and my writings. Anecdotes are short narratives about an interesting or amusing incident or event in the life of a real person. Carefully selected and told to drive home a point in a speech or writing, anecdotes can inspire, entertain, teach, and win over a reader or listener to your point of view. Quotations can produce the same results.

> I quote others only the better to express myself.
> *Michel de Montaigne (1533–92)*
> *French essayist*

A few authorities, some with considerable stature as writers and philosophers, argue against the use of quotations. Emerson was in this camp.

> Stay at home in your mind. Don't recite other people's opinions. I hate quotations. Tell me what you know.
>
> *Ralph Waldo Emerson (1803–82)*
> *American essayist and poet*

My own experience and that of most writers and public speakers point to the effectiveness of using the poignant, profound, and often witty words of acknowledged authorities and famous men and women in any persuasive communications.

> The wisdom of the wise and the experience of the ages are perpetuated by quotations.
>
> *Benjamin Disraeli (1804–81)*
> *British novelist and prime minister*

> It is the little writer rather than the great writer who seems never to quote, and the reason is that he is never really doing anything else.
>
> *Havelock Ellis (1859–1939)*
> *English psychologist and writer*

> To be amused by what you read—that is the great spring of happy quotations.
>
> *C. E. Montague (1867–1928)*
> *British journalist*

CREATING A BOOK OF QUOTATIONS FOR THE 1990S

Within arm's length of my desk are three prototypical components of the writer's world: a dictionary, thesaurus, and a copy of Bartlett's *Familiar Quotations*. All are timeworn, but Bartlett's the least of the three. My own experience has been that so many of the entries in this classic compilation first published in 1855 are difficult to convert into the language of today's audience. In some instances, the quotations from another era seem stilted and old-fashioned. In other cases, difficulty arises from the fact that many entries are verses of poetry rather than pithy sentences of prose from history's seminal thinkers. Finally, the broad focus of the compilation reduces the number of relevant topics for me. Quotation after quotation in Bartlett's simply failed the test on p. xi. So I began to compile my own collection, haphazardly at first, and then, over the past five years, in a much more systematic fashion.

My original intent was to limit the book's scope to organizations, the people who create and operate these organizations, and their own dreams. I sought depth by compiling the best and most complete collection of business-related quotations ever assembled.

First we will be best, and then we will be first.
Grant Tinker (1926–　)
American television executive

My conception of the book was couched in the broadest possible meaning of the word *business.* By focusing on organizations, people, and their dreams, I hoped to compile a text that would speak not only to the managers of profit-seeking enterprises but to people involved with any organization. After all, the goal of profitability is the only distinction between a local retailer and a church, a public-school system, a professional basketball team, the local chapter of the American Cancer Society, or a government organization. All of these organizations are guided by goals set and achieved by people and all serve customers, clients, patients, fans, citizens, or parishioners. Each of the twenty-five chapters provides nuggets of humor, wisdom, and instruction for persons in any type of organization.

QUOTATIONS VERSUS EFFECTIVE QUOTATIONS

> He wrapped himself in quotations—as a beggar would en-
> fold himself in the purple of emperors.
>
> *Rudyard Kipling (1865–1936)*
> *English novelist*

Readers will use the book again and again in one or more ways.
Quotations will be chosen for inclusion in a speech, a report, or
other written communication. Inevitably, many will be repeated
in conversation to add emphasis to topics being discussed. To
facilitate their use, information is included about the author of
each quotation to add context to the point being made in the
quotation. The dates of birth and death as well as a brief description of each author provide insights into the era in which the
person being quoted lived in his or her nationality and chief
occupation.

ORGANIZATION OF THE BOOK

The book's organization is aimed at easing the task of choosing
appropriate quotations. The book's five parts are further divided
into twenty-five chapters, and each chapter is subdivided into
sections. Every chapter and every section begins with an anec-
dote. Brief definitions of management concepts are included in
each section. The quotations themselves are arranged to produce
a logical flow of ideas, and controversial issues are typically
treated through the alternative sequencing of quotations favor-
ing different sides of an issue. To further aid the book's user,
detailed name and subject indexes are provided.

THE ATTRIBUTION PROBLEM

> The ideas I stand for are not mine. I borrowed them from
> Socrates. I swiped them from Chesterfield. I stole them
> from Jesus. And I put them in a book. If you don't like
> their rules, whose would you use?
>
> *Dale Carnegie (1888–1955)*
> *American writer and speaker*

The difficulty in matching a quotation with its author results
from the very nature of ideas. Great quotations are repeated by
the members of succeeding generations to produce agreement,
smiles, and marvel. Over time, the original authorship may become lost. For the collector of great quotations, the attribution
process becomes detective work of sorting through historical
writings in an attempt to match the statement with its original
utterer. The difficulty of the task is reflected in the number of
anonymous quotations included in a typical collection.

Modern celebrities, frequently called on for speechmaking
or simply to make comments on events for the news media,
often insert great quotations in their remarks. Frequently, however, the quotation is mistakenly attributed to the celebrity.
For example, the late U.S. senator Robert F. Kennedy was
fond of the following statement by George Bernard Shaw and
often used it (with minor changes in phrasing) in his own
speeches:

> You see things; and you say, "Why?" But I dream things
> that never were and say, "Why not?"

Dozens of news stories subsequently credited Kennedy with the
remark.

Misattribution of quotations is nowhere more common than
in the world of sports, where reporters must daily seek out quips
and newsworthy comments for the evening news. American
sports broadcaster Vin Scully was quoted a few years ago with
the remark "Statistics are used like a drunk uses a lamp post—

for support, not illumination." Scully was actually paraphrasing a much earlier quotation:

> He uses statistics as a drunken man uses lamp posts—for support rather than illumination.
>
> > *Andrew Lang (1844–1912)*
> > *Scottish scholar and author*

On occasion, such modern misattributions find themselves in print. A well-known quotation by one of America's greatest statesmen is one such example:

> I'm a great believer in luck, and I find the harder I work, the more I have of it.
>
> > *Thomas Jefferson (1743–1826)*
> > *3rd president of the United States*

Since such a statement produces agreement from most goal-oriented individuals, it is not surprising that it is frequently repeated. A few years ago, professional golfer Gary Player was enjoying considerable success in tournament after tournament. Every drive seemed to stay in the fairway, chip shots would invariably land near the hole, and long putts kept dropping in. Asked by reporters about this streak of luck, Player responded, "It's funny—the harder you work, the luckier you get." His comments made the next day's sports summaries. Eventually, Player discovered that he was being incorrectly identified as the source of the quotation in compilations such as *The Official MBA Handbook of Great Business Quotations*.

WHO SAID IT FIRST?

Never give a sucker an even break.
Edward F. Albee (1857–1930)
American author and dramatist

Few are likely to associate Albee with this quotation, a statement repeated and made famous by W.C. Fields. Likewise, most sports fans credit American football coach Vince Lombardi with the line "Winning isn't everything, it's the only thing." After all, it certainly sums up the philosophy of Lombardi, a stern disciplinarian and an inspirational leader who hated to lose. But Lombardi borrowed the line, knowingly or unknowingly, from Red Sanders, another college football coach, who first said it around 1948.

These instances are analogous to the association of computers with IBM Corporation. IBM did not build the first commercial computers; Sperry Rand did. But IBM's phenomenal success as the industry giant produced this immediate association of the firm and the computer to most persons.

In instances where the same quotation is attributed to more than one person, I have used the earliest-referenced author as the true source. Nineteenth-century British prime minister Benjamin Disraeli's "Never complain. Never explain" has also been attributed to Henry Ford II, but Ford's 1917 birth occurred thirty-six years after the death of Disraeli.

THEY NEVER SAID IT

In a great many instances, quotations are attributed to well-known persons because they sound like something they *might* have said or written. These occurrences are so frequent that Paul F. Boller and John George were able to compile an entire book of fake quotations, misquotes, and misleading attributions with the title *They Never Said It* (Oxford University Press, 1989).

The unfeeling remark "Let them eat cake," long attributed to Marie-Antoinette (1755–93) in response to the plight of French peasants who had no bread to eat, is one of the best-known examples of a false attribution. The saying was known in Europe long before the birth of the ill-fated queen.

American Expeditionary Forces general John Pershing was mistakenly credited with another famous line. On July 4, 1917, a contingent of AEF representatives was sent to visit the grave of Lafayette in Paris. Pershing sent Colonel Charles E. Stanton to make a speech on behalf of the U.S. forces fighting alongside the French in World War I. Stanton's brief announcement was memorable: "Lafayette, we are here!" Later, the words were attributed to Pershing himself, who always denied authorship, stating that he had never said "anything so splendid."

Perhaps no twentieth-century personages have been the recipient of more fake quotations than Hollywood movie producer Sam Goldwyn and baseball great Yogi Berra. Both men are notorious for ridiculous misuse of words, causing many to consider the term *malapropism* as a surrogate for their names and others to wonder whether English was, indeed, their first language.

Some of Goldwyn's quotes were never uttered by him. Here are some examples:

The next time I send a damn fool for something, I'll go myself. (The remark was actually made by Hungarian director Michael Curtiz.)

You've got to take the bull by the teeth.

When I see the pictures you play in that theater, it makes the hair stand on the edge of my seat. (Another Curtiz remark.)

It rolls off my back like a duck.

Never let that sonofabitch in this office again—unless we need him. (This remark of unknown origin was associated with a succession of Hollywood motion-picture producers, including Harry Cohn of Columbia Pictures and MGM's Louis B. Mayer.)

Yogi Berra, the butt of good-natured ribbing by his St. Louis schoolmate Joe Garagiola and subsequently by teammates and sportswriters, admits to difficulty with the English language. Over the years, the misquotes grew to the point that Yogi felt compelled to deny authorship. Don Lessem, author of *The Worst of Everything*, compiled a list of widely attributed Yogi-isms. Berra claims never to have said any of the following:

1. "If you can't imitate him, don't copy him." ("Stengel said that," says Yogi, "not me.")
2. When asked if he'd buy his kids an encyclopedia: "No, let them walk to school like I did."
3. When told by a mayor's wife, "You look cool": "You don't look so hot yourself."
4. When asked about Mickey Mantle's switch-hitting: "Mantle was naturally amphibious."
5. When asked if he had seen *Dr. Zhivago:* "No, I feel fine."

Acknowledgments

I am indebted to many individuals and institutions for invaluable assistance in gathering much of the material that appears in this book. Special thanks go to the Mobile Public Library and the University of South Alabama Library for their wonderful staffs. I am particularly grateful for my research assistants, Colleen Keleher, Tanya McGowan, Jeffrey Price, Gary Prish, and Phyllis Spruiell, who continued the seemingly unending search for authorships, birth dates, and other important and not-so-important bits of information inspired by the words of Sir Winston Churchill:

> It is no use saying, "We are doing our best." You have got to succeed in doing what is necessary.

I can never fully express my appreciation to my research associate, Jeanne Lowe, for her many contributions. It is her book, too.

Part I

THE ART AND SCIENCE OF MANAGING

Chapter 1

The Beginnings
of a Business

BUSINESS: *all profit-seeking activities and organizations that offer goods and services to customers, patients, or clients.*

The seeds of a successful business are sometimes the product of the inventor's inquisitive mind. George Westinghouse had such a mind. Among his four hundred patents was the automatic air brake. In 1869, the Westinghouse Air Brake Company was organized to manufacture air brakes that functioned more quickly and safely than the hand brakes then in use. Although highly successful with his invention, Westinghouse had trouble finding a sponsor for his idea in its early stages. Recognizing the invention's value to the rapidly growing railroad companies, he wrote to Cornelius Vanderbilt, president of the New York Central Railroad, detailing the advantages of the air brake. Vanderbilt returned his letter with a note scribbled on the bottom: "I have no time to waste on fools."

Westinghouse was not discouraged, and next contacted officials at the Pennsylvania Railroad. They were intrigued, and gave him the funds he needed to continue working on his invention. The tests were successful, and news of the breakthrough finally got back to Vanderbilt. He wrote a letter to Westinghouse, inviting him to meet with him. Westinghouse returned the letter with a note on the bottom: "I have no time to waste on fools. George Westinghouse."

Business is like sex. When it's good, it's very, very good; when it's not so good, it's still good.

> *George Katona (1901–81)*
> *American educator and*
> *economist*

If you can dream it, you can do it.

> *Walt Disney (1901–66)*
> *American film producer*

Business? That's very simple: it's other people's money.

> *Alexandre Dumas (1824–95)*
> *French novelist and*
> *dramatist*

A businessman is a hybrid of a dancer and a calculator.

> *Paul Valéry (1871–1945)*
> *French poet and*
> *philosopher*

Always remember that this whole thing was started by a mouse.

> *Walt Disney (1901–66)*
> *American film producer*

When two men in business always agree, one of them is unnecessary.

> *William Wrigley, Jr. (1861–*
> *1932)*
> *American business*
> *executive*

Genius begins great works, labor alone finishes them.

> *Joseph Joubert (1754–1824)*
> *French essayist and*
> *moralist*

Every man with an idea has at least two or three followers.

> *Brooks Atkinson (1894–*
> *1984)*
> *American drama critic and*
> *essayist*

Every accomplishment starts with the decision to try.

> *Anonymous*

Our greatest glory is not in never failing but in rising up every time we fail.

> *Ralph Waldo Emerson*
> *(1803–82)*
> *American essayist and poet*

A single idea, if it is right, saves us the labor of an infinity of experiences.

> *Jacques Maritain (1882–*
> *1973)*
> *French philosopher*

A new idea is delicate. It can be killed by a sneer or a yawn; it can be stabbed to death by a quip and worried to death by a frown on the right man's brow.

> *Charles Brower (1901–84)*
> *president, Batten, Barton,*
> *Durstine & Osborne*
> *advertising agency*

Management's job is to see the company not as it is . . . but as it can become.

> *John W. Teets (1933–   )*
> *chairman, Greyhound*
> *Corporation*

It may be those who do most, dream most.

> *Stephen Leacock (1869–*
> *1944)*
> *Canadian economist and*
> *humorist*

Great ideas need landing gear as well as wings.

> *C. D. Jackson (1902–64)*
> *American publisher*

The future belongs to those who believe in the beauty of their dreams.

> *Eleanor Roosevelt (1884–*
> *1962)*
> *American humanitarian and*
> *writer*

Dreams never hurt anybody if he keeps working right behind the

dreams to make as much of them become real as he can.

> *Frank W. Woolworth (1852–*
> *1919)*
> *American merchant*

Man's mind, stretched to a new idea, never goes back to its original dimensions.

> *Oliver Wendell Holmes*
> *(1809–94)*
> *American physician and*
> *author*

No one regards what is before his feet; we all gaze at the stars.

> *Quintus Ennius (239–169*
> *B.C.)*
> *Roman poet*

Dreams have as much influence as actions.

> *Stéphane Mallarmé*
> *(1842–98)*
> *French poet*

My favorite thing is to go where I've never been.

> *Diane Arbus (1923–71)*
> *American photographer*

I suppose the one quality in an astronaut more powerful than any other is curiosity. They have to get some place nobody's ever been.

> *John Glenn (1921–   )*
> *American astronaut and*
> *U.S. senator*

GOALS

GOAL: *a desired future state; the end toward which effort is directed.*

Sports fans are likely to associate the bumblebee with former heavyweight boxing champion Muhammad ("Float like a butterfly, sting like a bee") Ali. But in the corporate world, this insect has been chosen to reflect the goals of Dallas-based Mary Kay Cosmetics. The firm's founder, Mary Kay Ash, was so successful in her sales career that she was elected to the Direct Selling Hall of Fame, and has since retired to write a book on women in sales. Then, in 1963, she went back to work and founded Mary Kay Cosmetics, basing her cosmetic lines on a formula developed by a tanner for softening animal hides. Ash began with a team of ten saleswomen and a five-thousand-dollar investment. This modest beginning was combined with such enormous goals that she decided to choose the bumblebee as a symbol for her firm. As any aerodynamics engineer will explain, the bumblebee can't fly—its wings are too small to lift its body. But since none of the engineers bothered to tell the bumblebee, it flies anyway. Like the bumblebee, Mary Kay Cosmetics also soars, as a major component of the American skin-care industry, with beauty consultants in Canada, Australia, Europe, and Asia.

Samuel Gompers, the outspoken and often controversial first president of the American Federation of Labor, was asked what the union stood for—what were its goals. Gompers's point-blank response was one word: *More.*

Hit the ball over the fence and you can take your time going around the bases.

> *John W. Raper (1870–1950)*
> *American author*

First we will be best, and then we will be first.

> *Grant Tinker (1926–   )*
> *American television*
> *executive*

The idea in this game isn't to win popularity polls or to be a good guy to everyone. The name of the game is *win.*

> *Billy Martin (1928–89)*
> *American baseball player*
> *and manager*

Ah, but a man's reach should exceed his grasp—or what's a heaven for?

> *Robert Browning (1812–89)*
> *English poet*

Fixing your objective is like identifying the North Star—you sight your compass on it and then use it as the means of getting back on the track when you tend to stray.

> *Marshall E. Dimock*
> *(1903–)*
> *American author*

Go as far as you can see, and when you get there, you will see farther.

> *Anonymous*

It is a silly game where nobody wins.

> *Thomas Fuller (1608–61)*
> *English chaplain to*
> *Charles II*

Once you say you're going to settle for second, that's what happens to you in life, I find.

> *John F. Kennedy (1917–63)*
> *35th president of the United States*

Businesses planned for service are apt to succeed; businesses planned for profit are apt to fail.

> *Nicholas M. Butler (1862–1947)*
> *American educator and Nobel laureate*

There is something sick about a person whose only interest is money. And the same can be said, I think, for the company whose sole goal is profit.

> *Richard J. Haayen*
> *(1924–)*
> *chairman, Allstate Insurance Company*

If you chase two rabbits, both will escape.

> *Anonymous*

Men, like nails, lose their usefulness when they lose direction and begin to bend.

> *Walter Savage Landor*
> *(1775–1864)*
> *English poet and writer*

Management by objectives works if you know the objectives. Ninety percent of the time you don't.

> *Peter Drucker (1909–)*
> *American business philosopher and author*

Never promise more than you can perform.

> *Publilius Syrus (1st century B.C.)*
> *Latin writer of mimes*

I came, I saw, I conquered. [*Veni, vidi, vici.*]

> *Julius Caesar (100–44 B.C.)*
> *Roman general and emperor*

I find that the three major administrative problems on a campus are sex for the students, athletics for the alumni, and parking for the faculty.

> *Clark Kerr (1911–)*
> *president, University of California*

One cannot collect all the beautiful shells on the beach.

> Anne Morrow Lindbergh
> (1906–   )
> American author

In two words: *im possible*.

> Samuel Goldwyn (1882–
> 1974)
> American motion-picture
> producer

There are two things to aim at in life: first, to get what you want; and after that, to enjoy it. Only the wisest of mankind achieve the second.

> Logan Pearsall Smith
> (1865–1946)
> American essayist

We clamor for equality chiefly in matters in which we ourselves cannot hope to obtain excellence.

> Eric Hoffer (1902–83)
> American longshoreman
> and philosopher

To do all that one is able to do is to be a man; to do all that one would like to do is to be a god.

> Napoleon Bonaparte (1769–
> 1821)
> emperor of France

Let us not be too particular. It is better to have old secondhand diamonds than none at all.

> Mark Twain (1835–1910)
> American author

Every man takes the limits of his own field of vision for the limits of the world.

> Arthur Schopenhauer
> (1788–1860)
> German philosopher

Hell is paved with good Samaritans.

> William M. Holden
> (1918–81)
> American actor

My philosophy of life is that if we make up our mind what we are going to make of our lives, then work hard toward that goal, we never lose— somehow we win out. . . ."

> Ronald Reagan (1911–   )
> 40th president of the United
> States

The horizon is out there somewhere, and you just keep chasing it, looking for it, working for it. . . .

> Robert Dole (1923–   )
> U.S. senator

Without some goal and some efforts to reach it, no man can live.

> Fyodor Dostoevsky
> (1821–81)
> Russian author

Mere money-making has never been my goal.

> John D. Rockefeller (1839–
> 1937)
> American oil magnate and
> philanthropist

The greater thing in this world is not so much where we stand as in what direction we are going.

> *Oliver Wendell Holmes*
> *(1809–94)*
> *American physician and*
> *author*

The goal of all inanimate objects is to resist man and ultimately defeat him.

> *Russell Baker (1925–　)*
> *American author and*
> *humorist*

Institutions mistake good intentions for objectives. They say "health care"; that's an intention, not an objective.

> *Peter Drucker (1909–　)*
> *American business*
> *philosopher and author*

Any man who selects a goal in life which can be fully achieved has already defined his own limitations.

> *Cavett Robert*
> *American writer and*
> *speaker*

Nothing is so commonplace as to wish to be remarkable.

> *Oliver Wendell Holmes*
> *(1809–94)*
> *American physician and*
> *author*

Do not seek to follow in the footsteps of the men of old; seek what they sought.

> *Matsuo Basho (1644–94)*
> *Japanese poet*

The American lives even more for his goals, for the future, than the European. Life for him is always becoming, never being.

> *Albert Einstein (1879–1955)*
> *American physicist*

He who has a why to live for can bear almost any how.

> *Friedrich Nietzsche (1844–*
> *1900)*
> *German philosopher*

I think that I would still rather score a touchdown on a particular day than make love to the prettiest girl in the United States.

> *Paul Hornung (1935–　)*
> *American football player*

THE ENTREPRENEURIAL SPIRIT

ENTREPRENEUR: *one who assumes the financial risk of forming, operating, and managing a business or other undertaking.*

It seems that inventing something —anything—new has been the dream and lifelong work of humankind since the Neanderthals. Each year the number of patents issued by the U.S. Patent and Trademark Office seems to grow. In 1988, for example, 77,924 patents were issued in the United States alone. But obtaining the patent protection does not ensure success. Although about 60 percent of all patent applications are granted, fewer than one inventor in one hundred ever makes any money from an invention. One recent invention is another version of the "better mousetrap." In this new trap, the mouse trips a sensor that causes a chamber to lift up and dump the rodent into a plastic bag, causing suffocation. It is doubtful that this will be chosen as the Invention of the Year, leading some to wonder whether a patent should be issued to protect many inventors from themselves.

An irate banker demanded that Alexander Graham Bell remove "that toy" from his office. That toy was the telephone. A Hollywood producer scrawled a rejection note on a manuscript that became *Gone With the Wind.* Henry Ford's largest original investor sold all his stock in 1906. Roebuck sold out to Sears for $25,000 in 1895. Today, Sears may sell $25,000 of goods in 16 seconds.

> *United Technologies Corporation advertisement*

What would life be if we had no courage to attempt anything?

> *Vincent van Gogh (1853–90)*
> *Dutch painter*

To open a business is very easy; to keep it open is very difficult.

> *Chinese proverb*

Beware of enterprises that require new clothes.

> *Henry David Thoreau (1817–62)*
> *American naturalist and writer*

The creative person wants to be a know-it-all. He wants to know about all kinds of things: ancient history, nineteenth-century mathematics, current manufacturing techniques, flower arranging, and hog futures. Because he never knows when these ideas might come together to form a new idea. It may happen six minutes later or six months or six years down the road. But he has faith that it will happen.

> *Carl Ally (1924–   )*
> *founder, Ally & Gargano advertising agency*

If a man does not keep pace with his companions, perhaps it is because he hears a different drummer. Let him step to the music which he hears, however measured or far away.

> *Henry David Thoreau (1817–62)*
> *American naturalist and writer*

Never follow the crowd.

> *Bernard Baruch (1870–1965)*
> *American financier and statesman*

If I were to join a circle of any kind, it would be a circle that required its members to try something new at least once a month. The new thing could be very inconsequential: steak for breakfast, frog hunting, walking on stilts, memorizing a stanza of poetry. It could be staying up outdoors all night, making a dance and dancing it, speaking to a stranger, chinning yourself, milking a goat, reading the Bible—anything not ordinarily done.

> *Jessamyn West (1907–   )*
> *American author*

If a man goes into business with only the idea of making money, the chances are he won't.

> *Joyce Clyde Hall (1891–1982)*
> *founder, Hallmark Cards, Inc.*

Entrepreneurs are the forgotten heroes of America.

> *Ronald Reagan (1911–   )*
> *40th president of the United States*

Entrepreneurs are risk takers, willing to roll the dice with their money or reputations on the line in support of an idea or enterprise. They willingly assume responsibility for the success or failure of a venture and are answerable for all its facets. The buck not only stops at their desks, it starts there too.

> *Victor Kiam (1926–   )*
> *chairman, Remington Products Inc.*

A journey of a thousand miles must begin with a single step.

> *Chinese proverb*

Mrs. Thicknesse and I agreed that a business of his own was probably the only solution for him because he was obviously unemployable.

> *Peter DeVries (1910–   )*
> *American author*

The great majority of men are bundles of beginnings.

> *Ralph Waldo Emerson (1803–82)*
> *American essayist and poet*

We have lived through the age of big industry and the age of the giant corporation. But I believe that this is the age of the entrepreneur.

> *Ronald Reagan (1911–   )*
> *40th president of the United States*

Some men go through a forest and see no firewood.

> *English proverb*

The American system of ours, call it Americanism, call it capitalism, call it what you like, gives each and every one of us a great opportunity if we only seize it with both hands and make the most of it.

> *Al Capone (1899–1947)*
> *American gangster*

The secret of business is to know something that nobody else knows.

> *Aristotle Onassis*
> *(1906?–75)*
> *Greek shipping magnate*

Going into business for yourself, becoming an entrepreneur, is the modern-day equivalent of pioneering on the old frontier.

> *Paula Nelson (1945–   )*
> *American economist*

What entrepreneurs make and manage, not what economists measure, is the real economy.

> *George Gilder (1939–   )*
> *American author*

The best business you can go into you will find on your father's farm or his workshop. If you have no family or friends to aid you, and no prospect opened to you there, turn your face to the great West, and there build up a home and fortune.

> *attributed to Horace Greeley*
> *(1811–72)*
> *American journalist and*
> *politician*

A wise man will make more opportunities than he finds.

> *Francis Bacon (1561–1626)*
> *English philosopher*

Take the obvious, add a cupful of brains, a generous pinch of imagination, a bucketful of courage and daring, stir well and bring to a boil.

> *Bernard Baruch (1870–*
> *1965)*
> *American financier and*
> *statesman*

They say opportunity's only got one hair on its head and you got to grab it while it's going by.

> *William Demarest (1892–*
> *1983)*
> *American actor in Preston*
> *Sturges's 1944 motion*
> *picture* Hail the
> Conquering Hero

What on earth would a man do with himself if something didn't stand in his way?

> *H. G. Wells (1866–1946)*
> *English novelist and*
> *historian*

It is more admirable to be in business for yourself than to work for somebody else.

> *H. L. Mencken (1880–1956)*
> *American editor*

Being in your own business is working 80 hours a week so that you can avoid working 40 hours a week for someone else.

> *Ramona E. F. Arnett (1943–)*
> *president, Ramona Enterprises, Inc.*

The reason a lot of people do not recognize opportunity is because it usually goes around wearing overalls looking like hard work.

> *Thomas A. Edison (1847– 1931)*
> *American inventor*

The successful people are the ones who can think up stuff for the rest of the world to keep busy at.

> *Don Marquis (1878–1937)*
> *American humorist*

CREATIVITY

CREATIVITY: *human activity that produces original ideas or knowledge, frequently by testing combinations of data to produce unique results.*

People often exhibit their most inspired moments of creativity when they struggle to provide logical explanations for seemingly illogical behavior. Several years ago, officials at Metropolitan Life Insurance Company compiled a listing of explanations for accidents by auto-insurance claimants. Here are a few examples:

An invisible car came out of nowhere, struck my car, and vanished.

I had been driving my car for 40 years when I fell asleep at the wheel and had the accident.

As I reached the intersection, a hedge sprang up obscuring my vision.

I pulled away from the side of the road, glanced at my mother-in-law, and headed over the embankment.

The pedestrian had no idea which direction to go, so I ran over him.

The telephone pole was approaching fast. I attempted to swerve out of its path when it struck my front end.

The guy was all over the road. I had to swerve a number of times before I hit him.

Follow the crowd and you will never be followed by a crowd.

> *Anonymous*

In order to compose, all you need is to remember a tune that nobody else has thought of.

> *Robert Schumann (1810–56)*
> *German composer*

When Alexander the Great visited Diogenes and asked whether he could do anything for the famed teacher, Diogenes replied: "Only stand out of my light." Perhaps some day we shall know how to heighten creativity. Until then, one of the best things we can do for creative men and women is to stand out of their light.

> John W. Gardner (1912–)
> American writer and
> government official

It is better to light a candle than to curse the darkness.

> Chinese proverb
> (motto of the Christopher
> Society)

I had an immense advantage over many others dealing with the problem inasmuch as I had no fixed ideas derived from long-established practice to control and bias my mind, and did not suffer from the general belief that whatever is, is right.

> Sir Henry Bessemer
> (1813–98)
> English engineer (on his
> discovery of a new
> method of producing
> steel)

Creativeness often consists of merely turning up what is already there. Did you know that right and left shoes were thought up only a little more than a century ago?

> Bernice Fitz-Gibbon (1895–
> 1982)
> director of advertising,
> Macy's department stores

The nail that sticks up gets hammered down.

> Japanese proverb

Name the greatest of all inventors. Accident.

> Mark Twain (1835–1910)
> American author

Imagination is more important than knowledge.

> Albert Einstein (1879–1955)
> American physicist

We must either find a way or make one.

> attributed to Hannibal
> (247–183 B.C.)
> Carthaginian general

Every act of creation is first of all an act of destruction.

> Pablo Picasso (1881–1973)
> Spanish painter and
> sculptor

One has to look out for engineers— they begin with sewing machines and end up with the atomic bomb.

> Marcel Pagnol (1895–1974)
> French playwright

To think is to act.

> Ralph Waldo Emerson
> (1803–82)
> American essayist and
> poet

Inside myself is a place where I live all alone and that's where you renew your springs that never dry up.

> *Pearl S. Buck (1892–1973)*
> *American novelist and*
> *humanitarian*

Creative minds always have been known to survive any kind of bad training.

> *Anna Freud (1895–1982)*
> *Austrian psychoanalyst*

Creativity is so delicate a flower that praise tends to make it bloom, while discouragement often nips it in the bud. Any of us will put out more and better ideas if our efforts are appreciated.

> *Alexander F. Osborn (1888–*
> *1966)*
> *American advertising*
> *executive*

Innovators are inevitably controversial.

> *Eva Le Gallienne (1899–*
> *1990)*
> *American actress and*
> *director*

Every child is an artist. The problem is how to remain an artist once he grows up.

> *Pablo Picasso (1881–1973)*
> *Spanish painter and*
> *sculptor*

A person who walks in another's tracks leaves no footprints.

> *Anonymous*

Chapter 2

The Meaning of Management

MANAGEMENT: *process of coordinating human, informational, physical, and financial resources to accomplish organizational goals.*

Basketball Hall of Famer Hank Luisetti's lasting impact on the game came from his unique shooting style. Before Luisetti, any basketball goal attempt over five feet away was almost always a two-handed effort. Hank confessed that he didn't know why he started shooting one-handed, that for him it had just always seemed the natural way to do it. In high school, his coach allowed him to use one hand as long as the shot worked. Following graduation, though, he grew increasingly concerned that his unique style might not endear him to his college coach. When he discussed the matter with Stanford University coach Johnny Bunn and inquired about whether he would be allowed to use his one-handed style in college, Bunn asked him to demonstrate it. After watching Hank sink a series of outside one-handed jump shots in succession, Bunn said, "Stay with it." Luisetti's jumper revolutionized the game of basketball. As other players began to imitate the shot, higher scores resulted and defensive strategies changed. Some time later, Bunn reminisced about Luisetti's request and commented, "That's what makes a great coach—not changing a great player."

The secret of successful managing is to keep the five guys who hate you away from the five guys who haven't made up their minds.

> *American baseball manager*
> *Casey Stengel*
> *(1890–1975)*
> *American baseball manager*

A good manager is best when people barely know that he exists. Not so good when people obey and acclaim him. Worse when they despise him. Fail to honor people, they fail to honor you. But of a good manager, who talks little; when his work is done, his aim fulfilled, they will all say, "We did this ourselves."

> *Lao-tzu (6th century B.C.)*
> *Chinese philosopher and*
> *founder of Taoism*

I'll tell you what makes a great manager: a great manager has a knack for making ballplayers think they are better than they think they are. He forces you to have a good opinion of yourself. He lets you know he believes in you. He makes you get more out of yourself. And once you learn how good you really are, you never settle for playing anything less than your very best.

> *Reggie Jackson (1946–   )*
> *American baseball player*

To depend on the personnel department to do management development is basically a misunderstanding. A marriage counselor can help with a marriage, but it's your job.

> *Peter Drucker (1909–   )*
> *American business*
> *philosopher and author*

I find it rather easy to portray a businessman. Being bland, rather cruel, and incompetent comes naturally to me.

> *John Cleese (1939–   )*
> *British actor*

Few people do business well who do nothing else.

> *Philip Dormer Stanhope*
> *(1694–1773)*
> *Earl of Chesterfield*
> *English statesman and*
> *author*

By working faithfully eight hours a day, you may eventually get to be boss and work twelve hours a day.

> *Robert Frost (1874–1963)*
> *American poet*

If anything goes bad, I did it.
If anything goes semi-good, then we did it.
If anything goes real good, then you did it.
That's all it takes to get people to win football games.

> *Paul "Bear" Bryant*
> *(1913–83)*
> *American college football*
> *coach*

When you're right you take the bows, and when you're wrong you make the apologies.

> *Benjamin Ward (1926–   )*
> *police commissioner,*
> *New York City*

Effective management always means asking the right question.

Robert Heller (1933–   )
American editor

Show me a thoroughly satisfied man and I will show you a failure.

Thomas Edison
(1847–1931)
American inventor

I have learned a long time ago not to flinch when someone says they are going to hit you.

David M. Roderick
(1924–   )
chairman, USX Corporation

Nothing in the world is so powerful as an idea whose time has come.

Victor Hugo (1802–85)
French poet, novelist, and dramatist

I not only use all the brains I have, but all I can borrow.

Woodrow Wilson (1856–
1924)
28th president of the United States

I find business very relaxing. I look forward every day to going to the office.

Laurence Alan Tisch
(1923–   )
American hotel and theater executive and chairman, CBS, Inc.

A "tired businessman" is one whose business is usually not a successful one.

Joseph R. Grundy
(1863–1961)
U.S. senator

What's going to happen to the executive's job in the next ten years? Nothing. It is amazing how many jobs are exactly the same as they were in 1900.

Peter Drucker (1909–   )
American business philosopher and author

If he works for you, you work for him.

Japanese proverb

Remember this, if you work for a man, in Heaven's name, work for him. If he pays you wages which supply you bread and butter, work for him; speak well of him; stand by the institution he represents. If put to a pinch, an ounce of loyalty is worth a pound of cleverness. If you must vilify, condemn, and eternally disparage—resign your position, and when you are on the outside, damn to your heart's content, but as long as you are part of the institution do not condemn it.

Elbert Hubbard (1856–1915)
American writer

He [the business executive] is the only man who is forever apologizing for his occupation.

H. L. Mencken (1880–1956)
American editor

The executive's chief business is to organize, deputize, and supervise.

George Ripley (1802–80)
American literary critic

I don't want any yes-men around me. I want everyone to tell me the truth —even though it costs him his job.

Samuel Goldwyn (1882–
1974)
American motion-picture
producer

You people [his subordinates] are telling me what you think I want to know. I want to know what is actually happening.

Creighton Abrams
(1914–74)
commander of the American
forces in Vietnam

The best executive is the one who has the sense enough to pick good men to do what he wants done, and self-restraint enough to keep from meddling with them while they do it.

Theodore Roosevelt (1858–
1919)
26th president of the United
States

Managers are people who never put off till tomorrow that which they can get someone else to do today.

Anonymous

Good management consists in showing average people how to do the work of superior people.

John D. Rockefeller, Jr.
(1874–1960)
American oil magnate and
philanthropist

Be ever soft and pliable like a reed, not hard and unbending like a cedar.

the Talmud
(a compendium of Jewish
law, lore, and com-
mentary)

No "average" man or woman can be a successful manager. Average is a number. A number has:

No hands to reach out to help;
No heart to beat faster at the success of someone you have helped;
No soul to suffer a bit when one of your people suffers.
An average person lacks the disciplined mind to be tough and the self-confident strength to be gentle.

William A. Marsteller
(1914–   )
American advertising
agency executive

ADVICE (FROM KINDERGARTEN) FOR MANAGERS

Share everything.
Play fair.
Don't hit people.
Put things back where you found them.
Clean up your own mess.
Don't take things that aren't yours.
Say you're sorry when you hurt somebody.
Wash your hands before you eat.
Flush.
Warm cookies and cold milk are good for you.

Live a balanced life—learn some and think some and draw and paint and sing and dance and play and work every day some.
Take a nap every afternoon.
When you go out into the world, watch out for traffic, hold hands, and stick together.
Be aware of wonder.

> *Robert Fulghum (1937–   )*
> *American author*

There are times when even the best manager is like the little boy with the big dog waiting to see where the dog wants to go so he can take him there.

> *Lee Iacocca (1924–   )*
> *chairman, Chrysler*
> *Corporation*

A good manager is a man who isn't worried about his own career but rather the careers of those who work for him. My advice: Don't worry about yourself. Take care of those who work for you and you'll float to greatness on their achievements.

> *H.S.M. Burns (1900–71)*
> *president, Shell Oil*
> *Company*

THE LION TAMER SCHOOL OF MANAGEMENT

Keep them well fed and never let them know that all you've got is a chair and a whip.

> *Anonymous*

Lots of folks confuse bad management with destiny.

> *Frank McKinney (Kin)*
> *Hubbard (1868–1930)*
> *American humorist*

The management practices that can cure a troubled company could have kept it well.

> *John R. Whitney (1920–   )*
> *American educator*

For much of the trouble of the American economy, American management has to take the responsibility.

> *Akio Morita (1921–   )*
> *chairman, Sony*
> *Corporation*

If a manager spends more than 10 percent of his time on "human relations" the group is probably too large.

> *Peter Drucker (1909–   )*
> *American business*
> *philosopher and author*

If your desk isn't cluttered, you probably aren't doing your job.

> *Harold Geneen (1910–   )*
> *chairman, ITT Corporation*

No manager ever won no ballgames.

> *Sparky Anderson (1934–   )*
> *American baseball manager*

TIME MANAGEMENT

TIME MANAGEMENT: *method for scheduling time effectively.*

Henry Ford is well known for his appreciation of the value of time. In fact, many of his management techniques evolved from this concern for saving time. For instance, Ford preferred to visit a manager's office to discuss a problem rather than have the manager summoned to his office. Years later, Ford explained that he developed this method once he realized how much easier it was to leave the other person's office than it was to get him to leave his.

Next week there can't be any crisis. My schedule is already full.

> *Henry A. Kissinger*
> *(1923–)*
> *American scholar and U.S.*
> *secretary of state*

The time is always right to do what is right.

> *Martin Luther King, Jr.*
> *(1929–68)*
> *American clergyman and*
> *civil-rights leader*

Don't duck the most difficult problems. That just insures that the hardest part will be left when you're most tired. Get the big one done—it's downhill from then on.

> *Norman Vincent Peale*
> *(1898–)*
> *American clergyman and*
> *author*

Someday is not a day of the week.

> *Anonymous*

The day will happen whether or not you get up.

> *John Ciardi (1916–86)*
> *American poet and critic*

The sun has not caught me in bed in fifty years.

> *Thomas Jefferson (1743–*
> *1826)*
> *3rd president of the United*
> *States*

It isn't over till it's over.

> *Yogi Berra (1925–)*
> *American baseball player and*
> *manager*

Remember that time is money.

> *Benjamin Franklin*
> *(1706–90)*
> *American statesman and*
> *philosopher*

Those who make the worst use of their time are the first to complain of its brevity.

>Jean de La Bruyère
>(1645–96)
>French writer and
>novelist

Few men of action have been able to make a graceful exit at the appropriate time.

>Malcolm Muggeridge
>(1903–   )
>English editor and writer

Half the agony of living is waiting.

>Alexander Rose (1901–   )
>American writer

After all, tomorrow is another day.

>Scarlett O'Hara, in
>Gone With the Wind,
>by American novelist
>Margaret Mitchell
>(1900–49)

A man too busy to take care of his health is like a mechanic too busy to take care of his tools.

>Spanish proverb

There is time for work. And time for love. That leaves no other time.

>Coco Chanel (1883–1971)
>French fashion designer

Three o'clock is always too late or too early for anything you want to do.

>Jean-Paul Sartre (1905–80)
>French philosopher,
>dramatist, and novelist

It is difficult to live in the present, ridiculous to live in the future, and impossible to live in the past. Nothing is as far away as one minute ago.

>Jim Bishop (1907–87)
>American author and
>journalist

Effective managers live in the present—but concentrate on the future.

>James L. Hayes, (1895–
>1971)
>president and CEO,
>American Management
>Association

The trouble with being punctual is that nobody's there to appreciate it.

>Franklin P. Jones (1887–
>1929)
>American lawyer

Punctuality is one of the cardinal virtues. Always insist on it in your subordinates and dependents.

>Don Marquis (1878–1937)
>American humorist

Play it, Sam. Play "As Time Goes By."

>Ingrid Bergman (1915–82)
>in Michael Curtiz's 1942
>motion picture
>Casablanca

I have noticed that the people who are late are often so much jollier than the people who have to wait for them.

>E. V. Lucas (1868–1938)
>English author

People count up the faults of those who keep them waiting.

French proverb

If you're there before it's over, you're on time.

*James J. (Jimmy) Walker (1881–1946)
the "Midnight Mayor" of New York City*

Time always seems long to the child who is waiting—for Christmas, for next summer, for becoming a grown-up; long also when he surrenders his whole soul to each moment of a happy day.

*Dag Hammarskjöld (1905–61)
Swedish secretary general of the United Nations*

If it weren't for the last minute, nothing would get done.

Anonymous

I was expecting this, but not so soon.

*tombstone inscription
Boot Hill, Arizona*

Time! Time is one thing to a lawmaker, but, to a farmer, there is a time to plant and a time to harvest—and you cannot plant and harvest time.

*Marlon Brando (1924–   )
American actor in Elia Kazan's 1952 motion picture* Viva Zapata!

You may ask me for anything you like except time.

*Napoleon Bonaparte (1769–1821)
emperor of France*

I've been on a calendar, but never on time.

*Marilyn Monroe (1926–62)
American actress*

I definitely am going to take a course on time management . . . just as soon as I can work it into my schedule.

*Louis E. Boone (1941–   )
American educator and business writer*

Don't wait for your ship to come in; swim out to it.

Anonymous

It is better to begin in the evening than not at all.

English proverb

You can't escape the responsibility of tomorrow by evading it today.

*Abraham Lincoln (1809–65)
16th president of the United States*

Everything comes to him who hustles while he waits.

*Thomas Edison (1847–1931)
American inventor*

Most people put off till tomorrow that which they should have done yesterday.

> Ed Howe (1853–1937)
> American journalist

He who hesitates is sometimes saved.

> James Thurber (1894–1961)
> American writer

He who is late may gnaw the bones.

> Yugoslav proverb

The fox that waited for the chickens to fall off their perch died of hunger.

> Greek proverb

Procrastination is opportunity's natural assassin.

> Victor Kiam (1926–)
> chairman, Remington
> Products, Inc.

Tomorrow is often the busiest day of the week.

> Spanish proverb

ADVICE AND WISDOM

ADVICE: *opinions or recommendations offered as a guide to action or conduct.*

WISDOM: *understanding of what is true, right, or lasting.*

Frank Perdue, founder and chairman of Perdue Farms, is one of the giants in the American chicken industry. In less than three decades, Perdue has succeeded in taking an unbranded, unglamorous agricultural commodity and turning it into a familiar, recognizable, and sought-after branded product. Perdue accomplished this by combining top-quality products with superior marketing to build consumer awareness. He has become a recognizable celebrity in the Northeast and Mid-Atlantic states, where most of his chickens are marketed, as a result of his television ads featuring his Chesapeake Bay accent and the ingenious slogan "It takes a tough man to make a tender chicken." Even though Perdue is proud of his firm's product-quality levels, he knows that consumer satisfaction is the ultimate determiner of a firm's success. As he puts it, "Eighty percent of all newly advertised products fail. The manufacturer decides the consumer is a fool. That's why the product fails."

God grant me the serenity to accept the things I cannot change, courage to change the things I can, and the wisdom to know the difference.

> *attributed to Reinhold Niebuhr (1892–1971)*
> *American theologian*
> *(used as a prayer by Alcoholics Anonymous since 1940)*

If I have seen further it is by standing on the shoulders of giants.

> *Sir Isaac Newton (1642–1727)*
> *English mathematician and physicist*

Don't be irreplaceable. If you can't be replaced, you can't be promoted.

> *Anonymous*

A wise man will be master of his mind; a fool will be its slave.

> *Publilius Syrus (1st century B.C.)*
> *Latin writer of mimes*

'Tis the part of a wise man to keep himself today for tomorrow, and not venture all his eggs in one basket.

> *Miguel de Cervantes (1547–1616)*
> *Spanish novelist, dramatist, and poet*

Nothing is given so profusely as advice.

> *François Duc de La Rochefoucauld (1613–80)*
> *French writer and moralist*

Don't try to go too fast. Learn your job. Don't ever talk until you know what you're talking about. . . . If you want to get along, go along.

> *Sam Rayburn (1882–1961)*
> *speaker of the U.S. House of Representatives*

The cobra will bite you whether you call it cobra or Mr. Cobra.

> *Indian proverb*

Tell not all you know, believe not all you hear, do not all you are able.

> *Italian proverb*

No one wants advice—only corroboration.

> *John Steinbeck (1902–68)*
> *American novelist*

Wisdom is the power to put our time and our knowledge to the proper use.

> *Thomas J. Watson (1874–1956)*
> *founder and president, IBM Corporation*

A wise man knows everything; a shrewd one, everybody.

> *Anonymous*

Many receive advice, few profit by it.

> *Publilius Syrus (1st century B.C.)*
> *Latin writer of mimes*

I'm an owl. I hope to watch, to learn and be wise.

> Norman Schwarzkopf
> (1934–   )
> general, U.S. Army

The art of being wise is the art of knowing what to overlook.

> William James (1842–1910)
> American psychologist and
> philosopher

When a man seeks your advice he generally wants your praise.

> Philip Dormer Stanhope
> (1694–1773)
> Earl of Chesterfield
> English statesman and
> author

If you really want to advise me, do it on Saturday afternoon between 1 and 4 o'clock. And you've got 25 seconds to do it, between plays. Not on Monday. I know the right thing to do on Monday.

> Alex Agase (1922–   )
> American football coach

EXPERTS AND CONSULTANTS

EXPERT: *having a high degree of skill or knowledge of a certain subject.*

CONSULTANT: *specialist in any field of activity hired by an individual or organization to give professional or expert advice.*

Following the unsuccessful 1961 Bay of Pigs invasion of Cuba by Cuban exiles supported by the United States, President John F. Kennedy regretfully admitted, "All my life I've known better than to depend on the experts. How could I have been so stupid as to let them go ahead?"

Incomprehensible jargon is the hallmark of a profession.

> Kingman Brewster, Jr.
> (1919–88)
> president, Yale University
> and U.S. ambassador to
> Britain

All too many consultants, when asked "What is two and two?" respond, "What did you have in mind?"

> Norman R. Augustine
> (1935–   )
> American author and
> chairman, Martin
> Marietta Corporation

An expert is one who knows more and more about less and less.

> Nicholas M. Butler (1862–1947)
> American educator and Nobel laureate

Consultant: any ordinary guy more than fifty miles from home.

> Eric Sevareid (1912–)
> American news reporter and commentator

I can mend the break of day, heal a broken heart, and provide temporary relief to nymphomaniacs.

> Larry Lee (1947–)
> American singer

Make three correct guesses consecutively and you will establish a reputation as an expert.

> Laurence J. Peter (1919–90)
> American author

If you were a member of Jesse James's band and people asked you what you were, you wouldn't say, "Well, I'm a desperado." You'd say something like, "I work in banks," or "I've done some railroad work." It took me a long time to just say "I'm a writer." It's really embarrassing.

> Roy Blount, Jr. (1941–)
> American author

Show me a man who cannot bother to do little things and I'll show you a man who cannot be trusted to do big things.

> Lawrence D. Bell (1894–1956)
> American helicopter manufacturer

A consultant is a person who knows nothing about your business to whom you pay more to tell you how to run it than you could earn if you ran it right instead of the way he tells you.

> William A. Marsteller (1914–)
> American advertising agency executive

The man who knows only one subject is almost as tiresome as the man who knows no subject.

> Charles Dickens (1812–70)
> English author

Consultants are people who borrow your watch and tell you what time it is and then walk off with the watch.

> Robert Townsend (1920–)
> American business writer and former president, Avis-Rent-a-Car, Inc.

A professional is a man who can do his best at a time when he doesn't particularly feel like it.

> Alistair Cooke (1908–)
> American journalist and broadcaster

No man can be a pure specialist without being, in a strict sense, an idiot.

> *George Bernard Shaw*
> *(1856–1950)*
> *British playwright and*
> *social reformer*

My greatest strength as a consultant
is to be ignorant and ask a few questions.

> *Peter Drucker (1909–   )*
> *American business*
> *philosopher and author*

Chapter 3

Planning

PLANNING: *process by which people set objectives, assess the future, and develop courses of action to accomplish these objectives.*

Today, as throughout the ages, great works have always been the result of great plans. Michelangelo worked alongside physicians examining cadavers before he mastered the human anatomy and painted the Sistine Chapel in the Vatican. Ernest Hemingway lived in Spain and actually became a bullfighter before writing *The Sun Also Rises*. Robert De Niro put on fifty pounds to play the part of Jake LaMotta in *Raging Bull*.

No plan can prevent a stupid person from doing the wrong thing in the wrong place at the wrong time—but a good plan should keep a concentration from forming.

> *Charles E. Wilson (1890–1961)*
> *chairman, General Motors Corporation and U.S. secretary of defense*

The time to repair the roof is when the sun is shining.

> *John F. Kennedy (1917–63)*
> *35th president of the United States*

Victory often goes to the army that makes the least mistakes, not the most brilliant plans.

> *Charles de Gaulle (1890–1970)*
> *French general and president of the Fifth Republic*

You cannot run a business, or anything else, on a theory.

> *Harold S. Geneen (1910–   )*
> *chairman, ITT Corporation*

The other line moves faster.

> *Anonymous*

Once the toothpaste is out of the tube, it's hard to get it back in.

> *H. R. Haldeman (1926–   )*
> *White House chief of staff*

The opera ain't over till the fat lady sings.

> *Daniel J. Cook (1938–   )*
> *American sports broadcaster and writer (popularized in the late 1970s by coach Dick Motta of the Chicago Bulls professional basketball club)*

To do two things at once is to do neither.

> *Publilius Syrus (1st century B.C.)*
> *Latin writer of mimes*

If you wish to drown, do not torture yourself with shallow water.

> *Bulgarian proverb*

The mouse that hath but one hole is quickly taken.

> *George Herbert (1593–1633)*
> *English clergyman and poet*

Give a lot, expect a lot, and if you don't get it, prune.

> *Thomas J. Peters (1942–   )*
> *American business writer*

For want of a nail the shoe is lost, for want of a shoe the horse is lost, for want of a horse the rider is lost.

> *George Herbert (1593–1633)*
> *English clergyman and poet*

Hindsight is an exact science.

> *Guy Bellamy (1935–   )*
> *American journalist and writer*

Luck sometimes visits a fool, but never sits down with him.

> *German proverb*

Expect the worst and your surprises will always be pleasant ones.

> *Louis E. Boone (1941–   )*
> *American educator and business writer*

Eighty percent of all surprises are unpleasant. This includes bills, estimates, unkept promises, firings, birthday parties, and pregnancies.

> *William A. Marsteller*
> *(1914–)*
> *American advertising*
> *agency executive*

If a man dies and leaves his estate in an uncertain condition, the lawyers become his heirs.

> *Ed Howe (1853–1937)*
> *American journalist*

You only live once, but if you work it right, once is enough.

> *Joe E. Lewis (1902–71)*
> *American comedian*

To a gardener there is nothing more exasperating than a hose that just isn't long enough.

> *Cecil Roberts (1892–1976)*
> *English author*

The time not to become a father is 18 years before a World War.

> *E. B. White (1899–1985)*
> *American journalist and*
> *writer*

On to Little Big Horn for glory. We've caught them napping.

> *George A. Custer (1839–76)*
> *general, U.S. Cavalry*

If the alternative to dying is sitting in the sun for another summer, then that's not a bad alternative. I'm not rushing into battle. I'm not General Custer.

> *Norman Schwarzkopf*
> *(1934–)*
> *general, U.S. Army*

Plans are nothing; planning is everything.

> *Dwight D. Eisenhower*
> *(1890–1969)*
> *34th president of the United*
> *States*

Why is it that there is never enough time to do a job right, but always time enough to do it over?

> *Anonymous*

It is a bad plan that admits of no modification.

> *Publilius Syrus (1st century*
> *B.C.)*
> *Latin writer of mimes*

There is nothing so useless as doing efficiently that which should not be done at all.

> *Peter Drucker (1909–)*
> *American business*
> *philosopher and author*

Life is what happens while you are making other plans.

> *John Lennon (1940–80)*
> *English songwriter and*
> *singer*

If I had known I was going to live so long, I would have taken better care of myself.

>   *Anonymous*

It wasn't raining when Noah built the ark.

>   *Howard Ruff (1930–   )*
>   *American business*
>   *consultant*

You shouldn't take a fence down until you know the reason it was put up.

>   *G. K. Chesterton (1874–*
>   *1936)*
>   *English journalist and*
>   *author*

One should never wear one's best trousers to go out and battle for freedom and truth.

>   *Henrik Ibsen (1828–1906)*
>   *Norwegian poet and*
>   *dramatist*

Pick battles big enough to matter, small enough to win.

>   *Jonathan Kozol (1936–   )*
>   *American author*

Don't worry because a rival imitates you. As long as he follows in your tracks he cannot overtake you.

>   *Anonymous*

In investing money, the amount of interest you want should depend on whether you want to eat well or to sleep well.

>   *J. Kenfield Morley (1838–*
>   *1923)*
>   *British journalist*

Some people are making such thorough preparation for rainy days that they aren't enjoying today's sunshine.

>   *William Feather (1889–*
>   *1981)*
>   *American author and*
>   *publisher*

STRATEGY AND TACTICS

STRATEGIC PLANNING: *process of determining the major objectives of an organization and then choosing the course of action and allocating the resources necessary to achieve those objectives.*

TACTICAL PLANNING: *process of translating broad strategic goals and plans into specific goals and plans that are relevant to a single component of the organization,* *such as a functional area like human resources or marketing.*

Bureaucratic errors by government officials are prized stories for the news media. A good example is the UPI news wire report of a Beckley, West Virginia, bridge project: "State highway officials say they did not realize until too late they were building a two-lane bridge for a three-lane section of the West Virginia turnpike. Explained Joan Gallagher, a spokeswoman for the West Virginia Department of Highways, 'It sounds a lot worse than it is.' "

All men can see these tactics whereby I conquer, but what none can see is the strategy out of which victory is evolved.

> *Sun-tzu (4th century B.C.)*
> *Chinese military strategist*

Anyone who says businessmen deal in facts, not fiction, has never read old five-year projections.

> *Malcolm Forbes (1919–90)*
> *American publisher*

All strategy depends on competition.

> *Bruce D. Henderson*
> *(1915–   )*
> *American educator and*
> *founder of the Boston*
> *Consulting Group*

I have found that being honest is the best technique I can use. Right up front, tell people what you're trying to accomplish and what you're willing to sacrifice to accomplish it.

> *Lee Iacocca (1924–   )*
> *chairman, Chrysler*
> *Corporation*

You can't have a better tomorrow if you are thinking about yesterday all the time.

> *Charles F. Kettering (1876–*
> *1958)*
> *American electrical*
> *engineer and inventor*

Business is like war in one respect. If its grand strategy is correct, any number of tactical errors can be made and yet the enterprise proves successful.

> *General Robert E. Wood*
> *(1879–1969)*
> *president, Sears, Roebuck &*
> *Company*

The will to win is important, but the will to prepare is vital.

> *Joe Paterno (1926–   )*
> *American college football*
> *coach*

Plan your work and work your plan.

> *Anonymous*

I have studied the enemy all my life. I have read the memoirs of his generals and his leaders. I have even read his philosophers and listened to his music. I have studied in detail the account of every damned one of his battles. I know exactly how he will react under any given set of circumstances. And he hasn't the slightest idea of what I'm going to do. So when the time comes, I'm going to whip the hell out of him.

> *George S. Patton (1885–*
> *1945)*
> *general, U.S. Army*

In baiting a mouse trap with cheese, always leave room for the mouse.

> *Saki (1870–1916)*
> *Scottish writer*

Make no little plans; they have no magic to stir men's blood and probably themselves will not be realized. Make big plans; aim high in hope and work, remembering that a noble, logical diagram once recorded will not die.

Daniel H. Burnham (1846–1912)
American architect

If you are planning for one year, grow rice.
If you are planning for 20 years, grow trees.
If you are planning for centuries, grow men.

Chinese proverb

Chapter 4

Leadership

LEADERSHIP: *process of influencing people to direct their efforts toward the attainment of specific objectives.*

Although none of the teams Buddy Ryan coached ever made it to the Super Bowl, he certainly has been around the league. Prior to his recent position as head coach of the Philadelphia Eagles, Ryan was head coach for the New York Jets, Minnesota Vikings, and the Chicago Bears. A plaque on his desk reads, IF YOU AIN'T THE LEAD DOG, THE SCENERY NEVER CHANGES.

Eagles don't flock—you have to find them one at a time.

> *H. Ross Perot (1930–)*
> *American computer*
> *industry executive*
> *and philanthropist*

We take eagles and teach them to fly in formation.

> *D. Wayne Calloway (1935–)*
> *chairman, PepsiCo Inc.*

Rank times IQ is a constant.

> *Anonymous*

Habit is habit and not to be flung out of the windows by any man but coaxed downstairs a step at a time.

> *Mark Twain (1835–1910)*
> *American author*

Leadership appears to be the art of getting others to want to do something you are convinced should be done.

> *Vance Packard (1914–   )*
> *American journalist*

Those who apply themselves too closely to little things often become incapable of great things.

> *François Duc de La*
> *Rochefoucauld (1613–80)*
> *French writer and moralist*

A throne is only a bench covered with velvet.

> *Napoleon Bonaparte (1769–*
> *1821)*
> *emperor of France*

Behind an able man are always other able men.

> *Chinese proverb*

People are unreasonable, illogical and self-centered.
    Love them anyway.
If you do good, people will accuse you of selfish ulterior motives.
    Do good anyway.
If you are successful, you will win false friends and true enemies.
    Succeed anyway.
Honesty and frankness make you vulnerable.
    Be honest and frank anyway.
The good you do today will be forgotten tomorrow.
    Do good anyway.
The biggest people with the biggest ideas can be shot down by the smallest people with the smallest minds.
    Think big anyway.
People favor underdogs but always follow top dogs.

Fight for some underdogs anyway.
What you spend years building may be destroyed overnight.
    Build anyway.
Give the world the best you've got and you'll get kicked in the teeth.
    Give the world the best you've got anyway.

> *Dr. Robert Schuller*
> *(1926–   )*
> *American evangelist*

The man who goes alone can start today; but he who travels with another must wait till that other is ready.

> *Henry David Thoreau*
> *(1817–62)*
> *American naturalist and*
> *poet*

If two people ride the same horse, one must ride behind.

> *Anonymous*

Soldiers win battles and generals get the credit.

> *Napoleon Bonaparte (1769–*
> *1821)*
> *emperor of France*

I know even better than I used to that a lot of U.S. businesses are sinking in a sea of bureaucracy. What many need is a new skipper.

> *Carl Icahn (1936–   )*
> *CEO, Trans World Airlines*

Boss spelled backwards is double SOB.

> *Anonymous*

There's only two kinds of coaches: them that's been fired and them that's about to be fired.

> *Bum Phillips (1923–   )*
> *American professional*
> *football coach, formerly*
> *with the Houston Oilers*
> *and the New Orleans*
> *Saints*

It's the price of leadership to do the thing you believe has to be done at the time it must be done.

> *Lyndon B. Johnson*
> *(1908–73)*
> *36th president of the United*
> *States*

Managers are people who do things right, and leaders are people who do the right thing.

> *Warren G. Bennis (1925–   )*
> *and Burt Nanus (1936–   )*
> *American educators and*
> *business writers*

Leadership, like swimming, cannot be learned by reading about it.

> *Henry Mintzberg*
> *(1939–   )*
> *Canadian educator and*
> *management writer*

Two things are bad for the heart—running uphill and running down people.

> *Bernard Gimbel (1885–*
> *1966)*
> *American merchant*

The buck stops with the guy who signs the checks.

> *Rupert Murdoch (1931–   )*
> *Australian newspaper*
> *publisher*

The buck stops here.

> *Harry S Truman (1884–*
> *1972)*
> *33rd president of the United*
> *States*

If the blind lead the blind, both shall fall into the ditch.

> *Matthew 15:14*

In the country of the blind, the one-eyed man is King.

> *Desiderius Erasmus*
> *(1466?–1536)*
> *Dutch scholar and*
> *theologian*

We can't all be heroes because somebody has to sit on the curb and clap as they go by.

> *Will Rogers (1879–1935)*
> *American actor and*
> *humorist*

The office of President is such a bastardized thing, half royalty and half democracy, that nobody knows whether to genuflect or spit.

> *Jimmy Breslin (1930–   )*
> *American journalist and*
> *author*

The man with the best job in the country is the vice president. All he has to do is get up every morning and say, "How's the President?"

> Will Rogers (1879–1935)
> American actor and
> humorist

It is time for a new generation of leadership, to cope with new problems and new opportunities. For there is a new world to be won.

> John F. Kennedy (1917–63)
> 35th president of the United
> States

True leadership must be for the benefit of the followers, not the enrichment of the leaders.

> Robert Townsend (1920–   )
> American business writer
> and former president,
> Avis-Rent-a-Car, Inc.

Authority without wisdom is like a heavy ax without an edge, fitter to bruise than polish.

> Anne Bradstreet (1612–72)
> American author

When you look at it, anybody who runs a company, it's kind of like their own fiefdom. The other management people serve at the pleasure of the chairman, and the board of directors pretty well serves at the pleasure of the chairman. So who really watches the chairman?

> T. Boone Pickens (1928–   )
> president, Mesa Petroleum
> Company

If I were very lucky, I wouldn't have this job.

> Ronald Reagan (1911–   )
> 40th president of the United
> States

Now the guy that got to the top, the CEO, would obviously be stupid to have a number two guy who was a lot smarter than he is. So, by definition, since he's a survivor and he got to the top and he isn't that brilliant, his number two guy is going to always be a little worse than he is. So, as time goes on, it's anti-Darwinism, the survival of the unfittest.

> Carl Icahn (1936–   )
> CEO, Trans World Airlines

In America, anyone can become president. That's one of the risks you take.

> Adlai E. Stevenson
> (1900–65)
> American lawyer and
> diplomat

The best thing about this group of candidates is that only one of them can win.

> Will Rogers (1879–1935)
> American actor and
> humorist

The true worth of man is not to be found in man himself, but in the colors and texture that come alive in others.

> Albert Schweitzer (1875–
> 1965)
> French philosopher,
> physician, and music
> scholar

Leadership is an action, not a word.

> *Richard P. Cooley*
> *(1923–)*
> *American banker*

All mankind is divided into three classes: those who are immovable; those who are movable; and those who move.

> *Benjamin Franklin*
> *(1706–90)*
> *American statesman and*
> *philosopher*

THE GREAT MAN THEORY

GREAT MAN THEORY: *belief that only an exceptional person possessing unique personality traits, physical features, and/or work habits is capable of assuming a prominent leadership role.*

The early leadership researchers sought out traits of great leaders in the hope that they would serve as predictors of persons likely to succeed in leadership roles. They saw commonalities such as height in Abraham Lincoln and Charles de Gaulle, but a lack of the charac-teristic in others like Napoleon Bonaparte. They felt that the exceptional person would possess characteristics like those revealed in Benito Mussolini's command to his followers: "If I advance, follow me! If I retreat, kill me! If I die, avenge me!" Gradually, though, the researchers were forced to admit that different leadership styles were appropriate in different circumstances and that the key leadership issue lay in determining the circumstances under which a particular style might prove successful.

The question "Who ought to be boss?" is like asking "Who ought to be tenor in the quartet?" Obviously, the man who can sing tenor.

> *Henry Ford (1863–1947)*
> *American automobile*
> *manufacturer*

Great men are rarely isolated mountain peaks, they are the summits of ranges.

> *Thomas Wentworth Storrow*
> *Higginson (1823–1911)*
> *American clergyman, U.S.*
> *Army officer, and writer*

Great men are meteors designed to burn so that earth may be lighted.

> *Napoleon Bonaparte (1769–*
> *1821)*
> *emperor of France*

If an individual wants to be a leader and isn't controversial, that means he never stood for anything.

> *Richard M. Nixon (1913–)*
> *37th president of the United*
> *States*

Knowing is not enough; we must apply. Willing is not enough; we must do.

> Johann Wolfgang von Goethe
> (1749–1832)
> German poet and dramatist

Lead, follow, or get out of the way!

> Anonymous

You cannot manage men into battle. You manage things; you lead people.

> Grace Murray Hopper
> (1906–92)
> admiral, U.S. Navy

It is the weak man who urges compromise—never the strong man.

> Elbert Hubbard (1856–1915)
> American writer

Shallow men believe in luck... strong believe in cause and effect.

> Ralph Waldo Emerson
> (1803–82)
> American essayist and poet

Who rides a tiger cannot dismount.

> Chinese proverb

No one's a leader if there are no followers.

> Malcolm Forbes (1919–90)
> American publisher

There are no bad soldiers under a good general.

> Anonymous

When I was a boy, I was told that anybody could become President; I'm beginning to believe it.

> Clarence Darrow (1857–1938)
> American lawyer and author

Boy, the things I do for England.

> Prince Charles (1948–   )
> prince of Wales (on sampling snake meat)

Strong people always have strong weaknesses.

> Peter Drucker (1909–   )
> American business philosopher and author

To lead the people, walk behind them.

> Lao-tzu (6th century B.C.)
> Chinese philosopher and founder of Taoism

The graveyards are full of indispensable men.

> Charles de Gaulle (1890–1970)
> French general and president of the Fifth Republic

It often happens that I wake at night and begin to think about a serious problem and decide I must tell the Pope about it. Then I wake up completely and remember that I am the Pope.

> *Pope John XXIII (1881–1963)*

I would have made a good Pope.

> *Richard M. Nixon (1913–   )*
> *37th president of the*
> *United States*

I'd make a lousy President.

> *Lee Iacocca (1924–   )*
> *chairman, Chrysler*
> *Corporation*

A frightened captain makes a frightened crew.

> *Lister Sinclair (1921–   )*
> *Canadian author*

In calm water every ship has a good captain.

> *Swedish proverb*

O God, thy sea is so great, and my boat is so small.

> *prayer of Breton fisherman*
> *(plaque given to the commanding officer of each new Polaris submarine)*

Some are born great, some achieve greatness, and some have greatness thrust upon them.

> *William Shakespeare (1564–1616)*
> *English dramatist and poet*

You can't imagine the extra work I had when I was a god.

> *Hirohito (1901–89)*
> *emperor of Japan*

LEADERSHIP STYLES

LEADERSHIP STYLE: *distinctive manner or technique by which a leader uses available power to direct others.*

The choice of how to administer power possessed by a leader can range from an authoritative, threatening, and demanding style to pleading, cajoling, and begging. Ford Motor Company founder Henry Ford's leadership style leaned toward democratic. As U.S. Army General Brown described it, "Henry Ford could get anything out of men because he just talked and would tell them stories. He'd never say, 'I want this done.' He'd say, 'I wonder if we can do it.' "

If you hit a pony over the nose at the outset of your acquaintance, he may not love you, but he will take a deep interest in your movements ever afterwards.

> Rudyard Kipling (1865–1936)
> English novelist

You do not lead by hitting people over the head—that's assault, not leadership.

> Dwight D. Eisenhower (1890–1969)
> 34th president of the United States

Power is not revealed by striking hard or often, but by striking true.

> Honoré de Balzac (1799–1850)
> French novelist

Surround yourself with the best people you can find, delegate authority, and don't interfere as long as the policy you've decided upon is being carried out.

> Ronald Reagan (1911–   )
> 40th president of the United States

I have an absolute rule. I refuse to make a decision that somebody else can make. The first rule of leadership is to save yourself for the big decision. Don't allow your mind to become cluttered with the trivia. Don't let yourself become the issue.

> Richard Nixon (1913–   )
> 37th president of the United States

If thou art a master, be sometimes blind; if a servant, sometimes deaf.

> Thomas Fuller (1608–61)
> English clergyman and author

Sandwich every bit of criticism between two heavy layers of praise.

> Mary Kay Ash (1915–   )
> founder, Mary Kay Cosmetics

I praise loudly, I blame softly.

> Catherine II (The Great) (1729–96)
> empress of Russia

The most important words in the English language:
5 most important words: *I am proud of you!*
4 most important words: *What is your opinion?*
3 most important words: *If you please.*
2 most important words: *Thank you.*
1 most important word: *You.*"

> Anonymous

A mean streak is a very important quality of leadership.

> Charles E. Goodell (1926–87)
> American lawyer and U.S. senator

A leader is a dealer in hope.

> Napoleon Bonaparte (1769–1821)
> emperor of France

A leader has the vision and conviction that a dream can be achieved. He inspires the power and energy to get it done.

Ralph Lauren (1939–)
American clothing designer
and chairman, Polo/Ralph
Lauren Corporation

Any leader worth following gives credit easily where credit is due. He does not take someone's idea, dress it up and offer it as his own. He offers it as theirs. Otherwise, ideas will soon cease to flow his way. He plays fair with everyone and recognizes the strong points in people as well as the weak ones. He never takes advantage for his own selfish purposes.

Franklin J. Lundling
(1906–)
American lawyer

The weaker a man in authority ... the stronger his insistence that all his privileges be acknowledged.

Austin O'Malley (1858–
1932)
American writer

People should know what you stand for. They should also know what you won't stand for.

Anonymous

Can you imagine a petty person as a high official? After he gains the position, he is anxious about losing it. When he becomes anxious about losing it, there is nothing he will not do to keep it.

Confucius (551–479 B.C.)
Chinese philosopher and
teacher

Power corrupts, but lack of power corrupts absolutely.

Adlai E. Stevenson
(1900–65)
American lawyer and
diplomat

If you have no power, then having right on your side is useless.

Adolf Hitler (1889–1945)
German chancellor and
führer

Five things are requisite to a good officer—ability, clean hands, dispatch, patience, and impartiality.

William Penn (1644–1718)
English Quaker, founder of
Pennsylvania

The leader must know, must know that he knows, and must be able to make it abundantly clear to those around him that he knows.

Clarence B. Randall (1891–
1967)
chairman, Inland Steel
Corporation

If you command wisely, you'll be obeyed cheerfully.

Thomas Fuller (1608–1661)
English clergyman and
author

The first and great commandment is don't let them scare you.

Elmer Davis (1890–1958)
American writer and radio
news commentator

He's fair. He treats us all the same—like dogs.

> *Henry Jordan (1955–   )*
> *American football player*
> *(referring to Green Bay*
> *Packers coach Vince*
> *Lombardi)*

Treat 'em like dogs, and you'll have dogs' work and dogs' actions. Treat 'em like men, and you'll have men's works.

> *Harriet Beecher Stowe*
> *(1811–96)*
> *American author*

I never give them hell; I just tell the truth, and they think it's hell.

> *Harry S Truman (1884–*
> *1972)*
> *33rd president of the United*
> *States*

To command is to serve, nothing more, and nothing less.

> *André Malraux (1901–76)*
> *French novelist*

TEN WAYS TO BE A LEADER

1. Begin with praise and honest appreciation.
2. Call attention to people's mistakes indirectly.
3. Talk about your own mistakes before criticizing the other person.
4. Ask questions instead of giving direct orders.
5. Let the other person save face.
6. Praise the slightest improvement and praise every improvement.
7. Give the other person a fine reputation to live up to.
8. Use encouragement.
9. Make the fault easy to correct.
10. Make the other person happy about doing the thing you suggest.

> *Dale Carnegie (1888–1955)*
> *American writer and*
> *speaker*

It is much more secure to be feared than to be loved.

> *Niccolò Machiavelli (1469–*
> *1527)*
> *Italian political philosopher*

Keep away from people who try to belittle your ambitions. Small people always do that, but the really great make you feel that you, too, can become great.

> *Mark Twain (1835–1910)*
> *American author*

The top people of the biggest companies are, surprisingly, often the nicest ones in their company. I'm not sure, though, if they got there because they were good guys or that they're now good guys because they can afford to be.

> *Malcolm Forbes (1919–90)*
> *American publisher*

To be humble to superiors is a duty, to equals courtesy, to inferiors nobleness.

> *Benjamin Franklin*
> *(1706–90)*
> *American statesman and*
> *philosopher*

I think the American public wants a solemn ass as president. And I think I'll go along with them.

> *Calvin Coolidge (1872–*
> *1933)*
> *30th president of the*
> *United States*

A team should be an extension of the coach's personality. My teams were arrogant and obnoxious.

> *Al McGuire (1928–)*
> *American basketball coach*

I haven't changed my style in 20 years . . . and that style is to get mad when things go wrong.

> *Alexander Haig (1924–)*
> *president, United Technolo-*
> *gies Corporation, and U.S.*
> *secretary of state*

I don't chew people out. I remind them of their heritage, and who their parents were, and whether or not their parents were married, and a few things of that nature.

> *Donald Regan (1918–)*
> *American business*
> *executive and White*
> *House chief of staff*

Chapter 5

Motivation

MOTIVATION: *forces leading to behavior directed toward the satisfaction of some need.*

John H. Patterson, founder and owner of the National Cash Register Company (NCR), is renowned for his enlightened, people-oriented leadership during the decades prior to the emergence of the human-relations movement in Western industry. By locating his office on the factory floor, Patterson quickly recognized the need for changes as basic as improved lighting, a cleaner work area, and dressing rooms with showers and lockers for his employees. He redesigned NCR factories so that four fifths of the wall space was made of glass, and thus began the phrase *daylight factory*. A chance observation of an employee heating a cup of coffee on a radiator led Patterson to provide hot meals for all NCR employees. These changes were followed over time by such employee benefits as night classes, health clinics, lunch-hour movies, recreational facilities, and organized vacations. NCR's employee-created innovations proved to be a precursor to the human-resource management practices of today.

If you let conditions stop you from working, they'll always stop you.

> *James T. Farrell (1904–79)*
> *American novelist*

Only a mediocre writer is always at his best.

> *Somerset Maugham (1874–1965)*
> *English novelist and dramatist*

Heroism consists of hanging on one minute longer.

> *Norwegian proverb*

Anything you're good at contributes to happiness.

> *Bertrand Russell (1872–1970)*
> *English mathematician and philosopher*

Nothing so needs reforming as other people's habits.

> *Mark Twain (1835–1910)*
> *American author*

"Be yourself" is the worst advice you can give some people.

> *Tom Masson (1866–1934)*
> *American editor and author*

A great deal of talent is lost in the world for want of a little courage. Every day sends to their graves obscure men whom timidity prevented from making a first effort; who, if they could have been induced to begin, would in all probability have gone to great lengths in the career of fame. The fact is that to do anything in the world worth doing, we must not stand back shivering and thinking of the cold and danger, but jump in and scramble through as well as we can.

> *Sydney Smith (1771–1845)*
> *English essayist*

Remember, a dead fish can float downstream, but it takes a live one to swim upstream.

> *W. C. Fields (1880–1946)*
> *American actor and comedian*

Even if you're on the right track, you'll get run over if you just sit there.

> *Will Rogers (1879–1935)*
> *American actor and humorist*

Many things are lost for want of asking.

> *English proverb*

I love war and responsibility and excitement. Peace is going to be hell on me.

> *George S. Patton (1885–1945))*
> *general, U.S. Army*

A good deed never goes unpunished.

> *Gore Vidal (1925–   )*
> *American author and dramatist*

We know nothing about motivation. All we can do is write books about it.

> *Peter Drucker (1909–   )*
> *American business*
> *philosopher and author*

Nothing average ever stood as a monument to progress. When progress is looking for a partner it doesn't turn to those who believe they are only average. It turns instead to those who are forever searching and striving to become the best they possibly can. If we seek the average level we cannot hope to achieve a high level of success. Our only hope is to avoid being a failure.

> *A. Lou Vickery (1941–   )*
> *American business writer*

The man who can make others laugh secures more votes for a measure than the man who forces them to think.

> *Malcolm de Chazal*
> *(1902–   )*
> *French author*

It is easier to get out than to stay out.

> *Mark Twain (1835–1910)*
> *American author*

Don't fear failure so much that you refuse to try new things. The saddest summary of a life contains three descriptions: could have, might have, and should have.

> *Louis E. Boone (1941–   )*
> *American educator and*
> *business writer*

Because it's there.

> *George H. L. Mallory (1886–*
> *1924)*
> *English mountain climber*
> *(explaining why he wanted*
> *to climb Mount Everest)*

The difference between a rut and a grave is the depth.

> *Gerald Burrill (1906–   )*
> *Episcopal bishop of*
> *Chicago*

I like players to be married and in debt. That's the way you motivate them.

> *Ernie Banks (1931–   )*
> *American baseball player*
> *and coach*

MONEY AS A MOTIVATOR

NEED: *lack of something useful; a discrepancy between a desired state and the actual state.*

The high-paying contracts offered sports superstars still fill the headlines today, but it isn't a new sign of the times. Six decades ago, considerable controversy arose over how much salary a sports figure should be taking home. During the Great Depression of the early

1930s, New York Yankee great Babe Ruth was asked to take a cut in salary, but he held out for his eighty-thousand-dollar contract. One club official protested, "But

that's more money than Hoover got for being president last year."

"I know," said the Babe, "but I had a better year."

Why do you think I'm fighting? The glory? The agony of defeat? You show me a man says he ain't fighting for money, I'll show you a fool.

Larry Holmes (1949–)
American boxing champion

What's money? A man is a success if he gets up in the morning and gets to bed at night, and in between he does what he wants to.

Bob Dylan (1941–)
American singer and
songwriter

I don't want to make money. I just want to be wonderful.

Marilyn Monroe (1926–62)
American actress

I am not sending messages with my feet. All I ever wanted was not to come up empty. I did it for the dough and the old applause.

Fred Astaire (1899–1987)
American dancer and actor

A kleptomaniac is a person who helps himself because he helps himself.

Henry Morgan (1915–)
American comedian

A person usually has two reasons for doing something: a good reason and the real reason.

John Pierpont Morgan
(1837–1913)
American financier

I don't care a damn for the invention. The dimes are what I'm after.

Isaac M. Singer (1811–75)
American inventor
(referring to his sewing
machine)

Why rob banks? That's where the money is.

Willie Sutton (1901–80)
American bank robber

You never know what you can do without until you try.

Franklin Pierce Adams
(1881–1960)
American journalist

He who likes cherries soon learns to climb.

German proverb

One of the best ways to measure people is to watch the way they behave when something free is offered.

Ann Landers (1918–)
American advice columnist

No man does anything from a single motive.

> *Samuel Taylor Coleridge*
> *(1772–1834)*
> *English poet*

Every morning, I get up and look through the *Forbes* list of the richest people in America. If I'm not there, I go to work.

> *Robert Orben (1927–   )*
> *American humorist*

You can have your titular recognition. I'll take the money and power.

> *Helen Gurley Brown*
> *(1922–   )*
> *American publisher*

Call it what you will, incentives are the only way to make people work harder.

> *Nikita Khrushchev (1894–*
> *1971)*
> *Soviet premier*

THEORY X AND THEORY Y

THEORY X: *assumption that people are basically lazy and have to be coerced or threatened by autocratic leaders before they will work.*

THEORY Y: *assumption that people are creative and responsible and will work hard for democratic managers when encouraged to participate in organizational decisions.*

There are times when a manager has to give a shove to get desired

results, and although not everyone may need the push, it is often in the best interests of team unity to prod the entire group. Such was the case of Dave Bristol, San Francisco Giants manager, when he advised his lagging National League baseball team, "There'll be two buses leaving the hotel for the ballpark tomorrow. The two o'clock bus will be for those of you who need a little extra work. The empty bus will be leaving at five o'clock."

This is not Burger King! We do not do it your way. This is the county jail. You will do it our way!

> *sign in Chicago's Cook*
> *County Jail cafeteria*

I love long hair and beards and mustaches. Yes, sir. If you want to look like you want to look, dress like you

want to dress, act like you want to act, play like you want to play, shoot like you want to shoot, do your own thing, I say, "Great!" But you're sure as hell not coming to Indiana to play basketball. At Indiana, we're going to do my thing.

> *Bobby Knight (1940–   )*
> *American college basketball*
> *coach*

Man is a wanting animal—as soon as one of his needs is satisfied, another appears in its place. This process is unending. It continues from birth to death.

> Douglas McGregor
> (1906–64)
> American management
> writer

I must be cruel, only to be kind.

> William Shakespeare
> (1564–1616)
> English dramatist and poet

Nothing in the world can take the place of persistence. Talent will not; nothing is more common than unsuccessful men of talent. Genius will not . . . the world is full of educated derelicts. The slogan "Press on" has solved and always will solve the problems of the human race.

> attributed to Calvin Coolidge
> (1872–1933)
> 30th president of the United
> States

Fight one more round. When your feet are so tired that you have to shuffle back to the center of the ring, fight one more round. When your arms are so tired that you can hardly lift your hands to come on guard, fight one more round. When your nose is bleeding and your eyes are black and you are so tired that you wish your opponent would crack you one on the jaw and put you to sleep, fight one more round—remembering that the man who always fights one more round is never whipped.

> James J. Corbett (1866–
> 1933)
> American boxing champion

Four little words sum up what has lifted most successful individuals above the crowd: *a little bit more.* They did all that was expected of them and a little bit more.

> A. Lou Vickery (1941–   )
> American business writer

Illegitimati non carborundum— Don't let the bastards grind you down.

> Joseph W. Stilwell (1883–
> 1946)
> general, U.S. Army

Little man whip a big man every time if the little man's in the right and keeps on coming.

> Texas Rangers Baseball
> Club motto

"Involvement" in this context differs from "commitment" in the same sense as the pig's and the chicken's roles in one's breakfast of ham and eggs. The chicken was involved— the pig was committed.

> Anonymous

There are three classes of men—lovers of wisdom, lovers of honor, lovers of gain.

> Plato (ca. 428–348 or 347
> B.C.)
> Greek philosopher

There are no traffic jams when you go the extra mile.

> Anonymous

In order that people may be happy in their work, these three things are needed: They must be for it. They must not do too much of it. And they must have a sense of success in it.

John Ruskin (1819–1900)
English art critic and
historian

Showing up is 80 percent of life.

Woody Allen (1935–   )
American actor, film
director, and comedian

Sometimes it seems like this is the choice—either kick ass or kiss ass.

James Caan (1939–   )
American actor

Encouragement after censure is as the sun after a shower.

Johann Wolfgang von Goethe
(1749–1832)
German poet and dramatist

Our minds are lazier than our bodies.

François Duc de La Roche-
foucauld (1613–80)
French writer and moralist

Management is nothing more than motivating other people.

Lee Iacocca (1924–   )
chairman, Chrysler
Corporation

I have yet to find the man, however exalted his station, who did not do better work and put forth greater effort under a spirit of approval than under a spirit of criticism.

Charles Schwab (1862–
1939)
American industrialist

You can't push anyone up the ladder unless he is willing to climb himself.

Andrew Carnegie (1835–
1919)
American industrialist and
philanthropist

If you aren't fired with enthusiasm, you will be fired with enthusiasm.

Vince Lombardi (1913–
1970)
American professional
football coach

PHYSIOLOGICAL AND SAFETY NEEDS

PHYSIOLOGICAL NEEDS: *fundamental needs for basic life-giving elements such as food, water, and shelter that must be satisfied before higher-order needs can be considered.*

SAFETY NEEDS: *second level on psychologist Abraham Maslow's hierarchy of human needs; includes job security, protection from physical harm, and avoidance of the unexpected.*

Sports-news headlines today are filled with more than just the scores and the best plays. In fact, an entirely new direction taken by the media in recent years has been videos of fumbles and funny plays, as well as the actions and reactions of fans at the games. The playing field more frequently is becoming filled with spectators, storming the players not only in victory but also in defeat. Frank Layden, general manager of the National Basketball Association's Utah Jazz, once remarked, "We formed a booster club in Utah, but by the end of the season it had turned into a terrorist group."

Don't cross this field unless you can do it in 9.9 seconds. The bull can do it in 10.

sign in midwestern United States pasture

Jack, the python got loose again. Don't go in there alone. It takes two to handle him.

note on front door of hunter's isolated cabin in western United States

Natural man has only two primal passions: to get and to beget.

Sir William Osler (1849–1919)
Canadian physician

If you want to give me a present, give me a good life. That's something I can value.

Raymond Massey (1896–1983)
American actor in Elia Kazan's 1955 motion picture East of Eden

It has been well said that a hungry man is more interested in four sandwiches than four freedoms.

Henry Cabot Lodge, Jr. (1902–85)
American politician and diplomat

A hungry man is not a free man.

Adlai Stevenson (1900–65)
American lawyer and diplomat

Principles have no real force except when one is well fed.

Mark Twain (1835–1910)
American author

Those who have some means think that the most important thing in the world is love. The poor know that it is money.

Gerald Brenan (1894–1987)
English journalist

Every scarecrow has a secret ambition to terrorize.

Stanislaus J. Lec (1909–66)
Polish writer and aphorist

The best parachute folders are those who jump themselves.

Anonymous

To a man with an empty stomach, food is God.

Mohandas K. Gandhi
(1869–1948)
Indian nationalist leader

ESTEEM NEEDS

ESTEEM NEEDS: *human needs for a sense of accomplishment, a feeling of achievement, and the respect of others.*

For many people, one of the hardest things to do is to admit that they did not perform at their best, but it is even harder when they did give it all they had, and the results still did not meet expectations. Dallas Cowboys offensive end Larry Cole played eleven continuous seasons without making a touchdown. When the big day finally came, he was questioned about having finally scored after such a long time. Cole quipped, "Anybody can have an off decade."

I don't deserve this, but then, I have arthritis and I don't deserve that either.

Jack Benny (1894–1974)
American comedian (on receiving an award)

There is more credit and satisfaction in being a first-rate truck driver than a tenth-rate executive.

B. C. Forbes (1880–1954)
American publisher

It's better to be a lion for a day than a sheep all your life.

Sister Elizabeth Kenny
(1886–1952)
Australian nurse

The only prize much cared for by the powerful is power. The prize of the general is not a bigger tent, but command.

Oliver Wendell Holmes, Jr.
(1841–1935)
American jurist

I know better than to argue when the English talk about their duty.

Rudyard Kipling (1865–1936)
English author

Power is the ultimate aphrodisiac.

Henry A. Kissinger
(1923–   )
American scholar and U.S. secretary of state

What people say behind your back is your standing in the community.

> *Ed Howe (1853–1937)*
> *American journalist*

Loneliness and the feeling of being unwanted is the most terrible poverty.

> *Mother Teresa (1910–   )*
> *Roman Catholic nun and*
> *humanitarian*

I have always said that if I were a rich man I would employ a professional praiser.

> *Sir Osbert Sitwell (1892–*
> *1969)*
> *English author*

One of the greatest diseases is to be nobody to anybody.

> *Mother Teresa (1910–   )*
> *Roman Catholic nun and*
> *humanitarian*

The deepest principle in human nature is the craving to be appreciated.

> *William James (1842–1910)*
> *American psychologist and*
> *philosopher*

No one can make you feel inferior without your consent.

> *Eleanor Roosevelt (1884–*
> *1962)*
> *American humanitarian and*
> *writer*

No one is any better than you, but you are no better than anyone else until you do something to prove it.

> *Donald Laird (1897–1969)*
> *American psychologist*

If a man is called to be a street-sweeper, he should sweep streets even as Michelangelo painted, or Beethoven composed music, or Shakespeare wrote poetry.

He should sweep streets so well that all the host of heaven and earth will pause to say, "Here lived a great streetsweeper who did his job well."

> *Martin Luther King, Jr.*
> *(1929–68)*
> *American clergyman and*
> *civil-rights leader*

Only mediocrities rise to the top in a system that won't tolerate wavemaking.

> *Laurence J. Peter (1919–90)*
> *American author*

If you're knocked down, you can't lose your guts. You need to play with supreme confidence or else you'll lose again, and then losing becomes a habit.

> *Joe Paterno (1926–   )*
> *American college football*
> *coach*

It is far more impressive when others discover your good qualities without your help.

> *Judith S. Martin (1938–   )*
> *[Miss Manners] American*
> *advice columnist*

It's always worthwhile to make others aware of their worth.

> *Malcolm Forbes (1919–90)*
> *American publisher*

SELF-ACTUALIZATION NEEDS

SELF-ACTUALIZATION: *highest level on Abraham Maslow's hierarchy of human needs; includes the need for fulfillment, for realizing one's potential, and for totally using one's talents and capabilities.*

George Bernard Shaw, noted for his biting wit and often cruel sarcasm, invited Winston Churchill to the first-night performance of *Saint Joan.* Shaw enclosed two tickets, adding the snide remark, "One for yourself and one for a friend—if you have one." Of course, Churchill was also a man known for his quick thought and capable use of words. He sent a reply to Shaw expressing his regret at being unable to attend, but requested tickets for the second performance—"if there is one."

To be what we are, and to become what we are capable of becoming, is the only end of life.

> *Robert Louis Stevenson*
> *(1850–94)*
> *Scottish author*

When you cease to make a contribution you begin to die.

> *Eleanor Roosevelt (1884–*
> *1962)*
> *American humanitarian and*
> *writer*

You have reached the pinnacle of success as soon as you become uninterested in money, compliments, or publicity.

> *Dr. O. A. Battista (1917–   )*
> *American chemist*

Always bear in mind that your own resolution to succeed is more important than any other one thing.

> *Abraham Lincoln (1809–65)*
> *16th president of the United*
> *States*

Children, you must remember something. A man without ambition is dead. A man with ambition but no love is dead. A man with ambition and love for his blessings here on earth is ever so alive. Having been alive, it won't be hard in the end to lie down and rest.

> *Pearl Bailey (1918–90)*
> *American singer*

Man is not the sum of what he has but the totality of what he does not yet have, of what he might have.

> *Jean-Paul Sartre (1905–80)*
> *French philosopher,*
> *dramatist, and novelist*

There is at bottom only one problem in the world and this is its name. How does one break through? How does one get into the open? How does one burst the cocoon and become a butterfly?

> *Thomas Mann (1875–1955)*
> *German novelist*

Work out your own salvation. Do not depend on others.

> *Buddha (ca. 563–ca. 483 B.C.)*
> *Indian philosopher, founder*
> *of Buddhism*

Every calling is great when greatly pursued.

> *Oliver Wendell Holmes, Jr.*
> *(1841–1935)*
> *American jurist*

Genius is the ability to put into effect what is in your mind.

> *F. Scott Fitzgerald (1896–*
> *1940)*
> *American writer*

A man can succeed at almost anything for which he has unlimited enthusiasm.

> *Charles Schwab (1862–*
> *1939)*
> *American industrialist*

We work to become, not to acquire.

> *Elbert Hubbard (1856–*
> *1915)*
> *American writer*

There is only one success—to be able to spend your life in your own way.

> *Christopher Morley (1890–*
> *1957)*
> *American writer*

Chapter 6

Communication

COMMUNICATION: *transfer of information via an understandable message from one person to another.*

In his book *The Power of Words*, Stuart Chase emphasized the value of the KISS ("Keep it simple, stupid.") approach to effective communications by telling the story of the plumber who decided to use hydrochloric acid to clean drains but became concerned about possible harmful effects. His letter to the U.S. Bureau of Standards in Washington, D.C., produced this reply:

> The efficacy of hydrochloric acid is indisputable, but chlorine residue is incompatible with metallic permanence.

The plumber read the letter and then sent a follow-up letter to his correspondent in Washington, thanking him for responding and expressing his satisfaction in learning that his practice was a safe one. He received a brief note of alarm by return mail:

> We cannot assume responsibility for the production of toxic and noxious residues with hydrochloric acid, and suggest that you use an alternative procedure.

Again, the plumber responded, expressing his pleasure at the fact that the bureau still agreed with him. This produced an even briefer, more direct note from Washington:

Don't use hydrochloric acid; it eats hell out of the pipes.

The Persian Messenger Syndrome—killing the bearer of bad news—is frequently mentioned as a major reason why managers are kept in the dark concerning unexpected setbacks. The syndrome traces its origins to ancient Greece and Sophocles' tragedy *Antigone,* wherein a messenger fears for his life because he knows Creon, the king of Thebes, will be unhappy with the news he brings. The Persian Messenger Syndrome survives today in modern industry. General Motors Corporation is an organization well known for its hostility to bearers of bad news concerning the firm, its products, or its declining market share. The company joke is, "At GM, we not only shoot the messenger, we bayonet the stretcher carrier."

The right to be heard does not automatically include the right to be taken seriously.

> *Hubert Humphrey*
> *(1911–78)*
> *vice president of the United States*

No man would listen to you talk if he didn't know it was his turn next.

> *Ed Howe (1853–1937)*
> *American journalist*

If the house is on fire, forget the china, silver, and wedding album—grab the Rolodex.

> *Harvey MacKay (1933?–)*
> *American executive and business writer*

If I went back to college again, I'd concentrate on two areas: learning to write and to speak before an audience. Nothing in life is more important than the ability to communicate effectively.

> *Gerald R. Ford (1913–)*
> *38th president of the United States*

Learn to write. Never mind the damn statistics. If you like statistics, become a CPA.

> Jim Murray (1919–   )
> American sportscaster and writer

It's a pity to shoot the pianist when the piano is out of tune.

> René Coty (1882–1962)
> French statesman

All generalizations are false, including this one.

> Alexander Chase (1926–   )
> American journalist and editor

As I grow older, I pay less attention to what men say, I just watch what they do.

> Andrew Carnegie (1835–1919)
> American industrialist and philanthropist

It is impossible to defeat an ignorant man in an argument.

> William Gibbs McAdoo (1863–1941)
> U.S. senator and railroad executive

When someone tries to argue with you, say, "You are nothing if not accurate, and you are not accurate." Then escape from the room.

> Christopher Morley (1890–1957)
> American writer

Anger is just one letter short of *danger*.

> Anonymous

I have made this letter longer than usual, only because I have not had the time to make it shorter.

> Blaise Pascal (1623–62)
> French mathematician and philosopher

This report, by its very length, defends itself against the risk of being read.

> Winston Churchill (1874–1965)
> British statesman and prime minister

There is no quicker way for two executives to get out of touch with each other than to retire to the seclusion of their offices and write each other notes.

> R. Alec Mackenzie (1923–   )
> American management consultant

It is much easier to be critical than to be correct.

> Benjamin Disraeli (1804–81)
> British novelist and prime minister

Pay no attention to what the critics say. A statue has never been erected in honor of a critic.

> Jean Sibelius (1865–1957)
> Finnish composer

Critics are like eunuchs in a harem. They know how it's done; they've seen it done every day; but they're unable to do it themselves.

> *attributed to Brendan*
> *Behan (1923–64)*
> *Irish playwright*

The worse the news, the more effort should go into communicating it.

> *Andrew S. Grove (1936–   )*
> *chairman Intel Corporation*

Writing is easy. All you do is sit staring at a blank sheet of paper until the drops of blood form on your forehead.

> *Gene Fowler (1931–   )*
> *American writer*

The first Rotarian was the first man to call John the Baptist Jack.

> *H. L. Mencken (1880–1956)*
> *American editor*

Gossip is when you hear something you like about someone you don't.

> *Earl Wilson (1907–87)*
> *American newspaper*
> *columnist*

Vilify! Vilify! Some of it will always stick.

> *Pierre-Augustin Beau-*
> *marchais (1732–99)*
> *French dramatist and*
> *businessman*

The enemy came. He was beaten. I am tired. Good night.

> *message sent by Vicomte de*
> *Turenne (1611–75)*
> *marshal of France after the*
> *Battle of Dunen, 1658*

I don't care how much a man talks if he only says it in a few words.

> *Josh Billings (1818–85)*
> *American humorist*

Speech is a mirror of the soul; as a man speaks, so he is.

> *Publilius Syrus (1st century*
> *B.C.)*
> *Latin writer of mimes*

The fellow that agrees with everything you say is either a fool or he is getting ready to skin you.

> *Frank McKinney (Kin)*
> *Hubbard (1868–1930)*
> *American humorist*

MISCOMMUNICATION

MISCOMMUNICATION: *failure to communicate clearly.*

During his first term in the Oval Office, President Ronald Reagan attended a state dinner for French president François Mitterrand. Reagan entered the room, escorting Mrs. Mitterrand through the tables and trying to follow the butler's lead, when Mrs. Mitterrand abruptly stopped. "She calmly turned her head and said something to me in French," recalled Reagan, "which unfortunately I did not understand. And the butler was motioning for us to come on, and I motioned to her that we should go forward, that we were to go to the other side of the room. And again, very calmly, she made her statement to me."

An interpreter finally explained to Mr. Reagan that Madame Mitterrand was telling him he was standing on her gown.

———

I didn't say that I didn't say it. I said that I didn't say that I said it. I want to make that very clear.

> George Romney (1907–   )
> American industrialist and
> governor of Michigan

To improve communications, work not on the utterer, but the recipient.

> Peter Drucker (1909–   )
> American business
> philosopher and author

What we've got here is failure to communicate.

> Strother Martin (1919–80)
> American actor in Stuart
> Rosenberg's 1967 motion
> picture Cool Hand Luke

We always remember best the irrelevant.

> Peter Drucker (1909–   )
> American business
> philosopher and author

It is a luxury to be understood.

> Ralph Waldo Emerson
> (1803–82)
> American essayist and poet

The reports of my death are greatly exaggerated.

> Mark Twain (1835–1910)
> American author

I never fail to be amused by those figures of speech that the dictionary labels *oxymorons*: those combinations of contradictory terms like *jumbo shrimp* and *military intelligence*. But my two favorites are *postal service* and *sanitary landfill*.

> Louis E. Boone (1941–   )
> American educator and
> business writer

SPEECHES

SPEECH: *the power of expressing or communicating thoughts by speaking; a public discourse.*

I have never met anyone who listened to an entire political speech without becoming thoroughly bored at some point. More frequently, we catch the phrases that are emphasized, and the rest becomes a mumbo-jumbo of political innuendos. It is truly sad, however, when the speaker becomes so involved in reading his speech that he is unaware of what he is saying. Former Soviet leader Leonid Brezhnev, appearing in a nationally televised address, inadvertently read the same page twice, and no one seemed to even notice, including the premier himself.

My father gave me these hints on speech-making: "Be sincere . . . be brief . . . be seated."

> *James Roosevelt (1907–   )*
> *son of President Franklin D.*
> *Roosevelt, businessman,*
> *and politician*

An after-dinner speech should be like a lady's dress—long enough to cover the subject and short enough to be interesting.

> *Richard Austen Butler*
> *(1902–82)*
> *British politician*

He can compress the most words into the smallest idea of any man I ever met.

> *Abraham Lincoln (1809–65)*
> *16th president of the United*
> *States*

Man does not live by words alone, despite the fact that sometimes he has to eat them.

> *Adlai E. Stevenson*
> *(1900–65)*
> *American lawyer and*
> *diplomat*

It usually takes me more than three weeks to prepare a good impromptu speech.

> *Mark Twain (1835–1910)*
> *American author*

I have heard speakers use the phrase, "I can say without fear of contradiction. . . ." Anyone who says this in a modern democracy, or to the shareholders of a modern company, should see the doctor.

> *Oliver Lyttleton (1893–1972)*
> *British politician*

The ability to speak is a short cut to distinction. It puts a man in the limelight, raises him head and shoulders above the crowd, and the man who can speak acceptably is usually given credit for an ability out of all proportion to what he really possesses.

> Lowell Thomas (1892–1981)
> American radio broadcaster
> and journalist

I like the way you always manage to state the obvious with a sense of real discovery.

> Gore Vidal (1925–　)
> American author and
> dramatist

The best audience is intelligent, well-educated, and a little drunk.

> Alben W. Barkley (1877–
> 1956)
> vice president of the
> United States

A talk is a voyage with a purpose, and it must be charted. The man who starts out going nowhere, generally gets there.

> Dale Carnegie (1888–1955)
> American writer and
> speaker

A speech is a solemn responsibility. The man who makes a bad 30-minute speech to 200 people wastes only a half-hour of his own time. But he wastes 100 hours of the audience's time—more than four days—which should be a hanging offense.

> Jenkin Lloyd Jones
> (1911–　)
> American newspaper
> publisher

I do not object to people looking at their watches when I am speaking. But I strongly object when they start shaking them to make sure they are still going.

> Lord William Norman
> Birkett (1883–1962)
> British lawyer and judge

WRITING AND READING

WRITING: *the act or art of forming visible letters or characters that serve as visible signs of ideas, words, or symbols.*

READING: *learning from what one has seen or found in writing or printing.*

Playing for the Milwaukee Braves in 1957, future home-run king and Baseball Hall of Famer Hank Aaron was the National League's Most Valuable Player and led the league with 44 home runs and 132 runs batted in. That same year, Milwaukee came up against the New York Yankees in the World Series. As Hammerin' Hank approached the plate, bat in hand, Yankee catcher Yogi Berra noticed the way he was grasping the bat.

"Turn it around so you can see the trademark," Yogi advised Hank.

But Hank never flinched and said, "Didn't come up here to read. Came up here to hit."

I took a course in speed reading and was able to read *War and Peace* in twenty minutes. It's about Russia.

> *Woody Allen (1935–)*
> *American actor, film*
> *director, and comedian*

A recent government publication on the marketing of cabbage contains, according to one report, 26,941 words. It is noteworthy in this regard that the Gettysburg Address contains a mere 279 words while the Lord's Prayer comprises but 67.

> *Norman R. Augustine*
> *(1935–)*
> *American author and*
> *chairman, Martin*
> *Marietta Corporation*

When you take stuff from one writer, it's plagiarism; but when you take it from many writers, it's research.

> *Wilson Mizner (1876–1933)*
> *American author*

Words are, of course, the most powerful drug used by mankind.

> *Rudyard Kipling (1865–*
> *1936)*
> *English author*

Words pay no debts.

> *William Shakespeare (1564–*
> *1616)*
> *English dramatist and poet*

It's not the most intellectual job in the world, but I do have to know the letters.

> *Vanna White (1957–)*
> *American TV game-show*
> *hostess*

When you put down the good things you ought to have done, and leave out the bad things you did do—well, that's memoirs.

> *Will Rogers (1879–1935)*
> *American actor and*
> *humorist*

The hardest thing is writing a recommendation for someone we know.

> *Frank McKinney (Kin)*
> *Hubbard (1868–1930)*
> *American humorist*

Gutenberg made everybody a reader. Xerox makes everybody a publisher.

> *Marshall McLuhan*
> *(1911–80)*
> *Canadian educator and*
> *author*

Some books are to be tasted, others to be swallowed, and some few to be chewed and digested.

> *Francis Bacon (1561–1626)*
> *English philosopher*

If you want to get rich from writing, write the sort of thing that's read by persons who move their lips when they're reading to themselves.

> *Don Marquis (1878–1937)*
> *American humorist*

I'm a lousy writer; a helluva lot of people have got lousy taste.

> *Grace Metalious (1924–64)*
> *American novelist*

The best way to become acquainted with a subject is to write a book about it.

> *Benjamin Disraeli*
> *(1804–81)*
> *British novelist and prime*
> *minister*

I have always imagined that Paradise will be a kind of library.

> *Jorge Luis Borges (1899–*
> *1986)*
> *Argentine author*

No author is a man of genius to his publisher.

> *Heinrich Heine (1797–1856)*
> *German poet and critic*

That's not writing, that's typing.

> *Truman Capote (1924–84)*
> *American novelist*
> *(referring to the writing*
> *style of Jack Kerouac*
> *(1922–69), author of*
> On the Road)

Your manuscript is both good and original; but the parts that are good are not original and the parts that are original are not good.

> *Samuel Johnson (1709–84)*
> *English lexicographer and*
> *author*

I read part of it all the way through.

> *Samuel Goldwyn (1882–*
> *1974)*
> *American motion-picture*
> *producer*

The covers of this book are too far apart.

> *Ambrose Bierce (1842–*
> *ca. 1914)*
> *American author*

LISTENING AND SILENCE

LISTENING: *hearing something with thoughtful attention.*

SILENCE: *absence of sound or noise; forbearance from speech or noise.*

Perhaps no other president preferred listening over speaking more than the taciturn thirtieth president of the United States, Cal-vin Coolidge. Reporters waiting outside a church service attended by Coolidge sought a Monday news quotation by asking the president about the subject of the sermon he had just heard. "Sin," said Coolidge. The reporter's follow-up question was not surprising: "What did the preacher *say* about it?" "He was against it," replied Coolidge.

If you don't say anything you won't be called on to repeat it.

> *Calvin Coolidge (1872–1933)*
> *30th president of the United States*

Wise men say nothing in dangerous times.

> *John Selden (1584–1654)*
> *English jurist and antiquarian*

To avoid criticism, do nothing, say nothing, be nothing.

> *Elbert Hubbard (1856–1915)*
> *American author*

Once you get people laughing, they're listening and you can tell them almost anything.

> *Herbert Gardner (1872–1955)*
> *American author*

You have not converted a man because you have silenced him.

> *John Morley (1838–1923)*
> *English statesman and writer*

It is impossible to persuade a man who does not disagree, but smiles.

> *Muriel Spark (1918–   )*
> *Scottish author*

Too often the strong, silent man is silent because he does not know what to say.

> *Winston Churchill (1874–1965)*
> *British statesman and prime minister*

Nature has given to men one tongue, but two ears, that we may hear from others twice as much as we speak.

> *Epictetus (A.D. ca. 55–ca. 135)*
> *Greek philosopher*

Look wise, say nothing, and grunt. Speech was given to conceal thoughts.

> *Sir William Osler (1849–1919)*
> *Canadian physician*

No man pleases by silence; many please by speaking briefly.

> *Ausonius (A.D. ca. 310–ca. 395)*
> *Latin poet*

The only way to entertain some folks is to listen to them.

> *Frank McKinney (Kin) Hubbard (1868–1930)*
> *American humorist*

I like to listen. I have learned a great deal from listening carefully. Most people never listen.

> *Ernest Hemingway (1899–1961)*
> *American writer and journalist*

A closed mouth gathers no feet.

> *Anonymous*

Don't talk unless you can improve the silence.

> *New England proverb*

Silence is one of the hardest arguments to refute.

> *Josh Billings (1818–85)*
> *American humorist*

It takes two to speak the truth—one to speak and one to hear.

> *Henry David Thoreau (1817–82)*
> *American naturalist and writer*

I have never been hurt by anything I didn't say.

> *Calvin Coolidge (1872–1933)*
> *30th president of the United States*

Better to remain silent and be thought a fool than to speak out and remove all doubt.

> *Abraham Lincoln (1809–65)*
> *16th president of the United States*

Blessed is the man who, having nothing to say, abstains from giving in words, evidence of the fact.

> *George Eliot (1819–80)*
> *English novelist*

Ten persons who speak make more noise than ten thousand who are silent.

> *Napoleon Bonaparte (1769–1821)*
> *emperor of France*

A good listener is not only popular everywhere, but after a while he knows something.

> *Wilson Mizner (1876–1933)*
> *American author*

Look out for the fellow who lets you do all the talking.

> *Frank McKinney (Kin)*
> *Hubbard (1868–1930)*
> *American humorist*

One who never asks either knows everything or nothing.

> *Malcolm Forbes (1919–90)*
> *American publisher*

BORES, BOASTS, AND INSULTS

BORE: *a person who tires others with dullness, repetition, or tediousness.*

BOAST: *a statement of pride about one's own accomplishments, talents, or possessions.*

INSULT: *a callous or contemptuous statement or action; a verbal attack upon another person.*

Joe Louis was boxing's Heavyweight Champion of the World from 1937 until he retired in 1949, longer than any other boxer to date. In 1941, he defended his title eight times, including a thirteen-round knockout fight with Billy Conn. Five years later, in June of 1946, he again prepared to defend his title against Conn. Warned of Conn's tremendous speed and ability to quickly dart in, attack, and then move out of his opponent's range, Louis confidently replied, "He can run, but he can't hide." Louis KO'd Conn in eight rounds.

Known for his quick tongue and flamboyant phrases, American boxing champion Muhammad Ali always seems to have the last word in any conversation. So when a flight attendant instructed him to fasten his seat belt, Ali quipped, "Superman don't need no seat belt." To which the flight attendant replied, "Superman don't need no airplane, either."

Boredom is having to listen to someone talk about himself when I want to talk about me.

> *Tom Paciorek (1946–   )*
> *American baseball player*

The trouble with telling a good story is that it invariably reminds the other fellow of a bad one.

> *Sid Caesar (1922–   )*
> *American actor and*
> *comedian*

A gossip is one who talks to you about others; a bore is one who talks to you about himself, and a brilliant conversationalist is one who talks to you about yourself.

> *Lisa Kirk (1925–   )*
> *American musical-comedy*
> *entertainer*

Now when I bore people at a party, they think it's their fault.

> *Henry Kissinger (1923–   )*
> *American scholar and U.S.*
> *secretary of state*

The best way to be boring is to leave nothing out.

> *Voltaire (1694–1778)*
> *French writer*

If you haven't struck oil in the first three minutes—stop boring.

> *George Jessel (1898–1981)*
> *American comedian*

A bore is someone who follows your joke with a better one.

> *Anonymous*

A bore is a man who deprives you of solitude without providing you with company.

> *Gian Vincenzo Gravina*
> *(1664–1718)*
> *Italian jurist and writer*

George is bogged down in the history department. He's an old bog in the history department. That's what George is. A bog.

> *Elizabeth Taylor (1932–   )*
> *American actress in Mike*
> *Nichols's 1966 motion*
> *picture of Edward Albee's*
> Who's Afraid of Virginia
> Woolf?

The intelligent man who is proud of his intelligence is like the con-demned man who is proud of his large cell.

> *Simone Weil (1909–43)*
> *French philosopher and*
> *writer*

A fanatic is one who can't change his mind and won't change the subject.

> *Winston Churchill (1874–*
> *1965)*
> *British statesman and*
> *prime minister*

Suffer fools gladly. They may be right.

> *Holbrook Jackson (1874–*
> *1948)*
> *English journalist, editor,*
> *and author*

A man is like a phonograph with half-a-dozen records. You soon get tired of them all; and yet you have to sit at the table whilst he reels them off to every new visitor.

> *George Bernard Shaw*
> *(1856–1950)*
> *British playwright and*
> *social reformer*

Bragging may not bring happiness, but no man having caught a large fish goes home through an alley.

> *Anonymous*

It ain't braggin' if you can do it.

> *Jay Hanna ("Dizzy") Dean*
> *(1910–74)*
> *American baseball player*

I have my faults. But being wrong ain't one of them.

> *Jimmy Hoffa (1913–?75)*
> *American labor leader*

People hate me because I am a multifaceted, talented, wealthy, internationally famous genius.

> *Jerry Lewis (1926–   )*
> *American actor*

All the extraordinary men I have ever known were chiefly extraordinary in their own estimation.

> *Woodrow Wilson (1856–*
> *1924)*
> *28th president of the United*
> *States*

Early in life I had to choose between honest arrogance and hypocritical humility. I chose honest arrogance and have seen no occasion to change.

> *Frank Lloyd Wright (1867–*
> *1959)*
> *American architect*

Noise proves nothing. Often a hen who has merely laid an egg cackles as if she laid an asteroid.

> *Mark Twain (1835–1910)*
> *American author*

If I had not been born Perón, I would have liked to be Perón.

> *Juan Perón (1895–1974)*
> *president of Argentina*

One of my chief regrets during my years in the theater is that I couldn't sit in the audience and watch me.

> *John Barrymore (1882–*
> *1942)*
> *American actor*

You can always spot a well-informed man—his views are the same as yours.

> *Ilka Chase (1905–78)*
> *American actress, novelist,*
> *and playwright*

I'm not arrogant. I just believe there's no human problem that couldn't be solved—if people would simply do as I tell 'em.

> *Donald Regan (1918–   )*
> *American business executive and*
> *White House chief of staff*

Fans don't boo nobodies.

> *Reggie Jackson (1946–   )*
> *American baseball player*

Rudeness is the weak man's imitation of strength.

> *Eric Hoffer (1902–83)*
> *American longshoreman*
> *and philosopher*

If you can't say something good about someone, sit right here by me.

> *Alice Roosevelt Longworth*
> *(1884–1980)*
> *daughter of President*
> *Theodore Roosevelt*

Women and elephants never forget an injury.

> Saki (1870–1916)
> Scottish writer

Nobody ever forgets where he buried a hatchet.

> Frank McKinney (Kin)
> Hubbard (1868–1930)
> American humorist

Go, and never darken my towels again!

> Groucho Marx (1890–1977)
> American actor and come-
> dian in Leo McCarey's
> 1933 motion picture
> Duck Soup

He's a modest little man with much to be modest about.

> Winston Churchill (1874–
> 1965)
> British statesman and
> prime minister

An injury is much sooner forgotten than an insult.

> Philip Dormer Stanhope
> (1694–1773)
> Earl of Chesterfield
> English statesman and
> author

The only gracious way to accept an insult is to ignore it. If you can't ignore it, top it. If you can't top it, laugh at it. If you can't laugh at it, it's probably deserved.

> Joseph Russell Lynes, Jr.
> (1910–   )
> American author and editor

Men will take almost any kind of criticism except the observation that they have no sense of humor.

> Steve Allen (1921–   )
> American TV show host,
> author, and entertainer

I never forget a face, but in your case I'll be glad to make an exception.

> Groucho Marx (1890–1977)
> American actor and
> comedian

Chapter 7

Controlling

CONTROLLING: *evaluating performance to determine whether objectives are being accomplished; continual analysis and measurement of actual operations against standards developed during the planning process.*

George Washington's character is probably best exhibited in the many reports of his interactions with those who served under him and his respect for discipline. One story recounts an incident between Washington and his secretary. The secretary, who had arrived considerably late, apologized, explaining that his watch was the reason for his tardiness. Washington, in his calm, composed manner, replied, "Then you must find another watch, or I another secretary."

A young student, obviously enamored with the virtues of brevity, wrote the following essay on the life of Socrates: "Socrates was a philosopher. He went around pointing out errors in the way things were done. They fed him hemlock."

How would you like a job where, if you made a mistake, a big red light goes on and 18,000 people boo?

> *Jacques Plante (1929–86)*
> *National Hockey League*
> *goalie*

The handwriting on the wall may be a forgery.

> *Ralph Hodgson (1871–*
> *1962)*
> *English poet*

In God we trust—all others pay cash.

> *American business saying*

If you owe $50, you're a delinquent account.
If you owe $50,000, you're a small businessman.
If you owe $50 million, you're a corporation.
If you owe $50 billion, you're the government.

> *Lynn Townsend White, Jr.*
> *(1907–87)*
> *American historian*

They say a reasonable number of fleas is good fer a dog—keeps him from broodin' over bein' a dog.

> *E. N. Westcott (1846–98)*
> *American banker and*
> *novelist*

The man who complains about the way the ball bounces is likely the one who dropped it.

> *Lou Holtz (1937–   )*
> *American football coach*

You don't concentrate on risks. You concentrate on results. No risk is too great to prevent the necessary job from getting done.

> *Charles E. (Chuck) Yeager*
> *(1923–   )*
> *American test pilot*

In skating over thin ice, our safety is in our speed.

> *Ralph Waldo Emerson*
> *(1803–82)*
> *American essayist and poet*

The only way to solve the traffic problems of the country is to pass a law that only paid-for cars are allowed to use the highways.

> *Will Rogers (1879–1935)*
> *American actor and*
> *humorist*

The best way to keep children at home is to make the home atmosphere pleasant and let the air out of the tires.

> *Dorothy Parker (1893–1967)*
> *American writer and poet*

See everything, overlook a great deal, correct a little.

> *Pope John XXIII (1881–*
> *1963)*

Discipline is the soul of an army. It makes small numbers formidable, procures success to the weak, and esteem to all.

> *George Washington*
> *(1732–99)*
> *1st president of the United*
> *States*

I have built my organization upon
fear.

> *Al Capone (1899–1947)*
> *American gangster*

People react to fear, not love. They
don't teach that in Sunday school, but
it's true.

> *Richard M. Nixon (1913–   )*
> *37th president of the United*
> *States*

We are not looking for fear. We are
not looking for love. We are looking
for respect.

> *Lawrence Gibbs (1938–   )*
> *commissioner, U.S. Internal*
> *Revenue Service*

Music hath charm to soothe a savage
beast—but I'd try a revolver first.

> *Josh Billings (1818–85)*
> *American humorist*

You can get more with a kind word
and a gun than you can get with a
kind word.

> *Al Capone (1899–1947)*
> *American gangster*

If you're the boss and your people
fight you openly when they think
you're wrong, that's healthy. If your
people fight each other openly in
your presence for what they believe
in, that's healthy. But keep all conflict eyeball to eyeball.

> *Robert Townsend*
> *American business writer*
> *and former president,*
> *Avis-Rent-a-Car, Inc.*

If it moves, salute it,
If it doesn't move, pick it up.
If you can't pick it up, paint it.

> *U.S. Army saying*

There is no useful rule without an exception.

> *Thomas Fuller (1654–1734)*
> *English physician and*
> *writer*

A whipping never hurts so much as
the thought that you are being
whipped.

> *Ed Howe (1853–1937)*
> *American journalist*

Beat your child once a day. If you
don't know why, he does.

> *Chinese proverb*

There's some folks standing behind
the President that ought to get
around where he can watch 'em.

> *Frank McKinney (Kin)*
> *Hubbard (1868–1930)*
> *American humorist*

Catch-22 says they have a right to do
anything we can't stop them from
doing.

> *Joseph Heller (1923–   )*
> *American author*

Drive thy business or it will drive
thee.

> *Benjamin Franklin*
> *(1706–90)*
> *American statesman and*
> *philosopher*

Rules are prisons.

> *William Bernbach*
> *(1911–82)*
> *founder, Doyle Dane*
>   *Bernbach advertising*
>   *agency*

Rules are for the obedience of fools and the guidance of wise men.

> *David Ogilvy (1911–   )*
> *founder, Ogilvy & Mather*
> *advertising agency*

We must stop talking of profit as a reward. It is a cost. There are no rewards; only the costs of yesterday and tomorrow.

> *Peter Drucker (1909–   )*
> *American business*
>   *philosopher and author*

It's possible to own too much. A man with one watch knows what time it is; a man with two watches is never quite sure.

> *Lee Segall (1905–   )*
> *American communications*
>   *industry executive*

If it ain't broke, don't fix it.

> *Bert Lance (1931–   )*
> *American banker and*
>   *presidential adviser*

I don't believe the old statement, "If it ain't broke, don't fix it." If that's the case, then Cadillacs and Jaguars and Mercedes would never make a

change. I've always looked for ways to make things better.

> *Vic Bubas (1926–   )*
> *American basketball coach*
>   *and athletic conference*
>   *commissioner*

If you've got them by the balls, their hearts and minds will soon follow.

> *Charles Colson (1931–   )*
> *special assistant to*
>   *President Richard M.*
>   *Nixon*

When you have got an elephant by the hind legs and he is trying to run away, it is best to let him run.

> *Abraham Lincoln (1809–*
>   *1865)*
> *16th president of the United*
>   *States*

A man watches himself best when others watch him, too.

> *George Savile (1633–95)*
> *Marquis of Halifax*
> *English politician and*
>   *essayist*

Big Brother is watching you.

> *George Orwell (1903–50)*
> *English author*

Every organization has a Siberia.

> *Warren G. Bennis (1925–   )*
> *American educator and*
>   *business writer*

Exact scientific knowledge and methods are everywhere, sooner or later, sure to replace rule-of-thumb.

> *Frederick W. Taylor (1856–1915)*
> *American engineer and management writer*

Instead of a management science, which provides knowledge, concepts and discipline, we may be developing a gadget bag of techniques for the efficiency expert.

> *Peter Drucker (1909–   )*
> *American business philosopher and author*

The emphasis in sound discipline must be on *what's wrong*, rather than *who's to blame*.

> *George S. Odiorne (1920–92)*
> *American educator and business writer*

To err is human, but it is against company policy.

> *Anonymous*

I don't mean to sound arrogant, but it's my ass that's on the line.

> *Robert S. Hillman (1939–   )*
> *CEO, The Eyecare Company*

The doctor can bury his mistakes but an architect can only advise his client to plant vines.

> *Frank Lloyd Wright (1867–1959)*
> *American architect*

Without a yardstick, there is no measurement. And without measurement, there is no control.

> *Pravin M. Shah (1932–   )*
> *Indian management consultant*

We are drowning in information but starved for knowledge.

> *John Naisbitt (1929–   )*
> *American business writer and social researcher*

Torture the data long enough and they will confess to anything.

> *Anonymous*

One accurate measurement is worth a thousand expert opinions.

> *Grace Murray Hopper (1906–92)*
> *admiral, U.S. Navy*

Round numbers are always fake.

> *Samuel Johnson (1709–84)*
> *English lexicographer and author*

It isn't what we don't know that gives us trouble, it's what we know that ain't so.

> *Will Rogers (1879–1935)*
> *American actor and*
> *humorist*

Don't *expect. Inspect.*

> *American business saying*

Managers must have the discipline not to keep pulling up the flowers to see if their roots are healthy.

> *Robert Townsend (1920–)*
> *American business writer*
> *and former president,*
> *Avis-Rent-a-Car, Inc.*

BUDGETING

BUDGET: *financial plan that specifies revenues and expenses for a stated time period.*

When Philip K. Wrigley succeeded his father as chairman of the Chicago-based chewing-gum company, he continued the firm's practice of heavy spending on advertising to create and maintain consumer demand. During a trans-continental flight, a seatmate asked him why he continued to spend so much money on advertising a product that was already one of the best known in the world. Wrigley quickly replied, "For the same reason the pilot of this plane keeps the engine running when we're already twenty-nine thousand feet up."

I would rather have my people laugh at my economies than weep for my extravagance.

> *Oscar II (1829–1907)*
> *king of Sweden and Norway*

Why is there so much month left at the end of the money?

> *Anonymous*

Next to double-entry bookkeeping and the copying machine, budgets are the most commonly-used management tools.

> *Peter Drucker (1909–)*
> *American business*
> *philosopher and author*

In those days [in France during the Middle Ages], business people kept their money in a *bougette,* or small leather bag. Budgeting then consisted of counting the money in the bag to see if there was enough to pay expenses. As businesses grew to include many people, somebody had to keep track of the money, so there arose the *controlleur,* the one who kept a record of the *bougettes* in order to control the receipts and expenditures. So began the *controller* and *comptroller* as we know them today.

> *Louis A. Allen (1917–   )*
> *American management*
> *writer*

About the time we can make ends meet, somebody moves the ends.

> *Herbert Hoover (1874–*
> *1964)*
> *31st president of the United*
> *States*

When you can't make both ends meet, make one potatoes.

> *American saying*

A budget tells us what we can't afford, but it doesn't keep us from buying it.

> *William Feather (1889–*
> *1981)*
> *American author and*
> *publisher*

The only good budget is a balanced budget.

> *Adam Smith (1723–90)*
> *Scottish economist*

Any jackass can draw up a balanced budget on paper.

> *Lane Kirkland (1922–   )*
> *American labor leader*

My problem lies in reconciling my gross habits with my net income.

> *Errol Flynn (1909–59)*
> *American actor*

The reason most of us don't live within our income is that we don't consider that living.

> *Joe Moore (1941–   )*
> *American television news*
> *commentator*

I gave him an unlimited budget and he exceeded it.

> *Edward Bennett Williams*
> *(1920–88)*
> *American lawyer and former*
> *Washington Redskins foot-*
> *ball club owner (referring to*
> *former head coach George*
> *Allen)*

Chapter 8

Decision Making

DECISION MAKING: *choosing among two or more alternatives by following the steps of problem recognition, developing and analyzing alternative courses of action, selecting and implementing a course of action, and obtaining feedback to evaluate the effectiveness of the decision.*

Parables are often used to get a point across without having to name actual people, places, or events, although they generally apply to numerous situations. President Lyndon Johnson reportedly enjoyed telling the following railroad story:

A man applied for a job as a flagman at a railroad crossing and was told he would be given the job if he could pass a one-question test. Naturally, the man agreed. The applicant was told to imagine he was the flagman at a crossing having only one track, and approaching from the east at 95 mph was the Continental Express. At that same time, the Century Limited was speeding in at 100 mph from the west with only three hundred yards between the two fast-moving trains. The man was then asked what he would do in a case like this.

The applicant quickly responded, "I would run and get my brother-in-law." Not understanding the relevance of this answer, the railroad examiner asked him why. Replied the man, "He ain't never seen a train wreck."

Not to decide is to decide.

> *Harvey Cox (1929–)*
> *American theologian and*
> *author*

You don't save a pitcher for tomorrow. Tomorrow it may rain.

> *Leo Durocher (1906–91)*
> *American professional*
> *baseball manager*

If I had to sum up in one word what makes a good manager, I'd say decisiveness. You can use the fanciest computers to gather the numbers, but in the end you have to set a timetable and act. And I don't mean rashly. I'm sometimes described as a flamboyant leader and a hip-shooter, a fly-by-the-seat-of-the-pants operator. But if that were true, I could never have been successful in this business.

> *Lee Iacocca (1924–)*
> *chairman, Chrysler*
> *Corporation*

One day Alice came to a fork in the road and saw a Cheshire cat in a tree. "Which road do I take?" she asked. His response was a question: "Where do you want to go?" "I don't know," Alice answered. "Then," said the cat, "it doesn't matter."

> *Lewis Carroll (1832–98)*
> *English novelist*

If you do not know where you are going, every road will get you nowhere.

> *Henry Kissinger (1923–)*
> *American scholar and U.S.*
> *secretary of state*

When you see a snake, never mind where he came from.

> *William Gurney Benham*
> *(1859–1944)*
> *British author and poet*

One of our ironclad rules is "Never do business with anybody you don't like." If you don't like somebody, there's a reason. Chances are it's because you don't trust him, and you're probably right. I don't care who it is or what guarantees you get—cash in advance or whatever. If you do business with somebody you don't like, sooner or later you'll get screwed.

> *Henry V. Quadracci*
> *president, Quad/Graphics,*
> *Inc.*

He who builds according to every man's advice will have a crooked house.

> *Danish proverb*

An executive is someone who makes a decision quickly and gets somebody else to do the work.

> *Joe Moore (1941–)*
> *American television news*
> *commentator*

One cannot govern with buts.

> *Charles de Gaulle (1890–*
> *1970)*
> *French general and*
> *president of the Fifth*
> *Republic*

Take time to deliberate; but when the time for action arrives, stop thinking and go in.

> Andrew Jackson (1767–1845)
> 7th president of the United States

A mind all logic is like a knife all blade. It makes the hand bleed that uses it.

> Rabindranath Tagore (1861–1941)
> Bengali poet, novelist, and composer

What we think or what we believe is, in the end, of little consequence. The only thing of consequence is what we do.

> John Ruskin (1819–1900)
> English art critic and historian

Make every decision as if you owned the whole company.

> Robert Townsend (1920–   )
> American business writer and former president, Avis-Rent-a-Car, Inc.

Whenever I make a bum decision, I just go out and make another.

> Harry S Truman (1884–1972)
> 33rd president of the United States

All the mistakes I ever made were when I wanted to say "No" and said "Yes."

> Moss Hart (1904–61)
> American dramatist

Market research will always tell you why you can't do something. It's a substitute for decision making, for guts.

> Laurel Cutler (1926–   )
> vice chairman, FCB/Leber Katz Partners

Between two evils, I always pick the one I never tried before.

> Mae West (1892–1980)
> American actress

No great marketing decisions have ever been made on quantitative data.

> John Sculley (1939–   )
> chairman, Apple Computer Company

Next to knowing when to seize an opportunity, the most important thing in life is to know when to forego an advantage.

> Benjamin Disraeli (1804–81)
> British novelist and prime minister

There is a syndrome in sports called "paralysis by analysis."

> Arthur Ashe (1943–   )
> American tennis champion

If there are obstacles, the shortest line between two points may be the crooked line.

> Bertolt Brecht (1898–1956)
> German playwright

We know what happens to people who stay in the middle of the road. They get run over.

> *Aneurin Bevan (1897–1960)*
> *British politician*

There's nothing in the middle of the road but yellow stripes and dead armadillos.

> *James Allen (Jim)*
> *Hightower (1943–   )*
> *Texas agricultural*
> *commissioner*

Great crises produce great men and great deeds of courage.

> *John F. Kennedy (1917–63)*
> *35th president of the United States*

A crisis that recurs must not recur again.

> *Peter Drucker (1909–   )*
> *American business*
> *philosopher and author*

Assumption is the mother of screw-up.

> *Angelo Donghia (1935–85)*
> *American designer*

When you cannot make up your mind which of two evenly balanced courses of action you should take—choose the bolder.

> *W. J. Slim (1891–1970)*
> *general, British Army*

It is much easier to apologize than to ask permission.

> *Grace Murray Hopper*
> *(1906–92)*
> *admiral, U.S. Navy*

Whenever you see a successful business, someone once made a courageous decision.

> *Peter Drucker (1909–   )*
> *American business*
> *philosopher and author*

He who has a choice has trouble.

> *Dutch proverb*

When you come to a fork in the road, take it.

> *Yogi Berra (1925–   )*
> *American baseball*
> *player and manager*

When a three-engine Boeing 727 flying at 40,000 feet loses all three engines at once (under normal circumstances, the plane could glide for over 130 miles), the captain has ample time for quickly consulting with his copilot and flight engineer to get their ideas about the cause and remedy, and to discuss emergency procedures with the stewardesses. However, if a similar power loss occurred at 500 feet during a takeoff climb, the captain would be ill advised to practice such participative techniques.

> *J. Clayton Lafferty*
> *(1924–   )*
> *president, Human*
> *Synergistics, Inc.*

Decisions rise to the management level where the person making them is least qualified to do so.

> *Laurence J. Peter (1919–90) and Raymond Hull (1919–85) American authors of* The Peter Principle

If two friends ask you to be judge in a dispute, don't accept, because you will lose one friend; on the other hand, if two strangers come with the same request, accept, because you will gain one friend.

> *Saint Augustine (A.D. 354–430) bishop of Hippo*

It is a fine thing to be honest but it is also very important to be right.

> *Winston Churchill (1874– 1965) British statesman and prime minister*

You don't set a fox to watching the chickens just because he has a lot of experience in the hen house.

> *Harry S Truman (1884– 1972) 33rd president of the United States*

No amount of sophistication is going to allay the fact that all your knowledge is about the past and all your decisions are about the future.

> *Ian E. Wilson (1941–   ) chairman, General Electric Corporation*

One cool judgment is worth a thousand hasty councils.

> *Woodrow Wilson (1856– 1924) 28th president of the United States*

Decision making is the specific executive task.

> *Peter Drucker (1909–   ) American business philosopher and author*

You can use all the quantitative data you can get, but you still have to distrust it and use your own intelligence and judgment.

> *Alvin Toffler (1928–   ) American author*

PROBLEMS AND SOLUTIONS

PROBLEM: *any barrier preventing the accomplishment of an objective; a question or issue involving uncertainty, doubt, or difficulty.*

SOLUTION: *the answer to or disposition of a problem.*

It is often argued that the people who will be affected by a major decision should be involved in that decision. Paul Kruger (1825–1904), president of the Transvaal in southern Africa, once resolved a dispute between two brothers about a land inheritance they were to share. Kruger's decision: Let one brother divide the land, and let the other have first choice.

It is only in our decisions that we are important.

> *Jean-Paul Sartre (1905–80)*
> *French philosopher,*
> *dramatist, and novelist*

Please find me a one-armed economist so we will not always hear "on the other hand . . ."

> *Herbert Hoover (1874–*
> *1964)*
> *31st president of the United*
> *States*

Never go out to meet trouble. If you will just sit still, nine cases out of ten someone will intercept it before it reaches you.

> *Calvin Coolidge (1872–*
> *1933)*
> *30th president of the United*
> *States*

When I've heard all I need to make a decision, I don't take a vote. I make a decision.

> *Ronald Reagan (1911–   )*
> *40th president of the United*
> *States*

Getting the facts is the key to good decision making. Every mistake that I made—and we all make mistakes—came because I didn't take the time. I didn't drive hard enough. I wasn't smart enough to get the facts.

> *Charles F. Knight (1936–   )*
> *chairman, Emerson Electric*

All of us must become better informed. It is necessary for us to learn from others' mistakes. You will not live long enough to make them all yourself.

> *Hyman G. Rickover*
> *(1900–86)*
> *admiral, U.S. Navy, father*
> *of the nuclear navy*

If the only tool you have is a hammer, you tend to see every problem as a nail.

> *Abraham Maslow (1908–70)*
> *American psychologist*

The best way to escape from a problem is to solve it.

> *Anonymous*

It isn't that they can't see the solution. It is that they can't see the problem.

> *G. K. Chesterton (1874–*
> *1936)*
> *English journalist and*
> *author*

A problem well stated is a problem half solved.

> *Charles F. Kettering (1876–*
> *1958)*
> *American electrical*
> *engineer and inventor*

Never answer a question, other than an offer of marriage, by yes or no.

Susan Chitty (1929–   )
British writer

There is always an easy solution to every human problem—neat, plausible and wrong.

H. L. Mencken (1880–1956)
American editor

Problems are only opportunities in work clothes.

Henry J. Kaiser (1882–1967)
American industrialist

Even children learn in growing up that "both" is not an admissible answer to a choice of "which one?"

Paul A. Samuelson
(1915–   )
American economist

The guidelines that I like to follow [in decision making] include identification of all pertinent information and then a fast decision. And, I would emphasize the word "pertinent" and not the word "all." If you waited until you had every scrap of information, the world would pass you by while you were sorting out all the nitty-gritty.

Hicks Waldron (1923–   )
chairman, Avon Products

If a man mulls over a decision, they say, "He's weighing the options." If a woman does it, they say, "She can't make up her mind."

Barbara Proctor (1933–   )
American advertising
executive

You'll never have all the information you need to make a decision. If you did, it would be a foregone conclusion, not a decision.

David J. Mahoney, Jr.
(1923–   )
American corporate
executive

Part II

BUILDING A COMPETITIVE ORGANIZATION

Chapter 9

The Organization

ORGANIZATION: *structured grouping of people working together to accomplish objectives.*

The need for an organization to accomplish goals efficiently has long been recognized. In the Book of Exodus (18:17–23), Moses, grappling with the problem of how to get things done, received this advice from his father-in-law:

> The thing that thou doest is not good. Thou wilt surely wear away, both thou, and this people that is with thee: for this thing is too heavy for thee; thou are not able to perform it thyself alone.

> Hearken now unto my voice, I will give thee counsel . . . thou shalt provide out of all the people able men . . . and place such over them [the people], to be rulers of . . . tens. And let them judge the people at all seasons: and it shall be, that every great matter they shall bring unto thee, but every small matter they shall judge [themselves]: so shall it be easier for thyself, and they shall bear the burden with thee.

> If thou shalt do this thing, and God command thee so, then thou shalt be able to endure, and all this people shall also go to their place in peace.

Take my assets—but leave me my organization and in five years I'll have it all back.

> *Alfred P. Sloan (1875–1966)*
> *American automobile*
> *executive*

Our team is well balanced. We have problems everywhere.

> *Tommy Prothro (1941–   )*
> *American football coach*

If you assign people duties without granting them any rights, you must pay them well.

> *Johann Wolfgang von Goethe*
> *(1749–1832)*
> *German poet and dramatist*

For all the talk about a revolution in health care, the industry is still organized around medical specialties. Get a back problem and you see a neurologist here, an orthopedic surgeon there, a radiologist somewhere else. No one has ultimate responsibility for treatment. Wouldn't it make more sense to have a hospital with a department simply called "Backs" or "Feet"?

> *Regina Herzlinger*
> *(1944–   )*
> *American educator*

Business is never so healthy as when, like a chicken, it must do a certain amount of scratching around for what it gets.

> *Henry Ford (1863–1947)*
> *American automobile*
> *manufacturer*

The inevitable end of multiple chiefs is that they fade and disappear for lack of unity.

> *Napoleon Bonaparte (1769–*
> *1821)*
> *emperor of France*

Now an army is a team. It lives, eats, sleeps, fights, as a team. This individuality stuff is a bunch of crap. The bilious bastards who wrote that stuff about individuality for the *Saturday Evening Post* don't know any more about real battle than they do about fornicating.

> *George C. Scott (1927–   )*
> *American actor in Franklin*
> *Schaffner's 1970 motion*
> *picture* Patton

The important thing to recognize is that it takes a team, and the team ought to get credit for the wins and the losses. Successes have many fathers, failures have none.

> *Philip Caldwell (1920–   )*
> *chairman, Ford Motor*
> *Company*

Any job that has defeated two or three men in succession, even though each performed well in his previous assignments, should be deemed unfit for human beings and must be redesigned.

> *Peter Drucker (1909–   )*
> *American business*
> *philosopher and author*

On ships they are called barnacles; in radio they attach themselves to desks and are called vice presidents.

> *Fred Allen (1894–1956)*
> *American comedian*

The longer the title, the less important the job.

> *George McGovern*
> *(1922–　)*
> *American politician*

I don't mind when a private fails to salute me, but he must never forget to salute a second lieutenant.

> *John J. Pershing (1860–*
> *1948)*
> *general, U.S. Army*

Delegating work works, provided the one delegating works, too.

> *Robert Half (1918–　)*
> *American personnel-agency*
> *executive*

"My door is always open—bring me your problems." This is guaranteed to turn on every whiner, lackey and neurotic on the property.

> *Robert F. Six (1907–86)*
> *chairman, Continental*
> *Airlines*

The surest way for an executive to kill himself is to refuse to learn how, and when, and to whom to delegate work.

> *James Cash Penney (1875–*
> *1971)*
> *founder, JC Penney*

Next to doing a good job yourself, the greatest joy is in having someone else do a first-class job under your direction.

> *William Feather (1889–*
> *1981)*
> *American author and*
> *publisher*

The world is divided into people who do things—and people who get the credit.

> *Dwight Morrow (1873–*
> *1931)*
> *American lawyer*

Do you realize the responsibility I carry? I'm the only person standing between Nixon and the White House.

> *John F. Kennedy (1917–63)*
> *35th president of the United*
> *States*

Those who enjoy responsibility usually get it; those who merely like exercising authority usually lose it.

> *Malcolm Forbes (1919–90)*
> *American publisher*

... the easiest course would be for me to blame those to whom I delegated the responsibility.... In any organization the man at the top must bear the responsibility. That responsibility, therefore, belongs here in this office. I accept it.

> *Richard M. Nixon (1913–　)*
> *37th president of the United*
> *States*

I will not provide the rope for my own lynching.

> Clarence Thomas (1948–)
> U.S. Supreme Court justice
> (responding to charges of
> sexual harassment)

There's always room at the top—after the investigation.

> Oliver Herford (1863–1935)
> English writer and
> illustrator

Few things help an individual more than to place responsibility upon him, and to let him know you trust him.

> Booker T. Washington
> (1856–1915)
> American educator

Everyone's responsibility is no one's responsibility.

> Anonymous

The price of greatness is responsibility.

> Winston Churchill (1874–
> 1965)
> British statesman and
> prime minister

There can be no one best way of organizing a business.

> Joan Woodward (1916–71)
> English sociologist

Good organizations are living bodies that grow new muscles to meet challenges. [An organization] chart demoralizes people. Nobody thinks of himself as below other people. And in a good company, he isn't.

> Robert Townsend (1920–)
> American business writer
> and former president,
> Avis-Rent-a-Car, Inc.

In a hierarchy, every employee tends to rise to his level of incompetence.

> Laurence J. Peter (1919–90)
> American author

You don't get the breaks unless you play with the team instead of against it.

> Lou Gehrig (1903–41)
> American professional
> baseball player

Far too much reorganization goes on all the time. Organizitis is like a spastic colon.

> Peter Drucker (1909–)
> American business
> philosopher and author

If my boss calls, get his name.

> Anonymous

No man can serve two masters: for either he will hate the one and love the other; or else he will hold to the one and despise the other.

> Matthew 6:24

Every successful enterprise requires three men—a dreamer, a business-man, and a son-of-a-bitch.

> *Peter McArthur (1866–*
> *1924)*
> *Canadian author*

Be awful nice to 'em goin' up because you're gonna meet 'em all comin' down.

> *Jimmy Durante (1893–1980)*
> *American actor*

Routine is not organization, any more than paralysis is order.

> *Sir Arthur Helps (1813–75)*
> *English author and*
> *historian*

Nothing is particularly hard if you divide it into small jobs.

> *Henry Ford (1863–1947)*
> *American automobile*
> *manufacturer*

Any new venture goes through the following stages: enthusiasm, complication, disillusionment, search for the guilty, punishment of the innocent, and decoration of those who did nothing.

> *Anonymous*

Though this be madness, yet there is method in it.

> *William Shakespeare (1564–*
> *1616)*
> *English dramatist and poet*

An organization chart strangles profits and stifles people.

> *Robert Townsend (1920–   )*
> *American business writer*
> *and former president,*
> *Avis-Rent-a-Car, Inc.*

The system is the solution.

> *American Telephone &*
> *Telegraph advertisement*

Off the system!

> *American student radical,*
> *1968*

As to the EDP function being placed on a higher level in the organization, that's a lot of bullshit. I decide whether I want a washing machine. It's the mechanic's job to keep it running.

> *Peter Drucker (1909–   )*
> *American business*
> *philosopher and author*

The less important you are in the table of organization, the more you'll be missed if you don't turn up for work.

> *Bill Vaughan (1915–77)*
> *American writer and editor*

COMMITTEES

COMMITTEE: *group of people who render decisions or offer advice to management.*

It seems to be generally accepted that a decision made by many is superior to one made by an individual, reflecting the saying that two heads are better than one. Along these lines is the story of the company president who became ill and was admitted to the hospital. The board of directors quickly sent a get-well message wishing him a speedy return to work. At the bottom was the corporate secretary's notation: "Approved by a vote of 6 to 4."

————

Having served on various committees, I have drawn up a list of rules:

1. Never arrive on time; this stamps you as a beginner.
2. Don't say anything until the meeting is half over; this stamps you as being wise.
3. Be as vague as possible; this avoids irritating the others.
4. When in doubt, suggest that a subcommittee be appointed.
5. Be the first one to move for adjournment; this will make you popular; it's what everyone is waiting for.

> *Harry Chapman (1936–   )*
> *U.S. senator*

What is a committee? A group of the unwilling, picked from the unfit, to do the unnecessary.

> *Richard Harkness (1907–   )*
> *American radio-TV*
> *commentator and*
> *journalist*

There's a lot of administration which I'd suggest holds true in almost every situation. That is, if the boss presents his solution first and asks for opinions about it, a vote of approval will follow almost every time.

> *George S. Odiorne*
> *(1920–92)*
> *American educator and*
> *business writer*

I do not rule Russia; ten thousand clerks do.

> *Nicholas I (1796–1855)*
> *czar of Russia*

If you let other people do it for you, they will do it to you.

> *Robert A. Anthony*
> *(1931–   )*
> *American lawyer and*
> *educator*

Meetings are indispensable when you don't want to do anything.

> *John Kenneth Galbraith*
> *(1908–   )*
> *American economist*

No grand idea was ever born in a conference, but a lot of foolish ideas have died there.

> *F. Scott Fitzgerald (1896– 1940)*
> *American author*

I am a great believer, if you have a meeting, in knowing where you want to come out before you start the meeting. Excuse me if that doesn't sound very democratic.

> *Nelson Rockefeller (1908–79)*
> *vice president of the United States*

The first EDSer [Electronic Data Systems employee] to see a snake kills it. At GM, the first thing you do is organize a committee on snakes. Then you bring in a consultant who knows a lot about snakes. Third thing you do is talk about it for a year.

> *H. Ross Perot (1930–)*
> *American computer industry executive and philanthropist*

A committee is a cul-de-sac down which ideas are lured and then quietly strangled.

> *Sir Barnett Cocks (1907–)*
> *English scientist*

If a government commission had worked on the horse, you would have had the first horse who could operate his knee joint in both directions. The only trouble would have been that he couldn't stand up.

> *Peter Drucker (1909–)*
> *American business philosopher and author*

Committee—a group of men who keep minutes and waste hours.

> *Milton Berle (1908–)*
> *American actor and comedian*

I would not join a group which would have me as a member.

> *Groucho Marx (1890–1977)*
> *American actor and comedian*

Outside of traffic, there is nothing that has held this country back as much as committees.

> *Will Rogers (1879–1935)*
> *American actor and humorist*

A camel looks like a horse that was planned by a committee.

> *Anonymous*

If Columbus had had an advisory committee he would probably still be at the dock.

> *Arthur Goldberg (1908–90)*
> *American lawyer and associate justice, U.S. Supreme Court*

If you want to kill any idea in the world, get a committee working on it.

> *Charles F. Kettering (1876–1958)*
> *American electrical engineer and inventor*

Nothing is ever accomplished by committee unless it consists of three members, one of whom happens to be sick and the other absent.

> *Hendrik Van Loon (1892–1944)*
> *American historian and author*

BUREAUCRACY

BUREAUCRACY: *classical approach to organizing, emphasizing a structured, formal network of relationships among specialized positions in an organization characterized by set rules and procedures.*

As a young man, America's most prolific inventor, Thomas Edison, worked as a telegrapher. It was during this time that he first heard the story that later became one of his favorites. "Some linemen were busy putting up telephone poles through a farmer's fields. The farmer presently appeared and ordered them off his land, whereupon they showed him a paper giving them the right to plant poles wherever they pleased. Not long afterward a big and vicious bull charged the linemen, while the old farmer sat on a nearby fence and yelled: "Show him yer papers, darn ya, show him yer papers!"

GUIDELINES FOR BUREAUCRATS

(1) When in charge, ponder.
(2) When in trouble, delegate.
(3) When in doubt, mumble.

> *James H. Boren (1925–   )*
> *president, National Association of Professional Bureaucrats*

Things there are no solutions to: inflation, bureaucracy, and dandruff.

> *Malcolm Forbes (1919–90)*
> *American publisher*

The constable has three sons, two self-sustaining and one employed by the city.

> *Frank McKinney (Kin) Hubbard (1868–1930)*
> *American humorist*

The perfect bureaucrat everywhere is the man who manages to make no decisions and escapes all responsibility.

> *Brooks Atkinson (1894–1984)*
> *American drama critic and essayist*

It is the anonymous "they," the enigmatic "they," who are in charge. Who is "they"? I don't know. Nobody knows. Not even "they" themselves.

> *Joseph Heller (1923–   )*
> *American author*

If you build up a business big enough, it's respectable.

> *Will Rogers (1879–1935)*
> *American actor and*
> *humorist*

General Motors could buy Delaware if Du Pont were willing to sell it.

> *Ralph Nader (1934–   )*
> *American consumer*
> *advocate*

The only thing that saves us from the bureaucracy is its inefficiency.

> *Eugene McCarthy*
> *(1916–   )*
> *U.S. senator*

To grow faster than one is able to manage is flirting with disaster.

> *An Wang (1919–90)*
> *founder, Wang Laboratories*

The dinosaur's eloquent lesson is that if some bigness is good, an overabundance of bigness is not necessarily better.

> *Eric A. Johnston (1895–*
> *1963)*
> *director and president, U.S.*
> *Chamber of Commerce*

I sometimes believe that large corporations are not capable of real innovation. The giants . . . did not become a factor in the semiconductor industry even though they did spend most of the money on early development. They developed a good technical base, but small companies picked that up and made the applications.

> *W. A. Pieczonka*
> *president, Linear*
> *Technologies, Inc.*

The British created a civil service job in 1803 calling for a man to stand on the Cliffs of Dover with a spyglass. He was supposed to ring a bell if he saw Napoleon coming. The job was abolished in 1945.

> *Robert Townsend (1920–   )*
> *American business writer*
> *and former president*
> *Avis-Rent-a-Car, Inc.*

Chapter 10

People

HUMAN RESOURCE MANAGEMENT: *process of evaluating human-resource needs, finding people to fill those needs, and training, developing, motivating, and leading them in an organizational climate conducive to producing maximum employee efficiency and worker satisfaction.*

Job specialization is a familiar contemporary term but, contrary to belief, it does not always imply any particular talent or training, but rather a natural ability to perform the job. One story that is quite illustrative of this concerns a man who was driving down a country road and saw a small child, a girl of about six, leading a huge, hostile-looking bull. He stopped, concerned for her safety, and asked her what she was doing.

"I'm leading the bull down to the pasture to the cow," the little girl replied.

"But can't your father do that?" he asked.

"Nope," she replied flatly, "only the bull."

The person who knows *how* will always have a job. The person who knows *why* will always be his boss.

> *Diane Ravitch (1938–   )*
> *American educator*

The trouble with personnel experts is that they use gimmicks borrowed from manufacturing: recruiting, selecting, indoctrinating and training, machinery, job rotation, and appraisal programs. And this manufacturing of men is about as effective as Dr. Frankenstein was.

> *Robert Townsend (1920–   )*
> *American business writer*
> *and former president,*
> *Avis-Rent-a-Car, Inc.*

There's no way you can have consistent success without players. No one can win without material. But not everyone can win with material.

> *John Wooden (1910–   )*
> *American college basketball*
> *coach*

First-rate people hire first-rate people; second-rate people hire third-rate people.

> *Leo Rosten (1908–   )*
> *American writer*

Hire the best people and then delegate.

> *Carol A. Taber (1945–   )*
> *American magazine*
> *publisher*

The valuable person in any business is the individual who can and will cooperate with others.

> *Elbert Hubbard (1856–*
> *1915)*
> *American writer*

It's not the scarcity of money, but the scarcity of men and talents, which makes a state weak.

> *Voltaire (1694–1778)*
> *French writer*

If I had learned to type, I never would have made brigadier general.

> *Elizabeth P. Hoisington*
> *(1918–   )*
> *brigadier general, U.S.*
> *Army*

All the men on my staff can type.

> *Bella Abzug (1920–   )*
> *American politician*

If Hitler is moving Panzer divisions at you on the European plain, you'd better have some Sherman tanks.

> *Jack Bonner (1948–   )*
> *American lobbyist*

There may be luck in getting a job, but there's no luck in keeping it.

> *J. Ogden Armour (1863–*
> *1927)*
> *president, Armour Meat*
> *Packing Company*

You can dream, create, design, and build the most wonderful place in the world, but it requires people to make the dream a reality.

Walt Disney (1901–66)
American film producer

Treat people as if they were what they ought to be and you help them to become what they are capable of being.

Johann Wolfgang von Goethe
(1749–1832)
German poet and dramatist

Treat employees like partners, and they act like partners.

Fred Allen (1916–   )
chairman, Pitney-Bowes
Company

Sure, luck means a lot in football. Not having a good quarterback is bad luck.

Don Shula (1930–   )
American professional
football coach

Most managements complain about the lack of able people and go outside to fill key positions. Nonsense . . . I use the rule of 50 percent. Try to find somebody inside the company with a record of success (in any area) and with an appetite for the job. If he looks like 50 percent of what you need, give him the job. In six months, he'll have grown the other 50 percent and everybody will be satisfied.

Robert Townsend (1920–   )
American business writer
and former president,
Avis-Rent-a-Car, Inc.

The closest to perfection a person comes is when he fills out a job application form.

Stanley J. Randall
(1908–   )

Everybody looks good on paper.

John Y. Brown (1933–   )
American executive and
former governor of
Kentucky

A résumé is a balance sheet without any liabilities.

Robert Half (1918–   )
American personnel-agency
executive

Neither snow nor rain nor heat nor gloom of night stays these couriers [Persian post-riders] from the swift accomplishment of their appointed rounds.

Herodotus (5th century B.C.)
Greek "Father of History"
(adopted as the motto of
the U.S. Postal Service)

Put your personnel work first because it is the most important.

General Robert E. Wood
(1879–1969)
president, Sears, Roebuck &
Company

Here are all kinds of employers wanting all sorts of servants, and all sorts of servants wanting all kinds of employers, and they never seem to come together.

Charles Dickens (1812–70)
English novelist

You know, I think you and I have some of the same people working for each other.

Nikita Khrushchev (1894–1971)
Soviet premier
(speaking to Central Intelligence Agency director Allen Dulles)

Some people work just hard enough not to get fired, and some companies pay people just enough that they won't quit.

Louis E. Boone (1941–)
American educator and business writer

Fairness, justice, or whatever you call it—it's essential and most companies don't have it. Everybody must be judged on his performance, not on his looks or his manners or his personality or who he knows or is related to.

Robert Townsend (1920–)
American business writer and former president, Avis-Rent-a-Car, Inc.

If you're not a white male, consider sales seriously. Most employers, regardless of how sexist or racist they may be, will pay for any sales they can get. And they care little for the color or gender of the person who brings that business to the firm. Most will be glad to get the business even if it comes from a green, bisexual Martian. And in sales you're usually not exposed to subjective or biased performance appraisal systems. Either you're bringing in the business or you're not.

Ramona E. F. Arnett (1943–)
president, Ramona Enterprises, Inc.

The employer generally gets the employee he deserves.

Sir Walter Gilbey (1831–1914)
English agriculturist

I've met a few people in my time who were enthusiastic about hard work, and it was just my luck that all of them happened to be men I was working for at the time.

Bill Gold (1912–)
American newspaper reporter

WORKING

WORKING: *physical or mental effort or activity directed toward the production or accomplishment of something.*

Offspring of America's most distinguished families frequently find

themselves employed as investment bankers. In *Harrap's Book of Business Anecdotes*, Peter Hay recalls a story from the 1920s in which a Chicago banking firm wrote to a Boston investment banker for a letter of recommendation for a young Bostonian under consideration for a job. The response was immediate, and the Boston firm's letter spelled out that the young man's mother was a Lowell and his father was a Cabot. It also listed other relatives—the Appletons, Peabodys, and Saltonstalls—from among Boston's blue bloods.

The Chicago firm's acknowledgment letter was short, thanking the Boston firm for writing, but pointing out that the letter was not particularly helpful in the employment decision. As they pointed out, "We are not contemplating using the young man for breeding purposes."

In Boston they ask, How much does he know? In New York, How much is he worth? In Philadelphia, Who were his parents?

Mark Twain (1835–1910)
American writer and
humorist

Everyone thinks his sack heaviest.

George Herbert (1593–1633)
English clergyman and poet

Few great men could pass personnel.

Paul Goodman (1911–72)
American author and poet

Work is the curse of the drinking classes.

Oscar Wilde (1854–1900)
Irish poet, playwright, and
novelist

I get quiet joy from the observation of anyone who does his job well.

William Feather (1889–1981)
American author and publisher

In the tiny space of twenty years, we have bred a whole generation of working Americans who take it for granted that they will never be out of a job or go a single year without a salary increase.

Kenneth Keith Duvall (1900–)
American banker

I am a friend of the working man, and I would rather be his friend than be one.

Clarence Darrow (1857–1938)
American lawyer and author

We have a lot of players in their first year. Some of them are also in their last year.

Bill Walsh (1931–)
American professional football coach

Always mistrust a subordinate who never finds fault with his superior.

> *John Churton Collins*
> *(1848–1908)*
> *author and English*
> *professor*

A good horse should be seldom spurred.

> *Thomas Fuller (1608–61)*
> *English clergyman and*
> *author*

I am a true laborer: I earn that I eat, get that I wear, owe no man hate, envy no man's happiness, am glad of other men's good.

> *William Shakespeare (1564–1616)*
> *English dramatist and poet*

. . . it is time that we put aside such labels as "hard hat" and "blue collar" and gave our skilled workers their due—craftsman and craftswoman alike—for the pride they have in their products, their work place, their company, and their country.

> *Thomas A. Murphy*
> *(1915–)*
> *chairman, General Motors*
> *Corporation*

Work is for man and not man for work.

> *Pope John Paul II (1920–)*

A good farmer is nothing more nor less than a handyman with a sense of humor.

> *E. B. White (1899–1985)*
> *American journalist and*
> *writer*

The average male gets his living by such depressing devices that boredom becomes a sort of natural state to him.

> *H. L. Mencken (1880–1956)*
> *American editor*

The real problem is not whether machines think but whether men do.

> *B. F. Skinner (1904–90)*
> *American psychologist*

Times have changed. Forty years ago people worked 12 hours a day and it was called economic security. Now they work 14 hours a day, and it's called moonlighting.

> *Robert Orben (1927–)*
> *American humorist*

COMPENSATION

COMPENSATION: *monetary payments (wages or salaries) and nonmonetary items (goods/commodities, employee benefit programs) used to pay employees or other service providers or to pay for items purchased.*

Dozens of research studies have tried to link workers' levels of job involvement and performance with amounts and types of compensation they receive. Some studies have found that the less involved workers are with the overall performance of the company, the more importance they place on the amount of their wages. This point was clearly made in one instance when a newly elected chairman of a large corporate conglomerate first toured one of his company's steel mills. Several times during the tour he observed a worker running a hand-file over a huge bar of steel. Not wanting to reveal his unfamiliarity with the steel business, the CEO finally inquired of the worker, "What are you making?" Without hesitation the worker replied, "Eight dollars and sixty cents an hour. Why?"

I enjoy being a highly overpaid actor.

Roger Moore (1928–   )
English actor

We're overpaying him, but he's worth it.

Samuel Goldwyn (1882–1974)
American motion-picture producer

People who work sitting down get paid more than people who work standing up.

Ogden Nash (1902–71)
American writer of humorous verse

In the business world, everyone is paid in two coins: cash and experience. Take the experience first; the cash will come later.

Harold S. Geneen (1910–   )
chairman, ITT Corporation

The excellence of a gift lies in its appropriateness rather than in its value.

Charles Dudley Warner (1829–1900)
American editor and writer

A lot of it is the money, but I'd be playing if I was making $150,000.

Reggie Jackson (1946–   )
American baseball player

He is well paid that is well satisfied.

William Shakespeare (1564–1616)
English dramatist and poet

Stock option plans reward the executive for doing the wrong thing. Instead of asking, "Are we making the right decisions?" he asks, "How did we close today?" It is encouragement to loot the corporation.

Peter Drucker (1909–   )
American business philosopher and author

I understand why some American companies fail to gain the loyalty and dedication of their employees. Employees cannot care for an employer who is prepared to take their livelihood away at the first sign of trouble.

Sadami Wada (1932–   )
vice president, Sony of America

Pay peanuts and you get monkeys.

Anonymous

Too much of a good thing can be wonderful.

Mae West (1892–1980)
American actress

Pay your people the least possible and you'll get from them the same.

Malcolm Forbes (1919–90)
American publisher

Every man who takes office in Washington either grows or swells, and when I give a man office I watch him carefully to see whether he is growing or swelling.

Woodrow Wilson (1856–
1924)
28th president of the United
States

Pressed into service means pressed out of shape.

Robert Frost (1874–1963)
American poet

Firing people is unpleasant, but it really has to be done occasionally. . . . Purging the bad performers is as good a tonic for the organization as giving sizable rewards to the star performers.

Robert Townsend (1920–)
American business writer
and former president
Avis-Rent-a-Car, Inc.

It isn't the people you fire who will make your life miserable; it's the people you don't fire.

Harvey MacKay (1933–)
American executive and
business writer

Never hire someone who knows less than you do about what he's (or she's) hired to do.

Malcolm Forbes (1919–90)
American publisher

Always be smarter than the people who hire you.

Lena Horne (1917–)
American singer and actress

Tipping started when gratuities were dropped in a box marked T.I.P.S.— to insure prompt service.

Bertram Theodore Troy
(1932–)
president, Kayser-Roth
Corporation

There are highly successful businesses in the United States. There are also many highly paid executives. The policy is not to intermingle the two.

Philip K. Wrigley (1894–
1977)
American business and
baseball executive

No man can claim to be free unless he has a wage that permits him and his family to live in comfort.

Sidney Hillman (1887–
1946)
American labor leader

Maybe they call it take-home pay because there is no other place you can afford to go with it.

> Franklin P. Jones (1887–
> 1929)
> American lawyer

When I was in college I used to dream of the day when I might be earning the salary I can't get by on now.

> Louis E. Boone (1941–   )
> American educator and
> business writer

INCOMPETENCE

INCOMPETENCE: *state or quality of not being properly or well qualified.*

General Norman Schwarzkopf, head of coalition troops in the 1991 Persian Gulf War, thought very little of the military acumen of his adversary, Saddam Hussein. His summary of Hussein's strategic and tactical abilities left little to the imagination: "He is neither a strategist . . . nor is he a tactician, nor is he a general, nor is he a soldier. Other than that, he's a great military man."

The story goes that once there was a college running back who everyone agreed had the ability to be the best in the business. He was drafted early by the pros. Sadly, he never really performed up to his ability. His coach finally released him in favor of a player who had much less ability. Asked how he could do such a thing, the coach said the decision had been relatively simple: "That man has all the ability in the world, but the one I kept has all the touchdowns."

Organizations cannot make a genius out of an incompetent. On the other hand, disorganization can scarcely fail to result in efficiency.

> Dwight D. Eisenhower
> (1890–1969)
> 34th president of the United
> States

Some men are born mediocre, some men achieve mediocrity, and some men have mediocrity thrust upon them. With Major Major it has been all three.

> Joseph Heller (1923–   )
> American author
> (referring to a
>   character in his 1970
>   novel Catch-22)

A loafer always has the correct time.

> Frank McKinney (Kin)
> Hubbard (1868–1930)
> American humorist

Britain has invented a new missile. It's called the civil servant—it doesn't work and it can't be fired.

> *Sir Walter Walker (1912–   )*
> *British general*

Competence, like truth, beauty, and contact lenses, is in the eye of the beholder.

> *Laurence J. Peter (1919–90)*
> *and Raymond Hull*
> *(1919–85)*
> *American authors of* The
> Peter Principle

He started out at the bottom, and sort of likes it there.

> *Tennessee Ernie Ford*
> *(1919–   )*
> *American singer and*
> *comedian*

In time, every post tends to be occupied by an employee who is incompetent to carry out its duties . . . work is accomplished by those employees who have not yet reached their level of incompetence.

> *Laurence J. Peter (1919–90)*
> *American author*

He was a self-made man who owed his lack of success to nobody.

> *Joseph Heller (1923–   )*
> *American author*

People are rarely fired for incompetence. It's not getting along that's almost always the underlying reason for dismissal.

> *Stuart Margulies (1933–   )*
> *American industrial*
> *psychologist*

Titles distinguish the mediocre, embarrass the superior, and are disgraced by the inferior.

> *George Bernard Shaw*
> *(1856–1950)*
> *British playwright and*
> *social reformer*

The brain is a wonderful organ; it starts working the moment you get up in the morning and doesn't stop until you get into the office.

> *Robert Frost (1874–1963)*
> *American poet*

Doesn't it seem some days as though other people were put in the world for no other reason than to aggravate you?

> *Ed Howe (1853–1937)*
> *American journalist*

There is an enormous number of managers who have retired on the job.

> *Peter Drucker (1909–   )*
> *American business*
> *philosopher and author*

All organizations are at least 50 percent waste—waste people, waste effort, waste space, and waste time.

> *Robert Townsend (1920–   )*
> *American business writer*
> *and former president,*
> *Avis-Rent-a-Car, Inc.*

It isn't the incompetent who destroy an organization. The incompetent never get in a position to destroy it. It is those who have achieved something and want to rest upon their achievements who are forever clogging things up.

> *Charles Sorenson (1881–*
> *1968)*
> *American automobile*
> *manufacturing executive*

Why is it there are so many more horses' asses than there are horses?

> *G. Gordon Liddy (1930–   )*
> *American lawyer and FBI*
> *agent*

The average American thinks he isn't.

> *Anonymous*

UNEMPLOYMENT

UNEMPLOYMENT: *involuntary idleness of people who are actively seeking work.*

After years of rigorous commitment devoted to an education, university students about to graduate begin their job search by sending out résumés and letters of introduction and inquiry. A very high percentage of those attempts are rejected, as evidenced by the students at Arizona's American Graduate School of International Management. They pooled their rejection letters from would-be employers, reviewed them, and then voted on the company that had written the worst rejection letter. Here are excerpts from the five finalists:

- After most careful consideration of your qualifications and background, we are unable to identify anything you can do for us . . .
- We're certain you could be more useful someplace else . . .
- . . . but we're sure you will find something you can do.
- My conscience doesn't allow me to encourage you.
- Unfortunately, we have to be selective. . . .

Have you ever told a coal miner in West Virginia or Kentucky that what he needs is individual initiative to go out and get a job when there isn't any?

> *Robert F. Kennedy*
> *(1925–68)*
> *U.S. senator and attorney general*

A former executive of a company which had been taken over in a corporate merger gave this description of what had happened to his company's executive personnel: "We got the mushroom treatment. Right after the acquisition, we were left in the dark. Then they covered us with manure. Then they cultivated us. After that they let us stew awhile. Finally, they canned us."

> *Isadore Barmash (1921–   )*
> *American writer*

When a great many people are unable to find work, unemployment results.

> *Calvin Coolidge (1872–1933)*
> *30th president of the United States*

The rate of unemployment is 100 percent if it's you who is unemployed.

> *David L. Kurtz (1941–   )*
> *American educator and business writer*

The final solution for unemployment is work.

> *Calvin Coolidge (1872–1933)*
> *30th president of the United States*

If the unemployed could eat plans and promises, they would be able to spend the winter on the Riviera.

> *Anonymous*

A man willing to work, and unable to find work, is perhaps the saddest sign that fortune's inequality exhibits under this sun.

> *Thomas Carlyle (1795–1881)*
> *Scottish essayist and historian*

A lot of fellows nowadays have a B.A., M.D., or Ph.D. Unfortunately, they don't have a J.O.B.

> *Antoine "Fats" Domino (1928–   )*
> *American singer*

LABOR AND LABOR UNIONS

LABOR UNION: *employee organization that represents its members in employee-management bargaining about job-related issues such as compensation and working conditions.*

The following conversation took place between a Ford Motor Company official and the late United Auto Workers president Walter Reuther. The Ford official was escorting Reuther through an ultramodern auto plant. He stopped, pointed toward several robots, and turned to the UAW president and said, "How are you union people going to collect union dues from these guys?" Reuther answered, "How are you going to get them to buy Fords?"

Fairness and decency for American workers means more than simply keeping them alive and safe from injury and disease. It means an effort to make it possible for workers to live not just as robots or machines, but as men and women who are human beings. Additionally, making the assembly line more human and humane is a large and difficult task, but it is at the heart of everything we mean by social justice in America.

> *Edward M. Kennedy (1932–   )*
> *U.S. senator*

Back in the 1930's the unions were like a 21-year-old woman. She was beautiful, and had a gorgeous body, a sparkling personality, and she seduced a lot of people into the union movement. That's fine. The problem is that this twenty-one-year-old siren is now in her 60's and she's forty pounds overweight, needs a face lift, and has a terrible disposition.... The difficulty is that she still thinks she's 21.

> *Eric Hoffer (1902–83)*
> *American longshoreman*
> *and philosopher*

There is no right to strike against the public safety by anybody, anywhere, any time.

> *Calvin Coolidge (1872–1933)*
> *30th president of the United States*

Labor disgraces no man; unfortunately, you occasionally find men disgrace labor.

> *Ulysses S. Grant (1822–85)*
> *18th president of the United States*

We're supposed to be perfect our first day on the job, and then show constant improvement.

> *Ed Vargo (1923–   )*
> *American major-league*
> *baseball umpire*

Men have become the tools of their tools.

Henry David Thoreau
(1817–62)
American naturalist and
writer

And I'm convinced, beyond a shadow of a doubt, that you can work with the unions because the unions want to survive. If they are confronted simply with the question: "Do you want this company to survive or do you want it to be broken up?" they will listen. It's their livelihood.

Carl Icahn (1936–   )
CEO, Trans World Airlines

The biggest tragedy in America is not the waste of natural resources, though this is tragic. The biggest tragedy is the waste of human resources.

Oliver Wendell Holmes
(1809–94)
American physician and
author

The proletarians have nothing to lose but their chains. They have a world to win. Workers of the world, unite!

Karl Marx (1818–83) and
Friedrich Engels
(1820–95)
German political
philosophers

It is but a truism that labor is most productive where its wages are largest. Poorly paid labor is inefficient labor, the world over.

Henry George, Sr.
(1839–97)
American economist

Labor unions are the worst thing that ever struck the earth because they take away a man's independence.

Henry Ford (1863–1947)
American automobile
manufacturer

Management and union may be likened to that serpent of the fables who on one body had two heads that fighting each other with poisoned fangs killed themselves.

Peter Drucker (1909–   )
American business
philosopher and author

Chapter 11

Succeeding in a Competitive World

COMPETITION: *contest between rivals; the battle among business and nonprofit organizations for consumer acceptance.*

One day while hiking in the country two young boys came across a grizzly bear. One boy was understandably frightened, but he immediately sat down to put his sneakers back on so he could run from the bear. His companion, however, did not follow suit, but stood there and matter-of-factly said, "We've had it! I've read all there is to read about grizzly bears, and no man alive can outrun a grizzly." The first kid looked up and said, "I don't care about outrunning the bear. I just want to outrun you!"

When elephants fight, only the grass gets hurt.

> *Swahili proverb*

Most of our competitors were manufacturing-oriented, generations of fine pickle makers and proud of it. We came in exactly the opposite, as marketers who manufactured [in order] to have something to sell.

> *Robert J. Vlasic (1926–   )*
> *president, Vlasic Foods*

The underdog in many products . . . can pick and choose where it wants to hit the giant; the giant, by contrast, must defend itself everywhere.

> *George H. Lesch (1909–   )*
> *president, Colgate-Palmolive*
> *Company*

All wars are popular for the first thirty days.

> *Arthur Schlesinger, Jr.*
> *(1917–   )*
> *American author and*
> *historian*

Nobody talks more of free enterprise and competition and of the best man winning than the man who inherited his father's store or farm.

> *C. Wright Mills (1916–62)*
> *American sociologist*

Praises from an enemy imply real merit.

> *Thomas Fuller (1654–1734)*
> *English physician and*
> *writer*

The object of war is not to die for your country but to make the other bastard die for his.

> *George S. Patton (1885–*
> *1945)*
> *general, U.S. Army*

High pay does not equal good service, and, as McDonald's has shown, low pay need not result in poor service. . . . High-quality service depends on high-quality management. If U.S. providers fail to learn this lesson, they should not be surprised if Americans have accounts at Japanese banks, fly Singapore Airlines, or eat in French-owned restaurants.

> *Robert E. Kelley (1938–   )*
> *American educator*

We were fairly arrogant, until we realized the Japanese were selling quality products for what it cost us to make them.

> *Paul A. Allaire (1938–   )*
> *president, Xerox*
> *Corporation*

The hardest thing is to take less when you can get more.

> *Frank McKinney (Kin)*
> *Hubbard (1868–1930)*
> *American humorist*

I want this team to win, I'm obsessed with winning, with discipline, with achieving. That's what this country's all about.

> *George Steinbrenner*
> *(1930–   )*
> *American executive*
> *owner, New York Yankees*
> *professional baseball club*

We're eyeball to eyeball, and the other fellow just blinked.

> *Dean Rusk (1909–   )*
> *U.S. secretary of state*
> *(referring to Soviet prime minister Nikita Khrushchev's response to the U.S. naval blockade during the 1962 Cuban Missile Crisis)*

A man cannot be too careful in the choice of his enemies.

> *Oscar Wilde (1854–1900)*
> *Irish poet, playwright, and novelist*

The meek shall inherit the earth . . . but the strong shall retain the mineral rights.

> *Anonymous*

There are days when it takes all you've got just to keep up with the losers.

> *Robert Orben (1927–   )*
> *American humorist*

Forgive your enemies, but never forget their names.

> *John F. Kennedy (1917–63)*
> *35th president of the United States*

Always forgive your enemies—nothing annoys them so much.

> *Oscar Wilde (1854–1900)*
> *Irish poet, playwright, and novelist*

The man who is swimming against the stream knows the strength of it.

> *Woodrow Wilson (1856–1924)*
> *28th president of the United States*

Better make a weak man your enemy than your friend.

> *Josh Billings (1818–85)*
> *American humorist*

Whatever is not nailed down is mine. Whatever I can pry loose is not nailed down.

> *Ascribed to Collis P. Huntington (1821–1900)*
> *American railroad magnate*

War hath no fury like a noncombatant.

> *C. E. Montague (1867–1928)*
> *British journalist*

They Tore Out My Heart and Stomped That Sucker Flat

> *book title by Lewis Grizzard (1946–   )*
> *American humorist*

Competition, you know, is a lot like chastity. It is widely praised, but alas, too little practiced.

> *Carol Tucker (1943–   )*
> *American agricultural official*

If you can't stand the heat, get out of the kitchen.

> Harry S Truman (1884–1972)
> 33rd president of the United States

The business system is blessed with a built-in corrective, namely, that one executive's mistake becomes his competitor's assets.

> Leo Cherne (1912–   )
> American economist and humanitarian

In business, the competition will bite you if you keep running; if you stand still, they will swallow you.

> William Knudsen, Jr. (1925–   )
> chairman, Ford Motor Company

Live together like brothers and do business like strangers.

> Arabic proverb

The enemy advances, we retreat; the enemy camps, we harass; the enemy tires, we attack; the enemy retreats; we pursue.

> Mao Tse-tung (1893–1976)
> Chinese Communist leader of People's Republic of China

Carry the battle to them. Don't let them bring it to you. Put them on the defensive. And don't ever apologize for anything.

> Harry S Truman (1884–1972)
> 33rd president of the United States

Men, all this stuff you have heard about America not wanting to fight, wanting to stay out of the war, is a lot of horse dung. Americans, traditionally, love to fight. All real Americans love the sting of battle. When you were kids, you all admired the champion marble shooter, the fastest runner, the big-league ball player, the toughest boxer. Americans love a winner and will not tolerate a loser. Americans play to win all the time. I wouldn't give a hoot in hell for a man who lost and laughed. That's why Americans have never lost—and will never lose—a war, because the very thought of losing is hateful to Americans.

> George C. Scott (1926–   )
> American actor in Franklin Schaffner's 1970 motion picture Patton

Show me a good loser and I'll show you a loser.

> Anonymous

Show me a good and gracious loser, and I'll show you a failure.

> Knute Rockne (1888–1931)
> American college football coach

You can discover what your enemy fears most by observing the means he uses to frighten you.

> Eric Hoffer (1902–83)
> American longshoreman
> and philosopher

A difference of opinion is what makes horse racing and missionaries.

> Will Rogers (1879–1935)
> American actor and
> humorist

The race may not be to the swift nor the victory to the strong, but that's how you bet.

> Damon Runyon (1884–
> 1946)
> American author

What counts is not necessarily the size of the dog in the fight—it's the size of the fight in the dog.

> Dwight D. Eisenhower
> (1890–1969)
> 34th president of the United
> States

Don't wrestle with pigs; you get dirty and they enjoy it.

> Anonymous

WINNING

WINNING: *achieving success in an effort or venture; achieving victory over others in a competition.*

Eddie Erdelatz coached the Midshipmen, the varsity football team at the U.S. Naval Academy during the 1950s. When his team played its chief rival West Point to a 7–7 tie, Erdelatz was asked his reaction. "A tie game," he replied, "is like kissing your sister."

If winning isn't important, why do they keep score?

> Adolph Rupp (1901–77)
> American basketball coach

When you win, nothing hurts.

> Joe Namath (1943–)
> American football star

I never lost a game. I just ran out of time.

> Bobby Layne (1926–86)
> American professional
> football player

Nobody remembers who came in second.

> Charles Schulz (1922–)
> American cartoonist

I don't meet competition. I crush it.

> *Charles Revson (1906–75)*
> *chairman, Revlon, Inc.*

You're a hero when you win and a bum when you lose. That's the game.

> *Johnny Unitas (1933–)*
> *American professional*
> *football player*

Victory goes to the player who makes the next-to-last mistake.

> *Savielly Grigorievitch*
> *Tartakower (1837–1956)*
> *International Grand Master*
> *of Chess*

To finish first you must first finish.

> *Rick Mears (1951–)*
> *American race-car driver*

There is no finish line.

> *Nike Corporation motto*

If you think you can win, you can win. Faith is necessary to victory.

> *William Hazlitt (1778–1830)*
> *English essayist and critic*

It is better to lose the saddle than the horse.

> *Italian proverb*

People are always neglecting something they can do in trying to do something they can't do.

> *Ed Howe (1853–1937)*
> *American journalist*

War is a series of catastrophes that results in a victory.

> *Georges Clemenceau (1841–*
> *1929)*
> *French statesman*

Another such victory over the Romans and we are undone.

> *Plutarch (A.D. ca. 46–120)*
> *Greek biographer and*
> *moralist*

Glory is fleeting, but obscurity is forever.

> *Napoleon Bonaparte (1769–*
> *1821)*
> *emperor of France*

Every time you win, you're reborn; when you lose, you die a little.

> *George Allen (1922–)*
> *American college and*
> *professional football*
> *coach*

In a negotiation, he who cares less, wins.

> *Anonymous*

If you're going to be a bridge, you've got to be prepared to be walked upon.

> *Roy A. West (1932–)*
> *American educator*

If you are planning on doing business with someone again, don't be too tough in the negotiations. If you're going to skin a cat, don't keep it as a housecat.

> *Marvin S. Levin (1915–   )*
> *American financier*

Nice guys finish last.

> *Leo Durocher (1906–91)*
> *American professional*
> *baseball manager*

Let us never negotiate out of fear. But let us never fear to negotiate.

> *John F. Kennedy (1917–63)*
> *35th president of the United*
> *States*

Whoever said, "It's not whether you win or lose that counts," probably lost.

> *Martina Navratilova*
> *(1956–   )*
> *American tennis champion*

SUCCESS AND FAILURE

SUCCESS: *favorable completion of an endeavor.*

FAILURE: *condition or fact of not achieving the desired end.*

Few great leaders encountered defeats so consistently before enjoying ultimate victory as did this individual. A frequently reported listing of these failures includes the following:

Failed in business in 1831
Ran for the legislature and lost in 1832

Failed once again in business in 1834
Sweetheart died in 1835
Had a nervous breakdown in 1836
Lost a second political race in 1838
Defeated for Congress in 1843
Defeated for Congress in 1846
Defeated for Congress in 1848
Defeated for U.S. Senate in 1855
Defeated for Vice President in 1856
Defeated for U.S. Senate in 1858

The man was Abraham Lincoln, elected sixteenth president of the United States in 1860.

Notice the difference between what happens when a man says to himself, "I have failed three times," and what happens when he says, "I am a failure."

> *S. I. Hayakawa (1906–92)*
> *American semanticist and*
> *U.S. senator*

The minute you start talking about what you're going to do if you lose, you have lost.

> *George P. Shultz (1920–   )*
> *American industrialist and*
> *U.S. secretary of state*

The trouble with the rat race is that even if you win, you're still a rat.

> *Lily Tomlin (1939–   )*
> *American actress and*
> *comedienne*

If at first you don't succeed, try, try again. Then quit. There's no use being a damn fool about it.

> *W. C. Fields (1880–1946)*
> *American actor and*
> *comedian*

About the meanest thing you can say about a man is that he means well.

> *Harry S Truman (1884–*
> *1972)*
> *33rd president of the United*
> *States*

My formula for success? Rise early, work late, strike oil.

> *Jean Paul Getty (1892–*
> *1976)*
> *American oil magnate and*
> *philanthropist*

I don't know the key to success, but the key to failure is trying to please everybody.

> *Bill Cosby (1937–   )*
> *American actor and*
> *comedian*

The only way to succeed is to make people hate you.

> *Josef Von Sternberg (1894–*
> *1969)*
> *Austrian film director*

To succeed, it is necessary to accept the world as it is and rise above it.

> *Michael Korda (1933–   )*
> *American publishing*
> *executive and author*

Success is counted sweetest
By those who ne'er succeed.

> *Emily Dickinson (1830–86)*
> *American poet*

Some men succeed by what they know; some by what they do; and a few by what they are.

> *Elbert Hubbard (1856–*
> *1915)*
> *American writer*

Most of the trouble with most people in America who become successful is that they can really and truly get by on bullshit alone. They can survive on it.

> *Sammy Davis, Jr. (1925–90)*
> *American actor*

There is only one success—to be able to spend your life in your own way.

> *Christopher Morley (1890–*
> *1957)*
> *American writer*

Superior people never make long visits.

> *Marianne Moore (1887–*
> *1972)*
> *American poet*

The most important single ingredient in the formula of success is knowing how to get along with people.

> *Theodore Roosevelt (1858–1919)*
> *26th president of the United States*

Gross national product is our holy grail.

> *Stewart Udall (1920–   )*
> *U.S. secretary of the interior*

The toughest thing about success is that you've got to keep on being a success.

> *Irving Berlin (1888–1989)*
> *American composer*

Failure is never final and success is never-ending. Success is a journey, not a destination.

> *Dr. Robert Schuller (1926–   )*
> *American evangelist*

Success to me is having ten honeydew melons and eating only the top half of each one.

> *Barbra Streisand (1942–   )*
> *American actress and singer*

Success is never final.

> *Winston Churchill (1874–1965)*
> *British statesman and prime minister*

All you need in this life is ignorance and confidence, and then success is sure.

> *Mark Twain (1835–1910)*
> *American author*

Success is that old ABC—ability, breaks, and courage.

> *Charles Luckman (1909–   )*
> *American architect*

One must be a god to be able to tell successes from failures without making a mistake.

> *Anton Chekhov (1860–1904)*
> *Russian author*

Success generally depends upon knowing how long it takes to succeed.

> *Montesquieu (1689–1755)*
> *French lawyer and political philosopher*

To succeed in business it is necessary to make others see things as you see them.

> *John H. Patterson (1844–1922)*
> *founder, National Cash Register Company*

Success is simply a matter of luck. Ask any failure.

> *Earl Wilson (1907–87)*
> *American newspaper columnist*

The successful man is the one who has lived well, laughed often, and loved a great deal.

> *Arthur J. Stanley (1901–   )*
> *American jurist*

The first step towards success in any occupation is to become interested in it.

> *Sir William Osler (1849–1919)*
> *Canadian physician*

Too often it's not the most creative guys or the smartest. Instead, it's the ones who are best at playing politics and soft-soaping their bosses. Boards don't like tough, abrasive guys.

> *Carl Icahn (1936–   )*
> *CEO, Trans World Airlines*

The man who will use his skill and constructive imagination to see how much he can give for a dollar instead of how little he can give for a dollar is bound to succeed.

> *Henry Ford (1863–1947)*
> *American automobile manufacturer*

Ability is nothing without opportunity.

> *Napoleon Bonaparte (1769–1821)*
> *emperor of France*

Failure! There is no such word in all the bright lexicon of speech, unless you yourself have written it there! There is no such thing as failure except to those who accept and believe in failure.

> *Orison Swett Marden (1906–75)*
> *American lawyer*

There is the greatest practical benefit in making a few failures early in life.

> *Thomas H. Huxley (1825–95)*
> *English biologist*

There is no such thing as accident; it is fate renamed.

> *Napoleon Bonaparte (1769–1821)*
> *emperor of France*

It is a bad bargain where both are losers.

> *Anonymous*

The worst-tempered people I've ever met were the people who knew they were wrong.

> *Wilson Mizner (1876–1933)*
> *American author*

Wise men learn by other men's mistakes, fools by their own.

> *Anonymous*

In the depth of winter, I finally learned that within me there lay an invincible summer.

> *Albert Camus (1913–60)*
> *French novelist, essayist, and dramatist*

It takes less time to do a thing right than it does to explain why you did it wrong.

> *Henry Wadsworth Longfellow (1807–82)*
> *American poet*

Alas: early Victorian for *Oh, hell.*

> *Oliver Herford (1863–1935)*
> *English writer and illustrator*

RISK

RISK: *uncertainty regarding loss or injury or the outcome of an investment.*

William Randolph Hearst built the world's largest publishing empire of the late 1800s and early 1900s, consisting of nine magazines and eighteen newspapers in twelve cities. He was well known for buying distinctive talent and encouraging defections by employees of other papers through offers of high salaries and added prestige. True to his reputation, Hearst offered one of his best columnists, Arthur Brisbane, a six-month sabbatical, all expenses paid, in appreciation for his outstanding work. Surprisingly, Brisbane declined the offer. Hearst couldn't believe it and asked him why.

"First of all, I'm afraid," the journalist reasoned, "that if I quit for six months, the circulation of your newspapers may go down. And secondly, I'm afraid that it may not."

Capitalism without bankruptcy is like Christianity without hell.

> *Frank Borman (1928–   )*
> *American astronaut and business executive*

You can only become a winner if you are willing to walk over the edge.

> *Ronald E. McNair*
> *(1950–86)*
> *American astronaut*
> *(died in* Challenger *space shuttle explosion)*

In all human affairs, the odds are always six to five against.

> *Damon Runyon (1884–1946)*
> *American author*

I never gamble.

> *John Pierpont Morgan (1837–1913)*
> *American financier*

Take calculated risks. That is quite different from being rash.

> George S. Patton (1885–1945)
> general, U.S. Army

When in doubt, risk it.

> Holbrook Jackson (1874–1948)
> English journalist, editor, and author

I don't care how many boats I miss. I just don't want to catch the one that sinks me.

> Carl R. Pohlad (1915–   )
> chairman, MEI Corporation

Nine gamblers could not feed a single rooster.

> Yugoslav proverb

I want a priest, a rabbi, and a Protestant clergyman. I want to hedge my bets.

> Wilson Mizner (1876–1933)
> American author

We learn wisdom from failure much more than from success; we often discover what we will do by finding out what we will not do; and probably he who never made a mistake never made a discovery.

> Samuel Smiles (1812–1904)
> Scottish author

No one tests the depth of a river with both feet.

> Ashanti proverb

The gambling known as business looks with austere disfavor upon the business known as gambling.

> Ambrose Bierce (1842–ca. 1914)
> American author

Don't be afraid to take a big step. You can't cross a chasm in two small jumps.

> David Lloyd George (1863–1945)
> British statesman and prime minister

Being on the tightrope is living; everything else is waiting.

> Karl Wallenda (1905–78)
> American aerialist and circus performer

Unless you enter the tiger's den, you cannot take the cubs.

> Japanese proverb

Security is mostly a superstition. It does not exist in nature.... Life is either a daring adventure or nothing.

> Helen Keller (1880–1968)
> American essayist and lecturer

It is easy to be brave when far away from danger.

> Aesop (ca. 620–ca. 560 B.C.)
> Greek fabulist

Without risks we're all caretakers, and you can get a caretaker for very little money. . . . A leader has to have the vision that will let him take 2 and 2 and make 5.

> *Leonard N. Stern (1938–   )*
> *American corporate*
> *executive*

If you don't have some bad loans you are not in business.

> *Paul Volcker (1927–   )*
> *American economist and*
> *chairman, Federal*
> *Reserve System*

Behold the turtle. He makes progress only when he sticks his neck out.

> *James Bryant Conant*
> *(1893–1978)*
> *American chemist and*
> *educator*

He who can lick can bite.

> *French proverb*

Success tends to go not to the person who is error-free, because he also tends to be risk-averse. Rather it goes to the person who recognizes that life is pretty much a percentage business. It isn't making mistakes that's critical; it's correcting them and getting on with the principal task.

> *Donald Rumsfeld (1932–   )*
> *American pharmaceutical*
> *executive and U.S.*
> *secretary of defense*

The greatest mistake you can make in life is to be continually fearing you will make one.

> *Elbert G. Hubbard (1856–*
> *1915)*
> *American writer*

The man who insists upon seeing with perfect clearness before he decides, never decides. Accept life and you must accept regret.

> *Henri Frédéric Amiel*
> *(1821–81)*
> *Swiss philosopher and poet*

He that leaveth nothing to chance will do few things ill, but he will do very few things.

> *George Savile (1633–95)*
> *Marquis of Halifax*
> *English politician and*
> *essayist*

A little uncertainty is good for everything.

> *Henry Kissinger (1923–   )*
> *American scholar and U.S.*
> *secretary of state*

The better the gambler, the worse the man.

> *Publilius Syrus (1st century*
> *B.C.)*
> *Latin writer of mimes*

One throw of the dice will never abolish chance.

> *Stéphane Mallarmé*
> *(1842–98)*
> *French poet*

Most of us would rather risk catastrophe than read the directions.

> *Mignon McLaughlin*
> *(1918–   )*
> *American writer*

To win you have to risk loss.

> *Jean-Claude Killy (1943–   )*
> *French professional skier*

If you bet a horse, that's gambling. If you bet you can make three spades, that's entertainment. If you bet cotton will go up three points, that's business. See the difference?

> *William F. (Blackie)*
> *Sherrod (1920–   )*
> *American sportswriter*

Part III

KEYS TO BUSINESS SUCCESS

Chapter 12

Production Quality and Efficiency

PRODUCTION: *use of people and machinery to convert materials and resources into finished goods and services.*

Henry Ford's first inklings of the benefits and rewards of mass production came at an early age. After running away from home, Ford worked in a machine shop. He saved enough money to buy a three-dollar watch and immediately took it apart. Pricing each part, Ford deduced that if thousands of watches could be made exactly the same, the unit cost of the entire watch would be a mere thirty-seven cents. Even adding marketing expenses and a profit, the final price would be low enough to make it affordable for almost everyone. Ford later used the same philosophy in manufacturing automobiles, concluding that "anything that isn't good for everybody is no good at all." When he built his first horseless carriage in 1893, the price tag was nine thousand dollars. Every piece of the automobile was hand-designed, and the emphasis was on high prices for limited production runs.

Ford remembered his early experience with the watch and knew that the same approach would also work for automobiles. By turning to mass production, he could push down the costs and earn small profits on each car sold at a price that would fit the budget of most families. By 1908, his Model T carried a price tag of $850. In 1926, the price had dropped to $284. By that time, nearly 15 million Model T's had been sold, and the automobile had been converted from a plaything of the rich to a replacement of the horse for the public.

Don't tell me how hard you work. Tell me how much you get done.

> *James Ling (1922–   )*
> *American business*
> *executive*

The difficult we do at once; the impossible takes a bit longer.

> *inscription on the memorial*
> *to the SeaBees*
> *(U.S. Naval Construction*
> *Battalions)*

My father worked for the same firm for twelve years. They fired him. They replaced him with a tiny gadget this big. It does everything that my father does, only much better. The depressing thing is my mother ran out and bought one.

> *Woody Allen (1935–   )*
> *American actor, film*
> *director, and comedian*

It used to be that people needed products to survive. Now products need people to survive.

> *Nicholas Johnson (1934–   )*
> *American lecturer and*
> *writer*

Competition brings out the best in products and the worst in people.

> *David Sarnoff (1891–1971)*
> *American communications-*
> *industry pioneer, founder*
> *and president of RCA*

THE LAWS OF ROBOTICS

1. A robot may not injure a human being, or through inaction allow a human being to come to harm.
2. A robot must obey the orders given it by human beings, except where such orders would conflict with the First Law.
3. A robot must protect its own existence as long as such protection does not conflict with the First and Second Laws.

> *Isaac Asimov (1920–92)*
> *American novelist*

Every solution breeds new problems.
Every clarification breeds new questions.
A fail-safe circuit will destroy others.
If you improve or tinker with something long enough, eventually it will break malfunction.
A failure will not appear until a unit has passed final inspection.
Enough research will tend to support your conclusions.
After an instrument has been assembled, extra components will be found on the work bench.

> *Arthur Bloch (1882–1953)*
> *American merchant*

It costs me a dollar to make my product, and I can sell all I care to make for four dollars apiece. You just wouldn't believe the profit there is in that three percent.

Anonymous

Seek simplicity and distrust it.

*Alfred North Whitehead
(1861–1947)
English mathematician and
philosopher*

Large increases in cost with questionable increases in performance can be tolerated only for race horses and fancy women.

*William Thomson, Lord
Kelvin (1824–1907)
English scientist; president
of the Royal Society*

You can hype a questionable product for a little while, but you'll never build an enduring business.

*Victor Kiam (1926–   )
CEO, Remington Products,
Inc.*

Junk is the ultimate merchandise. The junk merchant does not sell his product to the consumer, he sells the consumer to the product. He does not improve and simplify his merchandise, he degrades and simplifies the client.

*William Burroughs
(1914–   )
American writer*

Every production must resemble its author.

*Miguel de Cervantes (1547–
1616)
Spanish writer*

Product testing should not be the basis for introducing a new product because 90 percent of the failures have had successful product test results.

*Richard H. Buskirk
(1927–   )
American educator*

The U.S. will not solve the competitiveness problem until it again becomes the place where the most advanced, highest quality goods and services are produced by the most skilled workers using the most advanced methods.

*Michael E. Porter (1947–   )
American educator*

Production is not the application of tools to materials, but logic to work.

*Peter Drucker (1909–   )
American business
philosopher and author*

It is not the employer who pays wages. He only handles the money. It is the product that pays wages and it is the management that arranges the production so that the product may pay the wages.

*Henry Ford (1863–1947)
American automobile
manufacturer*

Production is the goose that lays the golden egg. Payrolls make consumers.

> George Humphrey (1890–
> 1970)
> American industrialist and
> U.S. secretary of the
> treasury

Man produces in order to consume.

> Claude-Frédéric Bastiat
> (1801–50)
> French economist

One cannot walk through a mass-production factory and not feel that one is in hell.

> Wystan Hugh Auden
> (1907–73)
> American poet

As we all know, there ain't no Santa Claus. We're in a new day and age, and the public is demanding the best product at the lowest possible price. We are in a continuous fare war.

> Frank Lorenzo (1940–   )
> American airline-industry
> executive

The most popular labor-saving device today is still a husband with money.

> Joey Adams (1911–   )
> American comedian

You can't sell from an empty wagon.

> William Dillard (1914–   )
> founder and chairman,
> Dillard's department
> stores

Growth that adds volume without improving productivity is fat. Growth that diminishes productivity is cancer.

> Peter Drucker (1909–   )
> American business
> philosopher and author

Energy is beauty—a Ferrari with an empty tank doesn't run.

> Elsa Peretti (1940–   )
> American model and
> designer

When you turn the lights off we like to think you can't tell the difference between an Econo Lodge and a Hilton.

> Ben Douglas (1935–   )
> president, Econo Lodge
> hotel chain

QUALITY

QUALITY CONTROL: *measurement of goods and services against established standards of excellence.*

When Mikhail Gorbachev was chosen general secretary of the Communist party in 1985, he was the youngest member of the Politburo and signaled a change in Soviet leadership and economic, political, and social reforms. In an effort to increase the production and sale of Soviet products, Gorbachev emphasized the importance of better planning as a means of improving quality. To make his point quite clear, he authorized an exhibition of shoddy and defective goods produced by Soviet workers, including a whole consignment of boots with high heels attached to the toes.

The quality of a person's life is in direct proportion to their commitment to excellence, regardless of their chosen field of endeavor.

> *Vince Lombardi (1913–70)*
> *American professional*
> *football coach*

Excellence and size are fundamentally incompatible.

> *Robert Townsend (1920–)*
> *American business writer*
> *and former president,*
> *Avis-Rent-a-Car, Inc.*

It is a funny thing about life; if you refuse to accept anything but the best, you very often get it.

> *Somerset Maugham*
> *(1874–1965)*
> *English novelist and*
> *dramatist*

Anybody can cut prices, but it takes brains to make a better article.

> *Philip D. Armour*
> *(1832–1901)*
> *American industrialist*

People forget how fast you did a job —but they remember how well you did it.

> *Howard W. Newton*
> *(1903–51)*
> *American advertising*
> *executive*

If you don't do it excellently, don't do it at all. Because if it's not excellent, it won't be profitable or fun, and if you're not in business for fun or profit, what the hell are you doing there?

> *Robert Townsend (1920–)*
> *American business writer*
> *and former president,*
> *Avis-Rent-a-Car, Inc.*

WORK

WORK: *exertion or effort directed to producing or accomplishing something.*

———

My father taught me to work; he did not teach me to love it. I never did like to work, and I don't deny it. I'd rather read, tell stories, crack jokes, talk, laugh—anything but work.

> *Abraham Lincoln (1809–65)*
> *16th president of the United States*

The only place where success comes before work is in the dictionary.

> *Vidal Sassoon (1928–   )*
> *American hairstylist*

When I work I relax; doing nothing or entertaining visitors makes me tired.

> *Pablo Picasso (1881–1973)*
> *Spanish painter and sculptor*

We always admire the other fellow more after we have tried to do his job.

> *William Feather (1889–1981)*
> *American author and publisher*

Making play of the term *work,* when asked, "How many people work for you?" management quips, "Nearly half."

Of all the damnable waste of human life that ever was invented, clerking is the very worst.

> *George Bernard Shaw (1856–1950)*
> *British playwright and social reformer*

It's no credit to anyone to work too hard.

> *Ed Howe (1853–1937)*
> *American journalist*

The world is full of willing people, some willing to work, the rest willing to let them.

> *Robert Frost (1874–1963)*
> *American poet*

It is not enough to be busy; so are the ants. The question is: What are we busy about?

> *Henry David Thoreau (1817–62)*
> *American naturalist and writer*

Never mistake motion for action.

> *Ernest Hemingway (1899–1961)*
> *American writer and journalist*

You can't pick cherries with your back to the tree.

> *John Pierpont Morgan*
> *(1837–1913)*
> *American financier*

If you have two jobs and you're rich, you have diversified interests. If you have two jobs and you're poor, you're moonlighting.

> *Anonymous*

I never did anything worth doing by accident, nor did any of my inventions come by accident; they came by work.

> *Thomas Edison (1847–1931)*
> *American inventor*

Going to work for a large company is like getting on a train. Are you going sixty miles an hour, or is the train going sixty miles an hour and you're just sitting still?

> *Jean Paul Getty (1892–*
> *1976)*
> *American oil magnate and*
> *philanthropist*

EIGHT RULES FOR OFFICE WORKERS IN 1872

1. Office employees each day will fill lamps, clean chimneys, and trim wicks. Wash windows once a week.
2. Each clerk will bring in a bucket of water and a scuttle of coal for the day's business.
3. Make your pens carefully. You may whittle nibs to your individual taste.
4. Men employees will be given an evening off each week for courting purposes, or two evenings a week if they go regularly to church.
5. After thirteen hours of labor in the office, the employee should spend remaining time reading the Bible and other good books.
6. Every employee should lay aside from each pay day a goodly sum of his earnings for his benefit during his declining years so that he will not become a burden on society.
7. Any employee who smokes Spanish cigars, uses liquor in any form, or frequents pool and public halls or gets shaved in a barber shop, will give good reason to suspect his worth, intentions, integrity, and honesty.
8. The employee who has performed his labor faithfully and without fault for five years, will be given an increase of five cents per day in his pay, providing profits from business permit it.

> *Anonymous*

Farming looks mighty easy when your plow is a pencil and you're a thousand miles from a cornfield.

> *Dwight D. Eisenhower*
> *(1890–1969)*
> *34th president of the United*
> *States*

About the only thing on a farm that has an easy time is the dog.

> *Ed Howe (1853–1937)*
> *American journalist*

When you have a number of disagreeable duties to perform always do the most disagreeable first.

> *Josiah Quincy (1744–75)*
> *American lawyer*

If you want work well done, select a busy man; the other kind has no time.

> Elbert Hubbard (1856–1915)
> American writer

Amateurs hope. Professionals work.

> Garson Kanin (1912–   )
> American dramatist and theatrical director

Work is love made visible. And if you cannot work with love but only with distaste, it is better that you should leave your work and sit at the gate of the temple and take alms of those who work with joy.

> Kahlil Gibran (1883–1931)
> Lebanese novelist, poet, and artist

Work expands so as to fill the time available for its completion. General recognition of this fact is shown in the proverbial phrase, "It is the busiest man who has time to spare."

> C. Northcote Parkinson (1909–   )
> British historian and philosopher

Nobody works as hard for his money as the man who marries it.

> Frank McKinney (Kin) Hubbard (1868–1930)
> American humorist

Robinson Crusoe started the 40-hour week. He had all the work done by Friday.

> Leopold Fechtner (1916–   )

Nothing is really work unless you would rather be doing something else.

> James Matthew Barrie (1860–1937)
> Scottish novelist and dramatist

The man who does not work for the love of work, but only for money, is not likely to make money nor to find much fun in life.

> Charles Schwab (1862–1939)
> American industrialist

We have too many people who live without working; and we have altogether too many who work without living.

> Charles R. Brown (1862–1950)
> American clergyman, orator, and author

The hardest job of all is trying to look busy when you're not.

> William Feather (1889–1981)
> American author and publisher

The reason why worry kills more people than work is that more people worry than work.

> Robert Frost (1874–1963)
> American poet

It's just a job. Grass grows, birds fly, waves pound the sand. I beat people up.

> *Muhammad Ali (1942–)*
> *American boxing champion*

I consider myself blessed. I consider you blessed. We've all been blessed with God-given talents. Mine just happens to be beating people up.

> *Sugar Ray Leonard*
> *(1956–)*
> *American boxing champion*

Those who complain the most usually work the least.

> *Anonymous*

Work is the rent you pay for the room you occupy on earth.

> *Elizabeth II (1926–)*
> *queen of England*

My mistake was buying stock in the company. Now I worry about the lousy work I'm turning out.

> *Marvin Townsend*
> *(1915–)*
> *American cartoonist and*
> *illustrator*

Work is necessity for man. Man invented the alarm clock.

> *Pablo Picasso (1881–1973)*
> *Spanish painter and*
> *sculptor*

I like work; it fascinates me. I can sit and look at it for hours.

> *Jerome K. Jerome (1859–*
> *1927)*
> *English dramatist*

The best career advice given to the young is, "Find out what you like doing best and get someone to pay you for doing it."

> *Katharine Whitehorn*
> *(1928–)*
> *British columnist*

The test of a vocation is the love of the drudgery it involves.

> *Logan Pearsall Smith*
> *(1865–1946)*
> *American essayist*

One of the symptoms of an approaching nervous breakdown is the belief that one's work is terribly important.

> *Bertrand Russell (1872–*
> *1970)*
> *English mathematician and*
> *philosopher*

A company is known by the people it keeps.

> *Anonymous*

I have often maintained that I possess a rare talent and strong inclination to be a beachcomber ... if it were not for the demands made upon me by my business, I would provide living proof that a man can live quite happily for decades without even doing any work.

> Jean Paul Getty (1892–1976)
> American oil magnate and philanthropist

When people asked me what I did for a living, I told them, "I do pilots." They all thought I was a stewardess.

> Suzanne Somers (1946–)
> American actress

Everything considered, work is less boring than amusing oneself.

> Charles Baudelaire (1821–67)
> French poet

He and I had an office so tiny that an inch smaller and it would have been adultery.

> Dorothy Parker (1893–1967)
> American writer and poet

The only way I know to get somebody trained is on the job.

> Robert Townsend (1920–)
> American business writer and former president, Avis-Rent-a-Car, Inc.

If you have a job without aggravations, you don't have a job.

> Malcolm Forbes (1919–90)
> American publisher

We work not only to produce but to give value to time.

> Eugène Delacroix (1798–1863)
> French painter

The volume of paper expands to fill the available briefcase.

> Jerry Brown (1938–)
> governor of California

If the power to do hard work is not talent, it is the best possible substitute for it.

> James A. Garfield (1831–81)
> 20th president of the United States

When the going gets tough, everyone leaves.

> Lynch's Law

The difference between a job and a career is the difference between 40 and 60 hours a week.

> Robert Frost (1874–1963)
> American poet

I get satisfaction of three kinds. One is creating something, one is being paid for it, and one is the feeling that I haven't just been sitting on my ass all afternoon.

> William F. Buckley, Jr. (1925–)
> American editor and writer

Whatever is worth doing at all is worth doing well.

> Philip Dormer Stanhope
> (1694–1773)
> Earl of Chesterfield
> English statesman and
> author

If a thing isn't worth doing, it isn't worth doing well.

> Sydney J. Harris (1917–86)
> American newspaper
> columnist

Big shots are only little shots who keep shooting.

> Christopher Morley (1890–
> 1957)
> American writer

Work is the price you pay for money.

> Anonymous

The more I want to get something done, the less I call it work.

> Richard Bach (1936–   )
> American author

There is, of course, a certain amount of drudgery in newspaper work, just as there is in teaching classes, tunneling into a bank, or being President of the United States.

> James Thurber (1894–1961)
> American writer

I've had smarter people around me all my life, but I haven't run into one yet that can outwork me. And if they can't outwork you, then smarts aren't going to do them much good. That's just the way it is. And if you believe that and live by it, you'd be surprised at how much fun you can have.

> Woody Hayes (1913–87)
> American college football
> coach

The secret of joy in work is contained in one word—excellence. To know how to do something well is to enjoy it.

> Pearl Buck (1892–1973)
> American novelist

Small opportunities are often the beginning of great enterprises.

> Demosthenes (382–322 B.C.)
> Athenian orator and
> statesman

The most difficult part of getting to the top of the ladder is getting through the crowd at the bottom.

> Arch Ward (1882–1943)
> American sports editor

A man is not finished when he is defeated. He is finished when he quits.

> Richard M. Nixon (1913–   )
> 37th president of the United
> States

You have to perform at a consistently higher level than others. That's the mark of a true professional. Professionalism has nothing to do with getting paid for your services.

Joe Paterno (1926–   )
American college football
coach

If people knew how hard I had to work to gain my mastery, it wouldn't seem wonderful at all.

Michelangelo (1475–1564)
Italian sculptor, painter,
architect, and poet

Chapter 13

Customer Service

CUSTOMER SERVICE: *quality of service (in terms of timeliness, dependability, communication, and convenience) provided to a customer or client.*

In this day and age, finding a company that stands 100 percent behind its promises and still gives that extra 10 percent is a rare accomplishment. The airline industry has struggled to serve a growing number of travelers in an era of cut-rate fares, numerous discount programs, and a plethora of promotional gimmicks. During the 1980s, most airlines began offering various bonus-mileage programs to promote "brand" loyalty among frequent flyers, who comprise a sizable share of the overall business-traveler market. Soon it became a contest to determine the airline, rental car, and hotel-accommodation combinations that would generate maximum mileage. Perhaps the most unusual request for mileage credits came from Deborah Toga, wife of one of the hostages taken in the 1985 hijacking of TWA Flight 847, which was flown four times between Algeria and Beirut. Mrs. Toga inquired about whether those trips qualified under the TWA Frequent Flight Bonus Program. TWA marketing representatives immediately honored her request.

Rule 1: The customer is always right.
Rule 2: If the customer is ever wrong,
reread Rule 1.

> *Stew Leonard (1930–   )*
> *American merchant*

In all minor discussions between Statler employees and Statler guests, the employee is dead wrong.

> *Ellsworth M. Statler (1863–1928)*
> *American hotel-chain owner*

Use your own best judgment at all times.

> *entire contents of Nordstrom Corporation policy manual*

I solemnly promise and declare that every customer that comes within ten feet of me, I will smile, look them in the eye, and greet them, so help me Sam.

> *employee pledge, Wal-Mart discount stores*

A consumer is a shopper who is sore about something.

> *Harold Glen Coffin (1926–   )*
> *American scientific writer*

Customer service is American Express's patent protection. Our goal, simply stated, is to be the best.

> *James D. Robinson, III (1935–   )*
> *chairman, American Express Company*

Motivate them, train them, care about them and make winners out of them. . . . If we treat our employees correctly, they'll treat the customers right. And if customers are treated right, they'll come back.

> *J. W. Marriott, Jr. (1932–   )*
> *chairman, Marriott Corporation*

What Is a Customer?

A Customer is the most important person ever in this office . . . in person or by mail.
A Customer is not dependent on us . . . we are dependent on him.
A Customer is not an interruption of our work . . . he is the purpose of it. We are not doing a favor by serving him . . . he is doing us a favor by giving us the opportunity to do so.
A Customer is not someone to argue or match wits with. Nobody ever won an argument with a Customer.
A Customer is a person who brings us his wants.
It is our job to handle them profitably to him and ourselves.

> *sign posted at the Freeport, Maine, headquarters of L. L. Bean*

IBM always acts as if it were on the verge of losing every customer.

> *Jacques Maison-Rouge IBM executive*

Every company's greatest assets are its customers, because without customers there is no company.

> *Michael LeBoeuf (1942–   )*
> *American business writer*

There is only one boss: the customer. And he can fire everybody in the company, from the chairman on down, simply by spending his money somewhere else.

> *Sam Walton (1918–92)*
> *founder, Wal-Mart Stores*

Graduate school faculties are made up of people who have never been out working in organizations, who have never found out about the brilliant marketing strategy that doesn't work because the consumer does not behave the way you think he ought to.

> *Peter Drucker (1909–   )*
> *American business*
> *philosopher and author*

Every crowd has a silver lining.

> *Phineas Taylor (P. T.) Barnum*
> *(1810–91)*
> *American circus owner and*
> *showman*

In every instance, we found that the best-run companies stay as close to their customers as humanly possible.

> *Thomas J. Peters (1942–   )*
> *American business writer*

Forget words like "hard sell" and "soft sell." That will only confuse you. Just be sure your advertising is saying something with substance. Something that will inform and serve the consumer, and be sure you're saying it like it's never been said before.

> *William Bernbach*
> *(1911–82)*
> *founder, Doyle Dane*
> *Bernbach advertising*
> *agency*

There is no such thing as "soft sell" and "hard sell." There is only "smart sell" and "stupid sell."

> *Charles Brower (1901–84)*
> *president, Batten, Barton,*
> *Durstine & Osborn*
> *advertising agency*

Selling focuses on the need of the seller; marketing on the needs of the buyer. Selling is preoccupied with the seller's need to convert his product into cash; marketing with the idea of satisfying the needs of the customer by means of the product and the whole cluster of things associated with the creating, delivering, and finally consuming it.

> *Theodore Levitt (1925–   )*
> *American educator and*
> *author*

Spend whatever it takes to build the best. Then let people know about it. In New York, there is no limit to how much money people will spend for the very best, not second best, the very best."

> *Donald J. Trump (1946–   )*
> *American real estate*
> *executive*

If you give something worth paying for, they'll pay.

> *Thomas J. Peters (1943–   )*
> *American business writer*

A thing is worth whatever the buyer will pay for it.

> *Publilius Syrus (1st century*
> *B.C.)*
> *Latin writer of mimes*

There is a difference between getting what you pay for and what you hope for.

> Malcolm Forbes (1919–90)
> American publisher

Quality in a product or service is not what the supplier puts in. It is what the customer gets out and is willing to pay for. A product is not quality because it is hard to make and costs a lot of money, as manufacturers typically believe. This is incompetence. Customers pay only for what is of use to them and gives them value. Nothing else constitutes quality.

> Peter Drucker (1909–   )
> American business
> philosopher and author

Always give the customer quality, value, selection, and service.

> Fred G. Meyer (1917–   )
> American merchant

Fuel is not sold in a forest, nor fish on a lake.

> Chinese proverb

The only pretty store is one full of people.

> William Dillard (1914–   )
> founder and chairman,
> Dillard's department
> stores

How to improve goods or services? Learn to complain, politely and firmly, when you receive what you believe to be inferior goods or services. Don't register your complaint with the salesperson or the waiter, but with the boss or the owner. He'll listen.

> Stanley Marcus (1905–   )
> American merchant

Consumption is the sole end purpose of all production; and the interest of the producer ought to be attended to, only so far as it may be necessary for promoting that of the consumer.

> Adam Smith (1723–90)
> Scottish economist

People will buy anything that's one to a customer.

> Sinclair Lewis (1885–1951)
> American novelist and
> playwright

The critical element in selling a service comes in providing support *after* the sale, because, unlike other types of marketing, the customer can't really try the product until he's already bought it.

> Kay Knight Clarke
> (1938–   )
> chairman, Templeton, Inc.

We view a customer who is complaining as a real blessing in disguise. He or she is someone we can resell.

> Louis Carbone (1905–   )
> vice president, National Car
> Rental

APPLYING THE MARKETING CONCEPT

MARKETING CONCEPT: *philosophy of consumer orientation in which the organization first identifies unmet consumer needs and then designs a system for satisfying them.*

One key to effective customer service is close and continuing contacts with customers and clients. But problems frequently occur among the most customer-oriented organizations. When a truck operated by the U.S. Department of Agriculture accidentally killed a cow, an official responded with an apology and a form to be filled

out for loss compensation. It included a space for "disposition of the dead cow." The farmer responded, "Kind and gentle."

In a recent issue of the *Chronicle of Higher Education,* a West Coast track coach reported similar problems with responses to questionnaires sent to prospective recruits. When asked what he ran the mile in, one respondent wrote, "T-shirt and shorts." In response to a question asking for date of graduation, one athlete replied, "Emmy Lou Watson." And when the questionnaire asked for race, one student replied, "1,500 meters."

In our factory, we make lipstick. In our advertising, we sell hope.

> *Charles Revson (1906–75)*
> *chairman, Revlon, Inc.*

Nothing is so powerful as an insight into human nature . . . what compulsions drive a man, what instincts dominate his action . . . if you know these things about a man you can touch him at the core of his being.

> *William Bernbach*
> *(1911–82)*
> *founder, Doyle Dane*
> *Bernbach advertising*
> *agency*

Any article that does not fit well, is not the proper color or quality, does not please the folks at home, or for any reason is not perfectly satisfactory, should be brought back at once, and if returned as purchased within

10 days, we will refund the money. It is our intention always to give value for value in every sale we make, and those who are not pleased with what they buy do us a positive favor to return the goods and get their money back.

> *John Wanamaker (1838–*
> *1922)*
> *American merchant*

Let advertisers spend the same amount of money improving their product that they do on advertising and they wouldn't have to advertise it.

> *Will Rogers (1879–1935)*
> *American actor and*
> *humorist*

If a man write a better book, preach a better sermon, or make a better mousetrap than his neighbor, though he build his house in the woods, the world will make a beaten path to his door.

Ralph Waldo Emerson
(1803–82)
American essayist and poet

If you make a product good enough even though you live in the depths of the forest, the public will make a path to your door, says the philosopher. But if you want the public in sufficient numbers, you would better construct a highway. Advertising is that highway.

William Randolph Hearst
(1863–1951)
American newspaper
publisher

Today's mousetrap must go to market.

Norman Strouse (1906–   )
American advertising
executive

Anything that won't sell, I don't want to invent. Its sale is proof of utility and utility is success.

Thomas A. Edison (1847–
1931)
American inventor

The older we get, the more we realize that service to others is the only way to stay happy. If we do nothing to benefit others, we will do nothing to benefit ourselves.

Carl Holmes (1925–   )
African-American leader

. . . selling and marketing are antithetical rather than synonymous or even complementary. There will always, one can assume, be a need for some selling, but the aim of marketing is to make selling superfluous. The aim of marketing is to know and understand the customer so well the product or service fits him and sells itself.

Peter Drucker (1909–   )
American business
philosopher and author

Those who enter to buy, support me. Those who come to flatter, please me. Those who complain, teach me how I may please others so that more will come. Only those hurt me who are displeased but do not complain. They refuse me permission to correct my errors and thus improve my service.

Marshall Field (1834–1906)
American merchant

AVOIDING MARKETING MYOPIA

MARKETING MYOPIA: *term coined by Harvard Business School professor Theodore Levitt to describe the failure of executives in many industries to recognize the broad* scope *of their businesses, thereby endangering future growth.*

In a classic *Harvard Business Review* article published over thirty years ago, marketing professor Theodore Levitt used the term *marketing myopia* to describe the failure of management to recognize the scope of business. Levitt cited as examples many service industries, such as dry cleaning, electric utilities, movies, and railroads. For instance: "The railroads did not stop growing because the need for passenger and freight transportation declined. That grew.... They let others take customers away from them because they assumed themselves to be in the railroad business rather than in the transportation business. The reason they defined their industry wrong was because they were product-oriented instead of customer-oriented."

Last year our customers bought over one million quarter-inch drill bits and none of them wanted to buy the product. They all wanted quarter-inch holes.

Anonymous

There is only one valid definition of business purpose: to create a customer.

*Peter Drucker (1909–)
American business
philosopher and author*

Kodak sells film, but they don't advertise film. They advertise memories.

*Theodore Levitt (1925–)
American educator*

The magic formula that successful businesses have discovered is to treat customers like guests and employees like people.

*Thomas J. Peters (1942–)
American business writer*

Customers deserve the very best. It would be helpful if everyone in business could, to paraphrase the American Indian expression, walk a mile in their customer's moccasins. The author once asked a man pumping gas at a filling station why his station was always so busy while the one across the street selling comparable gas at an identical price was almost always empty. This sage businessman replied, "They're in a different business than us. They're a fillin' station —we're a service station." Ironically, at the other end of the spectrum, one wonders why patients visiting their doctors must struggle on their crutches through snow drifts from the back of the parking lot because all the spaces near the building are "reserved for doctors," not for the paying customers.

*Norman R. Augustine
(1935–)
American author and
chairman, Martin
Marietta Corporation*

Chapter 14

Marketing

MARKETING: *a process of planning and executing the conception, pricing, promotion, and distribution of persons, ideas, goods, and services to create exchanges that will satisfy individual and organizational objectives.*

At the height of the Great Sneaker Wars of the late 1980s and early 1990s, a Nike marketing executive chose an unusual setting and an even more unusual spokesperson to appear in a television ad for the firm's shoes. TV viewers were treated to the sight and sound of a traditionally dressed Samburu tribesman in Kenya delivering the phrase, *"Mayieu kuna. Ijooki inamuk sa-pukin."* Since few viewers were likely to be well versed in Maa, the local tongue used in the ad, Nike inserted the following English subtitle: *Just do it*. The phrase appearing on the screen also just happened to be the slogan from the current Nike advertising campaign.

As luck would have it, one of the few Westerners to speak Maa, a University of Cincinnati anthropology professor, saw the spot. Much to the chagrin of Nike marketers, he told news media what the African spokesperson was really saying: "I don't want these. Give me big shoes."

If I had my life to live over again, I would elect to be a trader of goods rather than a student of science. I think barter is a noble thing.

Albert Einstein (1879–1955)
American physicist

Because its purpose is to create a customer, the business has two—and only two—basic functions: marketing and innovation. Marketing and innovation produce results; all the rest are "costs."

Peter Drucker (1909–   )
American business
philosopher and author

If you sell diamonds, you cannot expect to have many customers. But a diamond is a diamond even if there are not customers.

Swami Prabhupada (1896–
1977)
Indian writer and leader of
U.S. Hare Krishna
movement

Put all your eggs in one basket, and watch the basket.

Mark Twain (1835–1910)
American author

No more good must be attempted than the people can bear.

Thomas Jefferson (1743–
1826)
3rd president of the United
States

Benjamin Franklin may have discovered electricity, but it was the man who invented the meter who made the money.

Earl Wilson (1907–87)
American newspaper
columnist

Marketing is merely a civilized form of warfare in which most battles are won with words, ideas, and disciplined thinking.

Albert W. Emery (1923–   )
American advertising
agency executive

Marketing is the delivery of a standard of living.

Paul Mazur (1892–1979)
American investment
banker

Fifty percent of Japanese companies do not have a marketing department, and ninety percent have no special section for marketing research. The reason is that everyone is considered to be a marketing specialist.

Hiroyuki Takeuchi (1934–   )
American educator and
business writer

Forgive us for frantic buying and selling, for advertising the unnecessary and coveting the extravagant, and calling it good business when it is not good for you.

United Presbyterian Church

One illusion is that you can industrialize a country by building factories. You don't. You industrialize it by building markets.

> Paul G. Hoffman (1891–1974)
> American business executive

When the product is right, you don't have to be a great marketer.

> Lee Iacocca (1924–   )
> chairman, Chrysler Corporation

It's the first company to build the mental position that has the upper hand, not the first company to make the product. IBM didn't invent the computer; Sperry Rand did. But IBM was the first to build the computer position in the prospect's mind.

> Al Ries (1929–   )
> chairman, Trout & Ries, Inc., advertising agency

Our economic understanding and models are simply not powerful enough to handle such a large and complex economic system better than the marketplace.

> C. Jackson Grayson (1923–   )
> American educator and productivity-center executive

The meek shall inherit the world, but they'll never increase market share.

> William G. McGowan (1927–   )
> American communications executive

We do not learn to know men through their coming to us. To find out what sort of persons they are, we must go to them.

> Johann Wolfgang von Goethe (1749–1832)
> German poet and dramatist

The idea that you can merchandise candidates for high office like breakfast cereal is, I think, the ultimate indignity of the democratic process.

> Adlai E. Stevenson (1900–65)
> American lawyer and diplomat

Marketing is a fashionable term. The sales manager becomes a marketing vice-president. But a grave digger is still a grave digger even when he is called a mortician—only the price of burial goes up.

> Peter Drucker (1909–   )
> American business philosopher and author

ADVERTISING

ADVERTISING: *paid, nonpersonal communication through electronic or print media by business firms, nonprofit organizations, and individuals who are identified in the advertising message and hope to inform or persuade members of a particular audience.*

Feedback from customers is often the most valuable tool an advertiser can use, not only in relation to the product advertised, but the advertisement itself. Campbell Soup marketers once decided to deliberately advertise twenty-one kinds of soup and to list them in the ad. The list, however, contained twenty-

two varieties. Variations of the ad were run for years thereafter. In some years, Campbell received over seven hundred customer letters about this discrepancy, which, of course, became a primary data source as to how carefully the ad was being read.

I know that half the money I spend on advertising is wasted; but I can never find out which half.

> *John Wanamaker (1838–1922)*
> *American merchant*

Advertisements contain the only truths to be relied on in a newspaper.

> *Thomas Jefferson (1743–1826)*
> *3rd president of the United States*

Advertising may be described as the science of arresting the human intelligence long enough to get money from it.

> *Stephen Leacock (1869–1944)*
> *Canadian economist and humorist*

Advertising is what you do when you can't go to see somebody. That's all it is.

> *Fairfax Cone (1903–77)*
> *founder, Foote, Cone & Belding advertising agency*

The philosophy behind much advertising is based on the old observation that every man is really two men—the man he is and the man he wants to be.

> *William Feather (1889–1981)*
> *American author and publisher*

If I were starting life all over again, I would go into the advertising business; it has risen with ever-growing rapidity to the dignity of an art.

> *Franklin D. Roosevelt (1882–1945)*
> *32nd president of the United States*

The codfish lays ten thousand eggs,
The homely hen lays one.
The codfish never cackles
To tell you what she's done.
And so we scorn the codfish,
While the humble hen we prize,
Which only goes to show you
That it pays to advertise.

> *Anonymous*

The American standard of living is due in no small measure to the imaginative genius of advertising, which not only creates and sharpens demand, but also by its impact upon the competitive process, stimulates the never-ceasing quest of improvement in quality of the product.

Adlai E. Stevenson
(1900–65)
American lawyer and diplomat

Advertising has annihilated the power of the most powerful adjectives.

Paul Valéry (1871–1945)
French poet and philosopher

IF YOU DON'T BUY THIS MAGAZINE, WE'LL KILL THIS DOG

January 1973 cover of National Lampoon

The most powerful element in advertising is the truth.

William Bernbach
(1911–82)
founder, Doyle Dane Bernbach advertising agency

You can tell the ideals of a nation by its advertisements.

Norman Douglas (1868–1952)
English author

Everybody sat around thinking about Panasonic, the Japanese electronics account. Finally, I decided, what the hell, I'll throw a line to loosen them up. . . . "The headline is: From Those Wonderful Folks Who Gave

You Pearl Harbor." Complete silence.

Jerry Della Femina
(1936–   )
American advertising agency executive

Join the army, see the world, meet interesting people, and kill them.

U.S. student anti–Vietnam War slogan

Nothing is real unless it happens on television.

Daniel J. Boorstin (1914–   )
American historian and librarian of Congress

Few people at the beginning of the nineteenth century needed an adman to tell them what they wanted.

John Kenneth Galbraith
(1908–   )
American economist

As to the idea that advertising motivates people, remember the Edsel.

Peter Drucker (1909–   )
American business philosopher and author

Advertising is the rattling of a stick inside a swill bucket.

George Orwell (1903–50)
English author

Doing business without advertising is like winking at a girl in the dark.

You know what you are doing, but nobody else does.

> *Steuart Henderson Britt*
> *(1907–79)*
> *American educator*

The faults of advertising are only those common to all human institutions. If advertising speaks to a thousand in order to influence one, so does the church. And if it encourages people to live beyond their means, so does matrimony. Good times, bad times, there will always be advertising. In good times, people want to advertise; in bad times, they have to.

> *Bruce Barton (1886–1967)*
> *American advertising*
> *executive and author*

When the client moans and sighs
Make his logo twice the size.
If he still should prove refractory,
Show a picture of his factory.
Only in the gravest cases
Should you show the clients' faces.

> *Anonymous*

If you think advertising doesn't pay —we understand there are 25 mountains in Colorado higher than Pikes Peak. Can you name one?

> *Anonymous*

Advertising is a valuable economic factor because it is the cheapest way of selling goods, particularly if the goods are worthless.

> *Sinclair Lewis (1885–1951)*
> *American novelist and*
> *playwright*

Advertising is legalized lying.

> *H. G. Wells (1866–1946)*
> *English novelist and historian*

Many a small thing has been made large by the right kind of advertising.

> *Mark Twain (1835–1910)*
> *American author*

Publicity is stronger than sanity: given the right PR, armpit hair on female singers could become a national fetish.

> *Lenny Bruce (1925–66)*
> *American social*
> *satirist*

They took a poll on Madison Avenue and here is what people in the advertising industry are worried about most: Inflation, unemployment, crime, and armpits . . . not necessarily in that order.

> *Robert Orben (1927–   )*
> *American humorist*

Advertising is a racket . . . its constructive contribution to humanity is exactly minus zero.

> *F. Scott Fitzgerald (1896–*
> *1940)*
> *American author*

Nothing except the mint can make money without advertising.

> *Thomas B. Macaulay*
> *(1800–59)*
> *English author, historian,*
> *and statesman*

If I were asked to name the deadliest subversive force within capitalism—the single greatest source of its waning morality—I would without hesitation name advertising.

> Robert L. Heilbroner
> (1919–   )
> American economist

Advertising is the most fun you can have with your clothes on.

> Jerry Della Femina
> (1936–   )
> American advertising
> agency executive

Advertising agency: eighty-five percent confusion and fifteen percent commission.

> Fred Allen (1894–1956)
> American comedian

Never write an advertisement which you wouldn't want your family to read. You wouldn't tell lies to your own wife. Don't tell them to mine. Do as you would be done by. If you tell lies about a product, you will be found out—either by the Government, which will prosecute you, or by the consumer, who will punish you by not buying your product a second time. Good products can be sold by honest advertising. If you don't think the product is good, you have no business to be advertising it.

> David M. Ogilvy (1911–   )
> founder, Ogilvy & Mather
> advertising agency

Advertising isn't a science. It's persuasion. And persuasion is an art.

> William Bernbach
> (1911–82)
> founder, Doyle Dane
> Bernbach advertising
> agency

Advertising is the principle of mass production applied to selling.

> Dr. John T. Dorrance (1873–
> 1930)
> American food industry
> executive and inventor of
> condensed soup

In science the credit goes to the man who convinces the world, not to the man to whom the idea first occurs.

> Sir William Osler (1849–
> 1919)
> Canadian physician

A promoter will provide the ocean if you will provide the ships.

> Anonymous

It is far easier to write ten passable effective sonnets, good enough to take in the not too inquiring critic, than one effective advertisement that will take in a few thousand of the uncritical buying public.

> Aldous Huxley (1894–1963)
> English author and critic

I sleep so much better at night, knowing that America is protected from thin pickles and fast ketchup.

> Orrin Hatch (1934–   )
> U.S. senator

SELLING

PERSONAL SELLING: *interpersonal influence process involving a seller's promotional presentation conducted on a person-to-person basis (either face-to-face or by telephone, video teleconferencing, or through interactive computer links) with the prospective buyer.*

For a man who has become one of the more notable investors of our time, Warren Buffet, owner of the ABC network, conducts most of his business out of Omaha, Nebraska, far away from major company head-quarters. Buffet likes to describe his view of customer-oriented personal selling with a story of a fisherman who goes into a sporting-goods store to buy a lure. The sales clerk shows him a wide array of colored feathers, plastic insects, and other ingenious enticements for the fisherman to use. Trying to select a lure that will be certain to increase his chances, the fisherman asks, "Do fish really like this sort of thing?"

To which the clerk flatly responds, "I don't sell to fish."

Everyone lives by selling something.

> *Robert Louis Stevenson*
> *(1850–94)*
> *Scottish author*

To sell something, tell a woman it's a bargain; tell a man it's deductible.

> *Earl Wilson (1907–87)*
> *American newspaper*
> *columnist*

When a man sells eleven ounces for twelve, he makes a compact with the devil, and sells himself for the value of an ounce.

> *Henry Ward Beecher*
> *(1813–87)*
> *American clergyman and*
> *writer*

The best way to get on in the world is to make people believe it's to their advantage to help you.

> *Jean de La Bruyère*
> *(1645–96)*
> *French writer and moralist*

A bashful beggar has an empty purse.

> *Hungarian proverb*

A little reciprocity goes a long way.

> *Malcolm Forbes (1919–90)*
> *American publisher*

When a man is trying to sell you something, don't imagine he is that polite all the time.

> *Ed Howe (1853–1937)*
> *American journalist*

A salesman is a fellow with a smile on his face, a shine on his shoes, and a lousy territory.

George Gobel (1919–91)
American actor and
comedian

Willy was a salesman. And for a salesman, there is no rock bottom to the life. He don't put a bolt to a nut, he don't tell you the law or give you medicine. He's a man way out there in the blue, riding on a smile and a shoeshine. And when they start not smiling back—that's an earthquake. . . . A salesman is got to dream, boy. It comes with the territory.

Arthur Miller (1915–   )
American dramatist
and novelist

Only a fool holds out for the top dollar.

Joseph P. Kennedy (1888–1969)
American businessman
and diplomat

There are more fools among buyers than among sellers.

French proverb

In the modern world of business it is useless to be a creative original thinker unless you can also sell what you create. Management cannot be expected to recognize a good idea unless it is presented to them by a good salesman.

David M. Ogilvy (1911–   )
founder, Ogilvy & Mather
advertising agency

I am the world's worst salesman; therefore, I must make it easy for people to buy.

Frank W. Woolworth (1852–1919)
American merchant

It is hard to believe that a man is telling the truth when you know that you would lie if you were in his place.

H. L. Mencken (1880–1956)
American editor

Whenever two people meet, there are really six people present. There is each man as he sees himself, each man as the other person sees him, and each man as he really is.

William James (1842–1910)
American psychologist and
philosopher

Agreement is brought about by changing people's minds—other people's.

S. I. Hayakawa (1906–92)
American semanticist and
U.S. senator

A salesman is one who sells goods that won't come back to customers who will.

Anonymous

If you can't convince 'em, confuse 'em.

Harry S Truman (1884–1972)
33rd president of the United
States

Some of the sharpest traders we know are artists, and some of the best salesmen are writers.

> *E. B. White (1899–1985)*
> *American journalist and*
> *writer*

A well-informed employee is the best salesperson a company can have.

> *Edwin J. Thomas (1947–   )*
> *American realtor*

It's no trick to be a successful salesman if you have what the people want. You never hear the bootleggers complaining about hard times.

> *Robert C. (Bob) Edwards*
> *(1864–1922)*
> *Canadian educator and*
> *humorist*

Salesmanship is an American specialty. It typifies the competitive spirit of our economy. Nowhere else in the world have so many executives come up through the selling ranks.

> *Robert A. Whitney (1888–*
> *1974)*
> *president of the New York*
> *Stock Exchange*

Nothing is as irritating as the fellow that chats pleasantly while he's overcharging you.

> *Frank McKinney (Kin)*
> *Hubbard (1868–1930)*
> *American humorist*

If we will not buy, we cannot sell.

> *William McKinley (1843–1901)*
> *25th president of the United*
> *States*

The buyer needs a hundred eyes, the seller not one.

> *George Herbert (1593–*
> *1633)*
> *English clergyman and poet*

We have something in this industry called the 10-3-1 ratio. This means that for every ten calls a salesperson makes, he will only get to make a presentation to three, and if he's got a good success rate, he'll make one sale. We need people who won't shrink from that kind of rejection.

> *Dennis Tamcsin (1938–   )*
> *senior vice president,*
> *Northwestern Mutual Life*
> *Insurance*

He that speaks ill of the mare will buy her.

> *Benjamin Franklin*
> *(1706–90)*
> *American statesman and*
> *philosopher*

There are worse things in life than death. Have you ever spent an evening with an insurance salesman?

> *Woody Allen (1935–   )*
> *American actor, film*
> *director, and comedian*

MARKETING MIDDLEMEN: RETAILERS AND WHOLESALERS

RETAILER: *marketing intermediary who sells or rents goods or provides services to ultimate consumers for personal use and not for resale.*

WHOLESALER: *marketing intermediary who sells products to retailers, other wholesalers, or businesses whose motive for purchase is to resell the goods or to use them in the operation of the business.*

During his five-year apprenticeship in a Massachusetts retail store, Marshall Field had many opportunities to learn how to handle a disgruntled customer. Several years later in Chicago, Field was walking through his own store and overhead a clerk arguing with a customer.

"What are you doing here?" Field demanded firmly.

"I'm settling a complaint," came the answer.

"No, you're not," Field corrected. "Give the lady what she wants." This phrase became his company motto, and is still used as a catchphrase today.

A customer looking for a particular item followed the shop owner into his store basement. He noticed that the walls were lined with sacks of salt. Curious, the customer commented, "You must sell lots of salt."

"Mister, I couldn't sell a pinch of salt, but the man who sells me salt —can he sell salt!"

The farmer is the only man in our economy who buys everything he buys at retail, sells everything he sells at wholesale, and pays the freight both ways.

> *John F. Kennedy (1917–63)*
> *35th president of the United States*

Today you can go to Sears and buy your stocks where you buy your socks.

> *Anonymous*

If you're over forty years old—mentally—you don't belong in retailing.

> *Cyril Magnin (1899–1988)*
> *American merchant*

Location, location, location.

> *William Dillard (1914–   )*
> *founder and chairman, Dillard's department stores*

I do not regard a broker as a member of the human race.

> *Honoré de Balzac (1790–1859)*
> *French novelist*

Let me have no lying; it becomes none but tradesmen.

> *William Shakespeare (1564–1616)*
> *English dramatist and poet*

I never knew an auctioneer to lie, unless it was absolutely necessary.

> *Josh Billings (1818–85)*
> *American humorist*

You can do away with the wholesaler but you can't do away with the functions he performs.

> *American business saying*

It is well known what a middleman is; he is the man who bamboozles one party and plunders the other.

> *Benjamin Disraeli*
> *(1804–81)*
> *British novelist and prime minister*

PRICE

PRICE: *exchange value of a good or service; the money or other considerations exchanged for the purpose or use of a product, idea, or service.*

From Here to Eternity (1951) was James Jones's first successful novel and, like many artists who finally achieve recognition, he exhibited

---

signs of moderate eccentricity. During that period, he was known to carry a pocketful of envelopes with sixty-seven cents in each one. When he ran into friends who had bought his book, he handed each of them an envelope, explaining, "That's my royalty on each copy. I don't want to make money on my friends."

What is a cynic? A man who knows the price of everything and the value of nothing. And a sentimentalist . . . is a man who sees an absurd value in everything, and doesn't know the market price of any single thing.

> *Oscar Wilde (1854–1900)*
> *Irish poet, playwright, and novelist*

People want economy, and they'll pay any price to get it.

> *Lee Iacocca (1924–   )*
> *chairman, Chrysler Corporation*

The value of anything is not what you get paid for it, nor what it cost to produce, but what you can get for it at an auction.

> *William Lyon Phelps*
> *(1865–43)*
> *American educator and writer*

You'd be surprised how much it costs to look this cheap.

> *Dolly Parton (1946–   )*
> *American singer*

Cutting prices is usually insanity if the competition can go as low as you can.

Michael E. Porter (1947–   )
American educator

There are two fools in every market; one asks too little, one asks too much.

Russian proverb

Inflation makes balloons larger and candy bars smaller.

David L. Kurtz (1941–   )
American educator and
business writer

A hamburger by any other name costs twice as much.

Evan Esar (1899–   )
American author

Cheat me in the price but not in the goods.

Thomas Fuller (1654–1734)
English clergyman and
author

There is hardly anything in the world that some men can't make a little worse and sell a little cheaper, and the people who consider price only are this man's lawful prey.

John Ruskin (1819–1900)
English art critic and
historian

I found the greater the volume, the cheaper I could buy and the better value I could give customers.

Frank W. Woolworth (1852–
1919)
American merchant

The only difference in a pigeon and the American farmer today is that a pigeon can still make a deposit on a John Deere.

James Allen (Jim)
Hightower (1943–   )
Texas agricultural
commissioner

Chapter 15

Money

MONEY: *anything generally accepted as a means of paying for goods and services.*

How much does it cost? is a question heard throughout the world. In France they ask, *Combien est-ce?* In Germany, *Wieviel kostet es?* In Italy, *Quanto costa? ¿Cuanto vale?* in Spain and in Russia, *Skok'ko eto stoit?*

The lack of money is the root of all evil.

> *George Bernard Shaw*
> *(1856–1950)*
> *British author and social*
> *reformer*

I'm living so far beyond my income that we may almost be said to be living apart.

> *e. e. cummings (1894–1962)*
> *American poet*

Dollars do better if they are accompanied by sense.

> *Earl Riney (1885–1955)*
> *American clergyman*

Money, it turned out, was exactly like sex. You thought of nothing else if you didn't have it and thought of other things if you did.

> *James Baldwin (1924–87)*
> *American novelist and*
> *essayist*

The chief value of money lies in the fact that one lives in a world in which it is overestimated.

> H. L. Mencken (1880–1956)
> American editor

Money, which represents the prose of life, and which is hardly spoken of in parlors without an apology, is, in its effects and laws, as beautiful as roses.

> Ralph Waldo Emerson
> (1803–82)
> American essayist and poet

Money is something you got to make in case you don't die.

> Max Asnas (1897–1968)
> Russian-American
> restaurateur

I've got all the money I'll ever need if I die by four o'clock.

> Henny Youngman (1906–)
> American comedian

I have enough money to last me the rest of my life, unless I buy something.

> Jackie Mason (1930–)
> American comedian

He was so broke he couldn't even pay attention.

> American saying

Bad money drives out good money.

> Thomas Gresham (1519–79)
> English financier

I don't want to be a millionaire, I just want to live like one.

> Bernard (Toots) Shor
> (1905–77)
> American restaurateur

A fool and his money are soon parted. What I want to know is how they got together in the first place.

> Cyril Fletcher (1904–)
> American educator

There was a time when a fool and his money were soon parted, but now it happens to everybody.

> Adlai E. Stevenson
> (1900–65)
> American lawyer and
> diplomat

I'd like to live like a poor man with lots of money.

> Pablo Picasso (1881–1973)
> Spanish painter and
> sculptor

Poor people are not poor because they're dumb or because they're lazy but because society has not provided opportunity.

> Andrew Young (1932–)
> mayor of Atlanta, Georgia

There are three faithful friends: an old wife, an old dog, and ready money.

> Benjamin Franklin
> (1706–90)
> American statesman and
> philosopher

Finance is the art of passing currency from hand to hand until it finally disappears.

> Robert W. Sarnoff
> (1918–   )
> American communications
> industry executive

In the bad old days, there were three easy ways of losing money—racing being the quickest, women the pleasantest, and farming the most certain.

> William Pitt Amherst
> (1773–1857)
> English diplomat

. . . remember, a billion dollars isn't worth what it used to be.

> Jean Paul Getty (1892–
> 1976)
> American oil magnate and
> philanthropist

A billion here, a billion there, and pretty soon you're talking about real money.

> attributed to Everett M.
> Dirksen (1896–1969)
> U.S. senator

The next time you see a headline about the government spending a billion dollars on some project, think about it this way: If you spent $100,000 every day of the week, it would take you more than 27 years to spend a billion dollars.

> Louis E. Boone (1941–   )
> American educator and
> business writer

If you can count your money, you don't have a billion dollars.

> Jean Paul Getty (1892–
> 1976)
> American oil magnate and
> philanthropist

The darkest hour of any man's life is when he sits down to plan how to get money without earning it.

> Horace Greeley (1811–72)
> American journalist and
> politician

Money is the barometer of society's virtue.

> Ayn Rand (1905–82)
> American writer

I do everything for a reason, most of the time the reason is for money.

> Suzy Parker (1933–   )
> American model and actress

Where large sums of money are concerned, it is advisable to trust nobody.

> Agatha Christie (1890–
> 1976)
> British mystery writer

It is better to have a permanent income than to be fascinating.

> Oscar Wilde (1854–1900)
> Irish poet, playwright, and
> novelist

If you want to know what a man is really like, take notice how he acts when he loses money.

> New England proverb

Money is the poor people's credit card.

> *Marshall McLuhan*
> *(1911–80)*
> *Canadian educator and*
> *author*

If a man runs after money, he's money-mad; if he keeps it, he's a capitalist; if he spends it, he's a playboy; if he doesn't get it, he's a ne'er-do-well; if he doesn't try to get it, he lacks ambition. If he gets it without working for it, he's a parasite; and if he accumulates it after a lifetime of hard work, people call him a fool who never got anything out of life.

> *Vic Oliver (1898–1964)*
> *English actor*

When I was young, I used to think that money was the most important thing in life; now that I am old, I know it is.

> *Oscar Wilde (1854–1900)*
> *Irish poet, playwright, and*
> *novelist*

Money is a stupid measure of achievement, but unfortunately it is the only universal measure we have.

> *Charles Steinmetz (1865–*
> *1923)*
> *American electrical*
> *engineer*

Gentility is what is left over from rich ancestors after the money is gone.

> *John Ciardi (1916–86)*
> *American poet and critic*

The man who damns money has obtained it dishonorably. The man who respects it has earned it.

> *Ayn Rand (1905–82)*
> *American author*

Money is like manure, of very little use except it be spread.

> *Francis Bacon (1561–1626)*
> *English philosopher*

Money is like manure. If you spread it around, it does a lot of good, but if you pile it up in one place, it stinks like hell.

> *Clint W. Murchison (1895–*
> *1969)*
> *Texas financier*

It is easier to make money than to save it; one is exertion, the other, self-denial.

> *Thomas C. Haliburton*
> *(1796–1865)*
> *English writer*

Money is a good servant, but a bad master.

> *Henry George Bohn (1796–*
> *1884)*
> *English publisher*

Mothers always tell you that honesty is the best policy, and money isn't everything. They're wrong about other things, too.

> *Anonymous*

I've been in trouble all my life; I've done the most unutterable rubbish,

all because of money. I didn't need it
... the lure of the zeroes was simply
too great.

> *Richard Burton (1925–84)*
> *Welsh actor*

If you want to know what God thinks
of money, look at the people he gives
it to.

> *Yiddish proverb*

Make money and the whole world
will conspire to call you a gentleman.

> *Mark Twain (1835–1910)*
> *American author*

With money in your pocket, you are
wise, and you are handsome, and you
sing well, too.

> *Yiddish proverb*

If you would know the value of
money, go and borrow some.

> *Benjamin Franklin*
> *(1706–90)*
> *American statesman and*
> *philosopher*

From birth to age 18, a girl needs
good parents; from 18 to 35 she needs
good looks; from 35 to 55 she needs
a good personality; and from 55 on
she needs cash.

> *Sophie Tucker (ca. 1884–*
> *1966)*
> *American actress*

Money is always there, but the pockets change.

> *Gertrude Stein (1874–1946)*
> *American writer*

Money is the only substance which
can keep a cold world from nicknam-
ing a citizen "Hey, you!"

> *Wilson Mizner (1876–1933)*
> *American author*

Money can't buy friends, but you can
get a better class of enemy.

> *Spike Milligan (1918–   )*
> *British actor and motion-*
> *picture director*

When a father gives to his son, both
laugh; when a son gives to his father,
both cry.

> *Yiddish proverb*

Money is power, freedom, a cushion,
the root of all evil, the sum of blessings.

> *Carl Sandburg (1878–1967)*
> *American author*

When a man says money can do anything, that settles it: he hasn't any.

> *Ed Howe (1853–1937)*
> *American journalist*

CREDIT AND BORROWING

CREDIT: *in* finance: *sales or purchases that are accomplished by a promise to pay later;*

in accounting: *a bookkeeping entry recording a decrease in an asset, an increase in a liability, or an increase in owners' equity;*

in banking: *funds remaining in a bank account (credit balance).*

BORROWING: *obtaining or receiving something on loan with the promise or understanding of returning it.*

Unfortunately, most artists realize that any fame and fortune bestowed upon them will more than likely be enjoyed by their heirs. Indeed, most live in debt their entire life. American painter James McNeill Whistler was not unlike this, but always treated his creditors with the utmost courtesy. It is said that one of them visited Whistler at his home to discuss payment of a long-overdue bill. The painter cordially invited him in and offered him a glass of champagne.

Shocked by this expensive and flamboyant gesture, the creditor demanded, "How can you afford champagne when you cannot even pay my bill?"

"My dear man, let me assure you," Whistler calmly replied, "I haven't paid for this either."

If you think nobody cares if you're alive, try missing a couple of car payments.

> *Earl Wilson (1907–87)*
> *American newspaper columnist*

A financier is a pawnbroker with imagination.

> *Arthur Wing Pinero (1855–1934)*
> *English dramatist*

If a man smiles at home, somebody is sure to ask him for money.

> *William Feather (1889–1981)*
> *American author and publisher*

There's no such thing as a free lunch.

> *Milton Friedman (1912–   )*
> *American economist*

Never call a man a fool; borrow from him.

> *Addison Mizner (1872–1933)*
> *American architect*

Interest works night and day, in fair weather and foul. It gnaws at a man's substance with invisible teeth.

> *Henry Ward Beecher (1813–87)*
> *American clergyman*

Creditors are a superstitious sect, great observers of set days and times.

*Benjamin Franklin
(1706–90)
American statesman and
philosopher*

The man who won't loan money isn't going to have many friends—or need them.

*Wilson Mizner (1876–1933)
American author*

Don't believe the world owes you a living; the world owes you nothing—it was here first.

*Robert Jones Burdette
(1844–1942)
American clergyman and
humorist*

It is better to give than to lend, and it costs about the same.

*Philip Gibbs (1877–1962)
English writer*

Credit is a system whereby a person who can't pay gets another person who can't pay to guarantee that he can pay.

*Charles Dickens (1812–70)
English novelist*

I have discovered the philosopher's stone, that turns everything into gold: It is, "pay as you go."

*John Randolph (1773–1833)
American statesman*

The foremost question before the nation today is, "How much is the down payment?"

*Joe Moore (1941–   )
American television news
commentator*

Remember when people worried about how much it took to buy something, instead of how long?

*Earl Wilson (1907–87)
American newspaper
columnist*

Bankruptcy is a legal proceeding in which you put your money in your pants pocket and give your coat to your creditors.

*Joey Adams (1911–   )
American comedian*

He that goes a borrowing goes a sorrowing.

*Benjamin Franklin
(1706–90)
American statesman and
philosopher*

Neither a borrower, nor a lender be; For loan oft loses both itself and friend.

*William Shakespeare (1564–1616)
English dramatist and poet*

A creditor is worse than a master; for a master owns only your person, a creditor owns your dignity, and can belabor that.

*Victor Hugo (1802–85)
French poet, novelist, and
dramatist*

Nowadays, people can be divided into three classes—the Haves, the Have-Nots, and the Have-Not-Paid-for-What-They-Haves.

> *Earl Wilson (1907–87)*
> *American newspaper*
> *columnist*

If it isn't the sheriff, it's the finance company. I've got more attachments on me than a vacuum cleaner.

> *John Barrymore (1882–*
> *1942)*
> *American actor*

Credit buying is much like being drunk. The buzz happens immediately and gives you a lift. . . . The hangover comes the day after.

> *Dr. Joyce Brothers*
> *(1928–)*
> *American psychologist*

No man's credit is as good as his money.

> *Ed Howe (1853–1937)*
> *American journalist*

Creditors have better memories than debtors.

> *James Howell (1594–1666)*
> *English author*

Acquaintance, *n.* A person whom we know well enough to borrow from, but not well enough to lend to.

> *Ambrose Bierce (1842–*
> *ca. 1914)*
> *American journalist, short-*
> *story author, and poet*

Everybody likes a kidder, but nobody lends him money.

> *Arthur Miller (1915–)*
> *American dramatist and*
> *novelist*

INVESTING

INVESTING: *putting to use money or other items of value, such as buildings, vehicles, or equipment, through purchase or expenditure, with the intention of earning profitable returns, especially interest or income.*

Dabbling in the stock market is a pastime of millions of serious and not-so-serious investors. Not surprisingly, investors frequently seek out advice from books, industry prognosticators, company executives, and from individuals known to have achieved fame and fortune from astute investments. J. P. Morgan, Sr., certainly fit the latter category. Asked by a would-be Wall Street winner what he expected the market to do in the near future, Morgan simply replied, "It will fluctuate."

It is not the return *on* my investment that I am concerned about; it is the return *of* my investment.

> *Will Rogers (1879–1935)*
> *American actor and*
> *humorist*

Never invest in anything that eats or needs repainting.

> *Billy Rose (1899–1966)*
> *American theatrical*
> *impresario and composer*

Bulls Can Make Money.
Bears Can Make Money.
Pigs Always Get Slaughtered.

> *American business saying*

Money is like an arm or a leg—use it or lose it.

> *Henry Ford (1863–1947)*
> *American automobile*
> *manufacturer*

The greatest waste of money is to keep it.

> *Jackie Gleason (1916–87)*
> *American actor and*
> *comedian*

Of all the mysteries of the stock exchange there is none so impenetrable as why there should be a buyer for everyone who seeks to sell.

> *John Kenneth Galbraith*
> *(1908–   )*
> *American economist*

What's good for the U.S. is good for the New York Stock Exchange. But what's good for the New York Stock Exchange might not be good for the United States.

> *William McChesney Martin,*
> *Jr. (1906–   )*
> *chairman, U.S. Federal*
> *Reserve System*

There are only two emotions in Wall Street—fear and greed.

> *William M. LeFevre, Jr.*
> *(1927–   )*
> *vice president, Granger &*
> *Company*

We make money the old fashioned way—we earn it.

> *Smith Barney advertising*
> *slogan*

Choose stocks the way porcupines make love—very carefully.

> *Anonymous*

Now I'm in real trouble. First, my laundry called and said they lost my shirt and then my broker said the same thing.

> *Leopold Fechtner (1916–   )*

When a company president is ready to buy you lunch, it's time to sell the stock. When he has something really good, you can't get him on the phone.

> *Phil Stoller (1952–   )*
> *American lawyer*

I wasn't affected by the crash of '29. I went broke in '28.

> Gerald F. Lieberman
> (1923–86)
> American author and
> humorist

They call him "Broker" because after you deal with him you are.

> Anonymous

If you hear that *everybody* is buying a certain stock, ask who is selling.

> James Dines (1935–   )
> American investment
> adviser

Now is always the most difficult time to invest.

> Anonymous

If stock market experts were so expert, they would be buying stocks not selling advice.

> Norman R. Augustine
> (1935–   )
> American author and
> chairman, Martin
> Marietta Corporation

Wall Street is a thoroughfare that begins in a graveyard and ends in a river.

> Anonymous

My father dealt in stocks and shares and my mother also had a lot of time on her hands.

> Hermione Gingold
> (1897–1987)
> English actress

The safest way to double your money is to fold it over and put it in your pocket.

> Frank McKinney (Kin)
> Hubbard (1868–1930)
> American humorist

There are two times in a man's life when he should not speculate: when he can't afford it and when he can.

> Mark Twain (1835–1910)
> American author

The best investment on earth is earth.

> Louis J. Glickman (1933–   )
> American business
> executive

Gentlemen prefer bonds.

> Andrew Mellon (1855–1937)
> American financier

With an evening coat and a white tie, anybody, even a stock broker, can gain a reputation for being civilized.

> Oscar Wilde (1854–1900)
> Irish poet, playwright, and
> novelist

October. This is one of the peculiarly dangerous months to speculate in stocks. The others are July, January, September, April, November, May, March, June, December, August and February.

> Mark Twain (1835–1910)
> American author

SPENDING AND SAVING

SPENDING: *paying out or disbursing money.*

SAVING: *safeguarding; preventing or reducing the waste, loss, or expenditure of something.*

Credit cards have long proven a boon to consumer spending. Somehow the cardholder is less reluctant to make credit card purchases; the awareness of how expensive an item is that is present in cash purchases isn't nearly so strong when the sales clerk simply charges it to a card number. Romanian tennis star Ilie Nastase was once asked why he waited over a year to report the theft of his wife's credit card. "Whoever had it," he explained, "was spending less than she was."

If only God would give me a clear sign! Like making a large deposit in my name in a Swiss bank.

> *Woody Allen (1935–)*
> *American actor, film*
> *director, and comedian*

Anyone who lives within his means suffers from a lack of imagination.

> *Lionel Stander (1909–)*
> *American actor*

The thrift industry is really in terrible shape. It has reached the point where if you buy a toaster, you get a free savings and loan.

> *Lloyd Bentsen (1921–)*
> *U.S. senator*

Put not your trust in money, but put your money in trust.

> *Oliver Wendell Holmes*
> *(1809–94)*
> *American physician and*
> *author*

Whoever said money can't buy happiness didn't know where to shop.

> *Anonymous*

Bargain: something you can't use at a price you can't resist.

> *Franklin P. Jones (1887–*
> *1929)*
> *American lawyer*

I haven't heard of anyone who wants to stop living on account of the cost.

> *Frank McKinney (Kin)*
> *Hubbard (1868–1930)*
> *American humorist*

Any man who has $10,000 left when he dies is a failure.

> *Errol Flynn (1909–59)*
> *American actor*

BANKING AND BANKERS

BANK: *profit-seeking business that receives deposits from individuals and organizations in the form of checking and savings accounts and uses some of these funds to make loans.*

American humorist James Thurber, like many other famous and not-so-famous people, was called in by the bank manager to straighten out his overdrawn bank account. After a few preliminary questions, the bank manager asked to see his check record. Thurber quite honestly confessed that he did not keep a record of the checks he wrote

"Then," asked the astonished bank manager, "how do you know how much money is in your account?"

"I thought that was *your* business," quipped Thurber.

Drive-in banks were invented so that automobiles could visit their real owners.

Anonymous

Banks do not raise or lower interest rates depending upon how they feel about it. A bank buys money like a grocer buys bananas—and then adds on salaries and rent and sells the product.

Llewellyn Jenkins (1919–   )
American banker

Banks will lend you money if you can prove you don't need it.

Mark Twain (1835–1910)
American author

Gentlemen, you are as fine a group of men as ever foreclosed a mortgage on a widow. I'm glad to be among you shylocks.

Will Rogers (1879–1935)
American actor and
humorist

A banker is a fellow who lends you his umbrella when the sun is shining and wants it back the minute it begins to rain.

Mark Twain (1835–1910)
American author

Will you please tell me what you do with all the vice presidents a bank has? I guess that's to get you discouraged before you can see the president. Why, the United States is the biggest institution in the world and they only have one vice president and nobody has ever found anything for him to do.

Will Rogers (1879–1935)
American actor and
humorist

It is rather a pleasant experience to be alone in a bank at night.

Willie Sutton (1901–80)
American bank robber

You know the difference between a dead skunk and a dead banker on the road? There are skid marks by the skunk.

Anonymous

Chapter 16

Numbers:
The Manager's Tool Kit

NUMBERS: *a series of symbols of unique meaning in a fixed order.*

D uring a meeting of the Continental Congress in 1787, Elbridge Gerry, who later became vice president of the United States, introduced a resolution to limit the size of the Continental Army, by law, to ten thousand people. With the Congress fearing that a large army might overpower a smaller government, the resolution seemed to be accepted fairly well until George Washington was heard to comment, "A very good idea. Let us also limit, by law, the size of any invading force to five thousand men." The resolution was defeated.

I don't know any CEO who doesn't love numbers.

> *Jeffrey Silverman (1945–)*
> *CEO, Ply Gem Industries,*
> *Inc.*

No amount of experimentation can ever prove me right; a single experiment can prove me wrong.

> *Albert Einstein (1879–1955)*
> *American physicist*

Results? Why man, I have gotten a lot of results. I know 50,000 things that won't work.

> *Thomas Edison (1847–1931)*
> *American inventor*

Companies were collapsing because of their bias for numeracy over action. Analysis paralysis.

> *Robert H. Waterman, Jr.*
> *American management*
> *consultant and business*
> *writer*

One of New York's leading cultural institutions was about to undertake a costly study to find out which of its many exhibits was the most popular with visitors. Just before the consulting contract was signed, a committee member suddenly suggested asking the janitor where he had to mop the most.

> *Marilyn Machlowitz*
> *(1952–   )*
> *American management*
> *consultant*

When you are drowning in numbers you need a system to separate the wheat from the chaff.

> *Anthony Adams (1940–   )*
> *vice president, Campbell*
> *Soup Company*

It is a capital mistake to theorize before one has data.

> *Sir Arthur Conan Doyle*
> *(1859–1930)*
> *British physician and*
> *novelist*

There is no sadder sight in the world than to see a beautiful theory killed by a brutal fact.

> *Thomas H. Huxley*
> *(1825–95)*
> *English biologist*

Man is a tool-using animal . . . without tools he is nothing, with tools he is all.

> *Thomas Carlyle (1795–*
> *1881)*
> *Scottish essayist and*
> *historian*

There are three kinds of lies: lies, damned lies, and statistics.

> *Benjamin Disraeli*
> *(1804–81)*
> *British novelist and prime*
> *minister*

The government are extremely fond of amassing great quantities of statistics. These are raised to the nth degree, the cube roots are extracted, and the results are arranged into elaborate and impressive displays. What must be kept ever in mind, however, is that in every case, the figures are first put down by a village watchman, and he puts down anything he damn well pleases.

> *Sir Josiah Stamp (1880–*
> *1941)*
> *English economist and*
> *banker*

STATISTICS

STATISTICS: *branch of mathematics dealing with the collection, analysis, interpretation, and presentation of masses of data.*

Mass-production pioneer Henry Ford occasionally conducted tours of his assembly plant. During one such tour, Ford pointed to a finished car and proudly stated, "There are exactly four thousand seven hundred and nineteen parts in that model car." One visitor was duly impressed with the technical data stored in the brain of the head of the Ford Motor Company. Later in the tour, the visitor had a chance to ask a plant engineer if the statement was factual. The engineer first shrugged and then replied, "I'm sure I don't know, but I can't think of a more useless piece of information."

A horse that can count to ten is a remarkable horse, not a remarkable mathematician.

> *Samuel Johnson (1709–84)*
> *English lexicographer and*
> *author*

Somewhere on this globe, every ten seconds, there is a woman giving birth to a child. She must be found and stopped.

> *Sam Levenson (1911–80)*
> *American humorist*

You cannot feed the hungry on statistics.

> *David Lloyd George (1863–*
> *1945)*
> *British statesman and*
> *prime minister*

When I am Premier, you will not have to look up figures to find out whether you are prosperous: you will know by feeling in your pockets.

> *Wilfred Laurier (1841–*
> *1919)*
> *Canadian statesman and*
> *prime minister*

Just try explaining the value of statistical summaries to the widow of the man who drowned crossing a stream with an average depth of four feet.

> *Anonymous*

It is now proved beyond a shadow of a doubt that smoking is one of the leading causes of statistics.

> *Fletcher Knebel (1911–   )*
> *American author and*
> *journalist*

Figures won't lie, but liars will figure.

> *Charles H. Grosvenor*
> *(1833–1917)*
> *American labor leader*

There are no facts, only interpretations.

> Friedrich Nietzsche (1844–
> 1900)
> German philosopher

How far would Moses have gone if he had taken a poll in Egypt?

> Harry S Truman (1884–
> 1972)
> 33rd president of the United
> States

There are two kinds of statistics, the kind you look up and the kind you make up.

> Rex Stout (1886–1975)
> American mystery writer

A single death is a tragedy, a million deaths is a statistic.

> Joseph Stalin (1879–1953)
> Soviet leader

The facts, all we want are the facts.

> Jack Webb (1920–82)
> American actor
> (as Sergeant Joe Friday in the
> 1950s television series
> Dragnet)

Facts do not cease to exist because they are ignored.

> Aldous Huxley (1894–1963)
> English author and critic

Reporting facts is the refuge of those who have no imagination.

> Luc de Clapiers (1715–47)
> Marquis de Vauvenargues
> French soldier and moralist

The weaker the data available upon which to base one's conclusion, the greater the precision which should be quoted in order to give the data authenticity.

> Norman R. Augustine
> (1935–   )
> American author and
> chairman, Martin
> Marietta Corporation

Get your facts first, then you can distort them as you please.

> Mark Twain (1835–1910)
> American author

Research is the process of going up alleys to see if they are blind.

> Marston Bates (1906–74)
> American zoologist

A theory has only the alternative of being right or wrong. A model has a third possibility—it may be right but irrelevant.

> Manfred Eigen (1927–   )
> German chemist

"Scientific" is not synonymous with quantification—if it were, astrology would be the queen of sciences.

> Peter Drucker (1909–   )
> American business
> philosopher and author

We don't ask research to do what it was never meant to do, and that is to get an idea.

> *William Bernbach*
> *(1911–82)*
> *founder, Doyle Dane*
> *Bernbach advertising*
> *agency*

Basic research is when I'm doing what I don't know I'm doing.

> *Wernher von Braun*
> *(1912–77)*
> *American engineer*

Research is to see what everybody else has seen, and to think what nobody else has thought.

> *Albert Szent-Gyorgyi*
> *(1893–1986)*
> *American biochemist*

"For example" is not proof.

> *Yiddish proverb*

ECONOMICS

ECONOMICS: *science concerned with analysis of production, distribution, and consumption of goods and services.*

The Republican campaign issues of the 1980 presidential election focused on economic ills, and Ronald Reagan spoke frequently of the dire straits America was headed toward. During a debate with then-president Jimmy Carter, Reagan referred to the approaching depression. Carter too quickly responded, "That shows how much he knows. This is a recession." To which Reagan appropriately defended with an attack, "If the president wants a definition, I'll give him one. Recession is when your neighbor loses his job, depression is when you lose yours. And recovery will be when Jimmy Carter loses his."

Economists are people who work with numbers but don't have the personality to be accountants.

> *Anonymous*

I believe that economists put decimal points in their forecasts to show they have a sense of humor.

> *William E. Simon (1927–)*
> *American business*
> *executive and U.S.*
> *secretary of the treasury*

The law of diminishing returns holds good in almost every part of our human universe.

> *Aldous Huxley (1894–1963)*
> *English author and critic*

Professor Galbraith is horrified by the number of Americans who have bought cars with tail fins on them, and I am horrified by the number of Americans who take seriously the proposals of Mr. Galbraith.

> *William F. Buckley, Jr.*
> *(1925–   )*
> *American editor and writer*

Literature was formerly an art and finance a trade; today it is the reverse.

> *Joseph Roux (1834–1905)*
> *French priest and writer*

It is an economic axiom as old as the hills that goods and services can be paid for only with goods and services.

> *Albert J. Nock (1870?–1945)*
> *American critic and*
> *publicist*

An economist is a guy with a Phi Beta Kappa key on one end of his watch chain and no watch on the other.

> *Alben W. Barkley (1877–*
> *1956)*
> *vice president of the United*
> *States*

Christmas is a time when kids tell Santa what they want and adults pay for it. Deficits are when adults tell the government what they want— and their kids pay for it.

> *Richard Lamm (1935–   )*
> *governor of Colorado*

If economists were any good at business, they would be rich men instead of advisers to rich men.

> *Kirk Kerkorian (1917–   )*
> *chairman, Metro-Goldwyn-*
> *Mayer film company*

No one in our age was cleverer than Keynes nor made less attempt to conceal it.

> *Roy Forbes Harrod*
> *(1900–78)*
> *British economist*

In all recorded history there has not been one economist who had to worry about where the next meal would come from.

> *Peter Drucker (1909–   )*
> *American business*
> *philosopher and author*

If all economists were laid end to end they would not reach a conclusion.

> *George Bernard Shaw*
> *(1856–1950)*
> *British author and social*
> *reformer*

If the nation's economists were laid end to end, they would point in all directions.

> *Arthur "Red" Motley*
> *(1900–84)*
> *American publisher and*
> *president, U.S. Chamber*
> *of Commerce*

An economist's guess is liable to be as good as anybody else's.

> *Will Rogers (1879–1935)*
> *American actor and*
> *humorist*

Economists think the poor need them to tell them that they are poor.

> *Peter Drucker (1909–   )*
> *American business*
> *philosopher and author*

"Other things being equal"—you can identify an economist by the number of times a person uses this particular phrase.

> *Anonymous*

An economist is an expert who will know tomorrow why the things he predicted yesterday didn't happen today.

> *Laurence J. Peter (1919–90)*
> *American author*

You can make even a parrot into a learned economist by teaching him two words: supply and demand.

> *Anonymous*

A study of economics usually reveals that the best time to buy anything is last year.

> *Marty Allen (1922–   )*
> *American comedian*

Practical men . . . are usually the slaves of some defunct economists.

> *John Maynard Keynes*
> *(1883–1946)*
> *English economist*

If ignorance paid dividends, most Americans could make a fortune out of what they don't know about economics.

> *Luther Hartwell Hodges*
> *(1898–1974)*
> *governor of North Carolina*
> *and U.S. secretary of*
> *commerce*

I learned more about economics from one South Dakota dust storm than I did in all my years in college.

> *Hubert Humphrey*
> *(1911–78)*
> *vice president of the United*
> *States*

[Economics] is a subject profoundly conducive to cliché, resonant with boredom. On few topics is an American audience so practiced in turning off its ears and minds. And . . . none can say that the response is ill advised.

> *John Kenneth Galbraith*
> *(1908–   )*
> *American economist*

To most of us, the leading economic indicator is our bank account.

> *Joe Moore (1941–   )*
> *American television news*
> *commentator*

The economist doll: You wind it up, ask it to forecast, and it shrugs its shoulders.

> *Eugene A. Birnbaum*
> *(1926–   )*
> *American economist and*
> *banker*

I do believe in supply-side economics.

> Ronald Reagan (1911–   )
> 40th president of the United
> States

Waiting for supply-side economics to work is like leaving the landing lights on for Amelia Earhart.

> Walter Heller (1915–87)
> American economist

In the long run we are all dead. Economists set themselves too easy, too useless a task if in tempestuous seasons they can only tell us that when the storm is long past the ocean is flat again.

> John Maynard Keynes
> (1883–1946)
> English economist

People don't eat in the long run—they eat every day.

> attributed to Harry L.
> Hopkins (1890–1946)
> director, Federal Emergency
> Relief Administration and
> U.S. secretary of commerce

It's a recession when your neighbor loses his job; it's a depression when you lose your own.

> Harry S Truman (1884–
> 1972)
> 33rd president of the United
> States

An economist is a man who states the obvious in terms of the incomprehensible.

> Alfred A. Knopf (1892–
> 1984)
> American publisher

Another difference between Milton [Friedman] and myself is that everything reminds Milton of the money supply. Well, everything reminds me of sex, but I keep it out of the paper.

> Robert Solow (1924–   )
> American economist and
> educator

Mathematics has given economics rigor, but alas, also mortis.

> Robert L. Heilbroner
> (1919–   )
> American economist

Whenever there are great strains or changes in the economic system, it tends to generate crackpot theories which then find their way into the legislative channels.

> David Stockman (1946–   )
> American economist and
> director of the Office of
> Management and Budget
> under President Ronald
> Reagan

Inflation means that your money won't buy as much today as it did when you didn't have any.

> Anonymous

One man's pay increase is another man's price increase.

> Harold Wilson (1916–   )
> British political leader and
> prime minister

The government fighting inflation is like the Mafia fighting crime.

> Laurence J. Peter (1919–90)
> American author

ACCOUNTING

ACCOUNTING: *recording, classifying, summarizing, interpreting, and communicating financial information to enable others inside and outside the organization to make informed decisions.*

Elgin Baylor, one of basketball's all-time greats, is second only to Wilt Chamberlain in average points scored per game in the National Basketball Association (NBA). Baylor was rooming with Rodney ("Hot Rod") Hundley in 1971 when he set a league record, scoring 71 points in one game. Hundley, notorious for his jokes and pranks, only scored two points that game, but as they got into the cab after the game, Hundley patted Baylor on the back and proudly boasted, "What a night we had, buddy! Seventy-three points between us!"

An accountant is a person hired to explain that you didn't make the money you thought you did.

Anonymous

Auditors are the people who go in after the war is lost and bayonet the wounded.

Paul Rubin (1903–80)
American investment
counsel

Specialists in finance must be on tap, but they should never be on top. Most think they can save their way to prosperity. Unless the CEO redirects their efforts, they're likely to spend as much time policing pennies and peanuts as they are managing or trying to make millions or billions of dollars. I've always tried to make it clear to the bean counters that they are a service department, not a police department. But they have trouble getting it.

Al Neuharth (1924–　)
American writer and
founder, USA Today

If you are truly serious about preparing your child for the future, don't teach him to subtract—teach him to deduct.

Fran Lebowitz (1950–　)
American author

Accountants can be smarter than anybody else or more ambitious or both, but essentially they are bean counters—their job is to serve the operation. They can't run the ship.

Robert Townsend (1920–　)
American business writer
and former president,
Avis-Rent-a-Car, Inc.

Accountants are the witch doctors of the modern world.

J. Harman (1894–1970)
English jurist

Kickbacks must always exceed bribes.

> John Peers
> president, Logical Machine
> Corporation and author
> of 1001 Logical Laws

Two and two continue to make four, in spite of the whine of the amateur for three, or the cry of the critic for five.

> James Abbott McNeill
> Whistler (1834–1903)
> American painter

The P/E ratio doesn't mean anything when there is no E.

> Raymond Rose (1948–   )
> chairman, Oliver Rose
> Securities

Absorption of overhead is one of the most obscene terms I have ever heard.

> Peter Drucker (1909–   )
> American business
> philosopher and author

Our accounting department is the office that has the little red box on the wall saying, "In case of emergency, break glass." And inside are two tickets to Brazil.

> Robert Orben (1927–   )
> American humorist

COMPUTERS

COMPUTER: *programmable electronic device that can store, retrieve, and process data.*

A Charleston, West Virginia, hospital sends a computer letter bearing this message: "Hello, there, I am the hospital's computer. As yet, no one but me knows that you have not been making regular payments on this account. However, if I have not processed a payment from you within 10 days, I will tell a human, who will resort to other means of collection."

First, get it through your head that computers are big, expensive, fast, dumb adding-machine-typewriters. Then realize that most of the computer technicians that you're likely to meet or hire are complicators, not simplifiers. They're trying to make it look tough. Not easy. They're building a mystique, a priesthood, their own mumbo-jumbo ritual to keep you from knowing what they—and you—are doing.

> Robert Townsend (1920–   )
> American business writer
> and former president,
> Avis-Rent-a-Car, Inc.

The factory of the future will have only two employees, a man and a dog. The man will be there to feed the dog. The dog will be there to keep the man from touching the equipment.

> *Warren G. Bennis (1925–)*
> *American educator and*
> *business writer*

I do not fear computers. I fear the lack of them.

> *Isaac Asimov (1920–92)*
> *American novelist*

Very few EDP people perform; in part because they are arrogant, in part because they are ignorant, and in part because they are too enamored of their god-damned tool.

> *Peter Drucker (1909–)*
> *American business*
> *philosopher and author*

To err is human but to really foul up requires a computer.

> *Paul Ehrlich (1932–)*
> *American biologist*

A computer does not substitute for judgment any more than a pencil substitutes for literacy. But writing without a pencil is no particular advantage.

> *Robert McNamara*
> *(1916–)*
> *American politician and*
> *statesman*

The real danger is not that computers will begin to think like men, but that men will begin to think like computers.

> *Sydney J. Harris (1917–86)*
> *American newspaper*
> *columnist*

Man is still the most extraordinary computer of all.

> *John F. Kennedy (1917–63)*
> *35th president of the United*
> *States*

One machine can do the work of fifty ordinary men. No machine can do the work of one extraordinary man.

> *Elbert Hubbard (1856–*
> *1915)*
> *American writer*

The computer revolution is the most advertised revolution in world history. Yet one of the funny things about it is that we probably still underestimate its impact.

> *Herman Kahn (1922–83)*
> *American futurist and*
> *author*

Computers are useless. They can only give you answers.

> *Pablo Picasso (1881–1973)*
> *Spanish painter and*
> *sculptor*

A computer isn't smart enough to make a mistake. Computers are dumb. Fast and efficient and dumb. No computer ever had an idea.

> *IBM advertisement*

Chapter 17

The Global Marketplace

INTERNATIONAL BUSINESS: *all economic activities that cross national boundaries.*

International business executives recognize that the Japanese have a cultural block against the word *no*. (Their most synonymous expression is "That will be very difficult.") In the book *Do's and Taboos Around the World,* one American traveler commented on this problem when asking directions of Tokyo taxi drivers.

> Nine times out of ten he will indicate "You bet!" and step on the gas. Consequently, many visitors to the Ginza have found themselves in Osaka. One man of the world thought he had solved the problem. When leaving his hotel, he would have the concierge write out his destination in Japanese characters. For his return, he would simply take a hotel matchbook and flash it at the driver. Late one night, he discovered that the matchbook had its drawback. As usual, the driver took one look and zoomed purposefully off. The ride had begun to seem unusually long, however, and downtown Tokyo was nowhere in sight when the cab stopped. All he saw were empty streets and darkened warehouses. The driver had taken him not to the Okura Hotel but to the matchbook factory.

Ever since the years of the Cold War, Americans have been hyped into being suspicious of anything to do with the Soviets. Boston Bruins heroes Phil Esposito and Bobby Orr were among the ice-hockey players who went to Moscow to play a series of exhibition games with the Soviets in the early 1970s. Assigned a hotel room, Esposito remembers how he and Orr suspected that the room was bugged: "We searched the room for microphones. In the center of the room, we found a funny-looking, round piece of metal imbedded in the floor, under the rug. We figured we had found the bug. We dug it out of the floor. And we heard a crash beneath us. We had released the anchor to the chandelier in the ceiling below."

A day will come when you, France; you, Russia; you, Italy; you, England; you, Germany—all of you nations of the continent, will, without losing your distinctive qualities, be blended into a ... European fraternity. ...

> *Victor Hugo (1802–85)*
> *French poet, novelist, and*
> *dramatist*

The U.S. puts its best young minds to work in staff jobs and has for years. Bright people have gotten the message. They avoid line jobs. Japan, on the other hand, wants its brightest men in line jobs. After all, that is what manufacturing is all about. Our people understand that while we may rotate them from line to staff, and vice versa, line jobs are critical for what you in America call fast-track executives.

> *chairman of a Japanese*
> *electrical manufacturing*
> *firm*

Immigration is the sincerest form of flattery.

> *Jack Paar (1918–   )*
> *American author*
> *and television-*
> *show host*

England and America are two countries separated by the same language.

> *attributed to*
> *George Bernard Shaw*
> *(1856–1950)*
> *British playwright and*
> *social reformer*

Things on the whole are much faster in America. People don't *stand for election*, they *run for office*. If a person says she's *sick*, it doesn't mean regurgitating, it means *ill*. *Mad* means angry, not insane. Don't ask for *left luggage*; it's called a *checkroom*. A *nice joint* is a good pub, not roast beef.

> *Jessica Mitford (1917–   )*
> *English author*

If you speak three languages, you are trilingual. If you speak two languages, you are bilingual. If you speak one language, you're American.

> *Anonymous*

They spell it *Vinci* and pronounce it *Vinchy;* foreigners always spell better than they pronounce.

> *Mark Twain (1835–1910)*
> *American author*

Boy, those French! They have a different word for everything.

> *Steve Martin (1945–   )*
> *American actor and*
> *comedian*

Continental people have sex lives; the English have hot-water bottles.

> *George Mikes (1912–87)*
> *Hungarian author*

There have been many definitions of hell, but for the English the best definition is that it is a place where the Germans are the police, the Swedish are the comedians, the Italians are the defence force, Frenchmen dig the roads, the Belgians are the pop singers, the Spanish run the railways, the Turks cook the food, the Irish are the waiters, the Greeks run the government, and the common language is Dutch.

> *David Frost (1939–   ) and*
> *Antony Jay*
> *English authors*

America looks 10 minutes ahead; Japan looks 10 years.

> *Akio Morita (1921–   )*
> *chairman, Sony*
> *Corporation*

Time. Time. What is time? Swiss manufacture it. French hoard it. Italians want it. Americans say it is money. Hindus say it does not exist. Do you know what I say? I say time is a crook.

> *Peter Lorre (1904–64)*
> *in John Huston's 1954*
> *motion picture* Beat the
> Devil

The secret of Japanese success is not technology, but a special way of managing people—a style that focuses a strong company philosophy, a distinct corporate culture, long-range staff development, and consensus on decision-making.

> *William Ouchi (1943–   )*
> *American educator and*
> *author*

A lot of Americans think if it's made in Japan, it's terrific, if it's made in America, it's lousy. It's time to peel off the Teflon kimono.

> *Lee Iacocca (1924–   )*
> *chairman, Chrysler*
> *Corporation*

From Montreal to Munich to Melbourne, the world is too large and filled with too many diverse people and firms for any single marketing strategy to satisfy everyone.

> *David L. Kurtz (1941–   )*
> *American educator and*
> *business writer*

A Canadian is someone who drinks Brazilian coffee from an English teacup and munches on French pastry while sitting on his Danish furniture having just come home from an Italian movie in his German car. He picks up his Japanese pen and writes to this member of Parliament to complain about the American takeover of the Canadian publishing business.

> *Campbell Hughes (1913–   )*
> *Canadian publisher*

Canada is a country whose main exports are hockey players and cold fronts. Our main imports are baseball players and acid rain.

> *Pierre Trudeau (1919–   )*
> *prime minister of Canada*

I traveled a good deal all over the world, and I got along pretty good in all these foreign countries, for I have a theory that it's their country and they got a right to run it like they want to.

> *Will Rogers (1879–1935)*
> *American actor and*
> *humorist*

They all come back to the same thing: We have got to decide what free and fair trade is all about, and we've got to level the playing field to be competitive. These are the gut issues.

> *Lee Iacocca (1924–   )*
> *chairman, Chrysler*
> *Corporation*

How can you govern a country with two hundred and forty-six varieties of cheese?

> *Charles de Gaulle (1890–*
> *1970)*
> *French general and*
> *president of the Fifth*
> *Republic*

Italians come to ruin most generally in three ways—women, gambling, and farming. My family chose the slowest one.

> *Pope John XXIII (1881–*
> *1963)*

There will be no veterans of World War III.

> *Walter Mondale (1928–   )*
> *vice president of the United*
> *States*

There is no security on this earth; there is only opportunity.

> *Douglas MacArthur (1880–*
> *1964)*
> *general, U.S. Army*

A nation is not in danger of financial disaster merely because it owes itself money.

> *Andrew Mellon (1855–1937)*
> *American financier*

No country has ever been ruined on account of its debts.

> *Adolf Hitler (1889–1945)*
> *German chancellor and*
> *führer*

No nation was ever ruined by trade.

> *Benjamin Franklin*
> *(1706–90)*
> *American statesman and*
> *philosopher*

It is an iron law of history that power passes from debtor to creditor.

> *Daniel Patrick Moynihan*
> *(1927–)*
> *U.S. senator*

The merchant has no country.

> *Thomas Jefferson*
> *(1743–1826)*
> *3rd president of the*
> *United States*

We will have differences. Men of different ancestries, men of different tongues, men of different colors, men of different environments, men of different geographies, do not see everything alike. Even in our own country we do not see everything alike. If we did, we would all want the same wife—and that would be a problem, wouldn't it?

> *Lyndon B. Johnson*
> *(1908–73)*
> *36th president of the United*
> *States*

As opposed to nations in the West, Asia is a growing market. By the year 2000, two-thirds of the world's consumers will live around the edge of the Pacific Rim.

> *Christopher Mill (1944–)*
> *vice president, Saatchi &*
> *Saatchi advertising*
> *agency*

Fools rush in where wise men fear to trade.

> *Peter Drucker (1909–)*
> *American business*
> *philosopher and author*

. . . interdependence re-creates the world in the image of a global village.

> *Marshall McLuhan*
> *(1911–80)*
> *Canadian educator and*
> *author*

I cannot forecast to you the action of Russia. It is a riddle wrapped in a mystery inside an enigma.

> *Winston Churchill (1874–*
> *1965)*
> *British statesman and*
> *prime minister*

There is a new awareness of style in the Soviet Union. The premier's wife recently appeared on the cover of *House and Tractor.*

> *Johnny Carson (1925–)*
> *American television-show*
> *host*

Gaiety is the most outstanding feature of the Soviet Union.

> *Joseph Stalin (1879–1953)*
> *Soviet leader*

Russians are very isolated from cultural differences. They're terribly uncomfortable and insecure around blacks, and every African knows it.

> *Andrew Young (1932–)*
> *mayor of Atlanta, Georgia*

Good Americans, when they die, go to Paris.

> *attributed to*
> *Oliver Wendell Holmes*
> *(1809–94)*
> *American physician and*
> *author*

France is a country where the money falls apart and you can't tear the toilet paper.

> *Billy Wilder (1906–   )*
> *American motion-picture*
> *director and producer*

The Chinese use two brush strokes to write the word "crisis." One brush stroke stands for danger; the other for opportunity. In a crisis, beware of danger—but recognize the opportunity.

> *Richard M. Nixon (1913–   )*
> *37th president of the United*
> *States*

The British tourist is always happy abroad so long as the natives are waiters.

> *Robert Morley (1908–   )*
> *British actor and*
> *playwright*

Nachman's Rule: When it comes to foreign food, the less authentic the better.

> *Gerald Nachman (1938–   )*
> *American author*

In an underdeveloped country, don't drink the water; in a developed country, don't breathe the air.

> *Jonathan Raban (1942–   )*
> *British writer*

Mass transportation is doomed to failure in North America because a person's car is the only place where he can be alone and think.

> *Marshall McLuhan*
> *(1911–80)*
> *Canadian educator and*
> *author*

Who gives a [expletive deleted] about the lira?

> *Richard Nixon (1913–   )*
> *37th president of the United*
> *States*

You can divide the countries of the world into two types—the ones that have all the oil and the ones that do not. We have oil.

> *José Lopez Portillo*
> *(1920–   )*
> *president of Mexico*

For my sins, I worked with the Nigerians when they became independent. I told them that what they needed was a late eighteenth-century English mechanic who could design a better hoe. They asked me, "Is that what they do at MIT?" I said no, of course not. They said, "We are going to do what they do at MIT! Anything else is second-class."

> *Peter Drucker (1909–   )*
> *American business*
> *philosopher and author*

In Italy, for thirty years under the Borgias, they had warfare, terror, murder, and bloodshed, but they produced Michelangelo, Leonardo da Vinci, and the Renaissance. In Switzerland, they had brotherly love; they had five hundred years of democracy and peace—and what did that produce? The cuckoo clock.

Orson Welles (1915–85)
American actor and motion-
picture producer
in Graham Greene's 1949
motion picture The Third
Man

The dollar has become like a hydrant at an international convention of dogs.

Eliot Janeway (1913–   )
American author

In the old days, we used to say that when the U.S. economy sneezed the rest of the world went to bed with pneumonia. Now when the U.S. economy sneezes the other countries say "Gesundheit."

Walter Heller (1915–87)
American economist

If people outside Italy have the impression that Italy is always on strike, that is because it is.

Paul A. Samuelson
(1915–   )
American economist

Don't overlook the importance of worldwide thinking. A company that keeps its eye on Tom, Dick, and Harry is going to miss Pierre, Hans, and Yoshio.

Al Ries (1929–   )
chairman, Trout & Ries,
Inc., advertising agency

To hear the Japanese plead for free trade is like hearing the word love on the lips of a harlot.

Lane Kirkland (1922–   )
American labor leader

VIEWS ON AMERICA

MULTINATIONAL CORPORATION: *firm that operates production and marketing facilities on an international level and considers the world its market.*

Some of the most difficult questions come from the most delicate minds, as can be attested by former

U.S. Secretary of Education William Bennett. When a seventh-grader queried how he could tell a good country from a bad one, Bennett offered this allegory: "I apply the 'gate' test. When the gates of a country are open, watch which way the people run. Do they run into the country or out of the country?"

My folks are immigrants and they fell under the spell of the American legend that the streets were paved with gold. When Papa got here he found out three things: (1) The streets were not paved with gold; (2) the streets were not paved at all; (3) he was supposed to do the paving.

> *Sam Levenson (1911–80)*
> *American humorist*

Intellectually I know America is no better than any other country; emotionally I know she is better than every other country.

> *Sinclair Lewis (1885–1951)*
> *American novelist and*
> *playwright*

Our national flower is the concrete cloverleaf.

> *Lewis Mumford (1895–*
> *1990)*
> *American writer*

It is not possible for this nation to be at once politically internationalist and economically isolationist. This is just as insane as asking one Siamese twin to high dive while the other plays the piano.

> *Adlai E. Stevenson*
> *(1900–65)*
> *American lawyer and*
> *diplomat*

America is the country where you buy a lifetime supply of aspirin for one dollar and use it up in two weeks.

> *John Barrymore (1882–*
> *1942)*
> *American actor*

Americans: people who laugh at . . . African witch doctors and spend 100 million dollars on fake reducing systems.

> *Leonard Louis Levinson*
> *(1904–74)*
> *American radio and*
> *television writer*

It's a scientific fact that if you stay in California, you lose one point of IQ every year.

> *Truman Capote (1924–84)*
> *American novelist*

The further he went West the more convinced he felt that the Wise Men came from the East.

> *Sydney Smith (1771–1845)*
> *English essayist*

It is veneer, rouge, aestheticism, art museums, new theaters, etc., that make America important. The good things are football, kindness, and jazz bands.

> *George Santayana (1863–*
> *1952)*
> *American poet and*
> *philosopher*

This is America. You can do anything here.

> *Robert Edward (Ted)*
> *Turner, III (1938–   )*
> *American cable-television*
> *pioneer*

How do the French see America? As an attractive, animated drawing that tends to be simplistic, just like any image that one people conjures up about another. Pell-mell you would doubtless see the landing of the GIs in Normandy, Roosevelt, Ike, and Kennedy, Wall Street, cavalcades of Indians in the Far West, Al Capone, Marilyn Monroe, Marlon Brando, Muhammad Ali, pretty majorettes, *West Side Story,* bourbon and Coca-Cola, man's first steps on the moon— with a musical background of Louis Armstrong and Duke Ellington.

Valéry Giscard d'Estaing
(1926–   )
prime minister of France

One of the special beauties of America is that it is the only country in the world where you are not advised to learn the language before entering. Before I ever set out for the United States, I asked a friend if I should study American. His answer was unequivocal. "On no account," he said. "The more English you sound, the more likely you are to be believed."

Quentin Crisp (1908–   )
British author and film
critic

Whoever wants to know the heart and mind of America had better learn baseball.

Jacques Barzun (1907–   )
American educator

The Americans never walk. In winter, too cold; in summer, too hot.

W. B. Yeats (1865–1939)
Irish poet and dramatist

Anyone who believes that the competitive spirit in America is dead has never been in a supermarket when the cashier opens another checkout line.

Ann Landers (1918–   )
American advice columnist

Part IV

A BROADER
PERSPECTIVE

Chapter 18

Ethical and Social Obligations

ETHICS: *standards of conduct and moral values.*

Unfortunately, the determination of what is and what is not ethical is frequently influenced by stereotypes, generalizations, and even trends in the climate of public sentiment. When the ABC movie *The Children of Times Square* was criticized as unsympathetic to minorities, NBC's senior vice president in charge of movies, Stephen White, was compelled to defend not only his competitor's film, but the industry as a whole. Forcing a broader awareness on the issue, he stated, "We don't get letters from white businessmen, but they're really the ones who should protest. A majority of them are shown to be villainous . . . because no one will object."

Live in such a way that you would not be ashamed to sell your parrot to the town gossip.

> *Will Rogers (1879–1935)*
> *American actor and*
> *humorist*

Fool me once, shame on you.
Fool me twice, shame on me.

> *American Indian expression*

I am proud of the fact that I never invented weapons to kill.

> Thomas A. Edison (1847– 1931)
> American inventor

I would rather be the man who bought the Brooklyn Bridge than the one who sold it.

> Will Rogers (1879–1935)
> American actor and humorist

The ability to adapt and adjust tactics while sticking to principles is extremely important. One of the biggest problems with CEOs is that they are flexible on principle and inflexible on plans.

> Eugene E. Jennings (1926–   )
> American educator and business writer

One man with courage makes a majority.

> Andrew Jackson (1767– 1845)
> 7th president of the United States

They [corporations] cannot commit treason, nor be outlawed nor excommunicated, for they have no souls.

> Sir Edward Coke (1552– 1634)
> English jurist

What is good for the country is good for General Motors, and what is good for General Motors is good for the country.

> Charles E. Wilson (1890– 1961)
> chairman, General Motors Corporation and U.S. secretary of defense

I am responsible for my actions, but who is responsible for those of General Motors?

> Ralph Nader (1934–   )
> American consumer advocate

A corporation is an artificial being, invisible, intangible, and existing only in contemplation of law.

> John Marshall (1755–1835)
> Chief Justice, U.S. Supreme Court

A corporation cannot blush.

> Anonymous

It is truly enough said that a corporation has no conscience. But a corporation of conscientious men is a corporation with a conscience.

> Henry David Thoreau (1817–62)
> American naturalist and writer

We demand that big business give people a square deal; in return we must insist that when anyone engaged in big business honestly endeavors to do right, he shall himself be given a square deal.

> *Theodore Roosevelt (1858–1919)*
> *26th president of the United States*

When asked by anthropologists what the Indians called America before the white man came, an Indian said simply, "Ours."

> *Vine Deloria (1933–   )*
> *American author*

What do I care about the law? H'aint I got the power?

> *Cornelius Vanderbilt (1794–1877)*
> *American shipping and railroad magnate*

First, there is the law. It must be obeyed. But the law is the minimum. You must act ethically.

> *IBM employee guidelines*

All that is necessary for the triumph of evil is that good men do nothing.

> *attributed to Edmund Burke (1729–97)*
> *British statesman and orator*

I think greed is healthy. You can be greedy and still feel good about yourself.

> *Ivan Boesky (1937–   )*
> *American investor and lawyer*

Greed . . . is good. Greed is right. Greed clarifies, cuts through and captures the essence of the evolutionary spirit. . . . Greed—mark my words— will save . . . the U.S.A.

> *Michael Douglas (1944–   )*
> *American actor in Oliver Stone's 1988 motion picture* Wall Street

Nothing is illegal if a hundred businessmen decide to do it.

> *Andrew Young (1932–   )*
> *mayor of Atlanta, Georgia*

Every man has his price.

> *Robert Walpole (1676–1745)*
> *English statesman*

I am like any other man. All I do is supply a demand.

> *Al Capone (1899–1947)*
> *American gangster*

The louder he talked of his honor, the faster we counted our spoons.

> *Ralph Waldo Emerson (1803–82)*
> *American essayist and poet*

Golden rule principles are just as necessary for operating a business profitably as are trucks, typewriters, or twine.

> *James Cash Penney (1875–1971)*
> *founder, JCPenney Company*

To imitate one's enemy is to dishonor.

> Thomas Hobbes (1588–1679)
> English philosopher

Living with a conscience is like driving a car with the brakes on.

> Budd Schulberg (1914–   )
> American writer

Confession may be good for the soul, but it is bad for the reputation.

> Thomas R. Dewar (1864–1930)
> British distiller

Everybody has a little bit of Watergate in him.

> Billy Graham (1918–   )
> American evangelist

The best way to keep one's word is not to give it.

> Napoleon Bonaparte (1769–1821)
> emperor of France

A promise made is a debt unpaid.

> Robert W. Service (1874–1958)
> Canadian writer

Nature knows no indecencies; man invents them.

> Mark Twain (1835–1910)
> American author

So the question is, do corporate executives, provided they stay within the law, have responsibilities in their business activities other than to make as much money for their stockholders as possible? And my answer to that is, no they do not.

> Milton Friedman (1912–   )
> American economist

Man is the only animal that blushes —or needs to.

> Mark Twain (1835–1910)
> American author

If it ever came to a choice between compromising my moral principles and the performance of my duties, I know I'd go with my moral principles.

> Norman Schwarzkopf (1934–   )
> general, U.S. Army

It's a matter of having principles. It's easy to have principles when you're rich. The important thing is to have principles when you're poor.

> Ray A. Kroc (1902–84)
> founder, McDonald's Corporation

A thing worth having is a thing worth cheating for.

> W. C. Fields (1880–1946)
> American actor and comedian

Most men only commit great crimes because of their scruples about petty ones.

> Cardinal de Retz (1613–79)
> French ecclesiastic and
> politician

Anyone who sells butter containing stones or other things (to add to the weight) will be put into our pillory, then said butter will be placed on his head until entirely melted by the sun. Dogs may lick him and people offend him with whatever defamatory epithets they please without offense to God or King. If the sun is not warm enough, the accused will be exposed in the hall of the gaol in front of a roaring fire, where everyone will see him.

> edict of Louis XI (1423–83)
> king of France

Behind every great fortune there is a crime.

> Honoré de Balzac (1799–
> 1850)
> French novelist

Conscience is the little voice that tells you you shouldn't have done it after you did.

> Anonymous

Never believe anything until it has been officially denied.

> Claud Cockburn (1904–81)
> British journalist

There is no crime in the cynical American calendar more humiliating than to be a sucker.

> Max Lerner (1902–   )
> American author and
> columnist

The world has achieved brilliance without conscience. Ours is a world of nuclear giants and ethical infants.

> Omar Bradley (1893–1981)
> general, U.S. Army

The first duty of a revolutionary is to get away with it.

> Abbie Hoffman (1936–89)
> American author and
> political activist

You are not here merely to make a living. You are here in order to enable the world to live more amply, with greater vision, with a finer spirit of hope and achievement. You are here to enrich the world, and you impoverish yourself if you forget the errand.

> Woodrow Wilson (1856–
> 1924)
> 28th president of the United
> States

Those who stand for nothing fall for anything.

> Alexander Hamilton (1755–
> 1804)
> American statesman

The nature of business is swindling.

> August Bebel (1840–1913)
> German political leader and
> writer

All the things I really like to do are either immoral, illegal, or fattening.

> *Alexander Woollcott (1887–1943)*
> *American writer*

I believe that every right implies a responsibility; every opportunity, an obligation; every possession, a duty.

> *John D. Rockefeller, Jr. (1874–1960)*
> *American oil magnate and philanthropist*

Grub first, then ethics.

> *Bertolt Brecht (1898–1956)*
> *German dramatist*

I gave 'em a sword. And they stuck it in, and they twisted it with relish. And I guess if I had been in their position, I'd have done the same thing.

> *Richard M. Nixon (1913–   )*
> *37th president of the United States*

Man is the only animal that can remain on friendly terms with the victims he intends to eat until he eats them.

> *Samuel Butler (1835–1902)*
> *English novelist and satirist*

The tyrant dies and his rule is over; the martyr dies and his rule begins.

> *Søren Kierkegaard (1813–55)*
> *Danish philosopher and theologian*

Whenever a man has cast a longing eye on offices, a rottenness begins in his conduct.

> *Thomas Jefferson (1743–1826)*
> *3rd president of the United States*

People of the same trade seldom meet together, even for merriment and diversion, but the conversation ends in a conspiracy against the public, or in some contrivance to raise prices.

> *Adam Smith (1723–90)*
> *Scottish economist*

Industrial relations are like sexual relations. It's better between two consenting parties.

> *Lord (Vic) Feather (1908–76)*
> *British trade-union official*

He who goes with wolves learns to howl.

> *Spanish proverb*

Goodness consists not in the outward things we do, but in the inward things we are.

> *Edwin Hubbell Chapin (1814–80)*
> *American clergyman and author*

I do the best I know how, the very best I can, and I mean to keep doing so until the end.

> *Abraham Lincoln (1809–65)*
> *16th president of the United States*

You and I can never do a kindness too soon, for we never know how soon it will be too late.

> *Ralph Waldo Emerson*
> *(1803–82)*
> *American essayist and poet*

Here's the rule for bargains: Do other men, for they would do you. That's the true business precept.

> *Charles Dickens (1812–70)*
> *English novelist*

Ethics stays in the preface of the average business science book.

> *Peter Drucker (1909–   )*
> *American business*
>   *philosopher and author*

Our deeds determine us, as much as we determine our deeds.

> *George Eliot (1819–80)*
> *English novelist*

We should keep the Panama Canal. After all, we stole it fair and square.

> *S. I. Hayakawa (1906–92)*
> *American semanticist and*
>   *U.S. senator*

Start with what is right rather than what is acceptable.

> *Peter Drucker (1909–   )*
> *American business*
>   *philosopher and author*

When Fortune means to men most good, she looks upon them with a threatening eye.

> *William Shakespeare (1564–*
>   *1616)*
> *English dramatist and poet*

The good die young—because they see it's no use living if you've got to be good.

> *John Barrymore (1882–*
>   *1942)*
> *American actor*

Our charity begins at home, and mostly ends where it begins.

> *Horace Smith (1808–93)*
> *American inventor and*
>   *manufacturer*

When you say that you agree to a thing on principle, you mean that you have not the slightest intention of carrying it out in practice.

> *Otto von Bismarck*
> *(1815–98)*
> *first chancellor of the*
>   *German Empire*

Conscience is the inner voice that warns us that someone may be looking.

> *H. L. Mencken (1880–1956)*
> *American editor*

SOCIAL RESPONSIBILITY

SOCIAL RESPONSIBILITY: *business philosophies, policies, procedures, and actions that have the enhancement of society's welfare as a primary objective.*

After five long and glorious years fighting along side General George Washington in the American Revolution, the marquis de Lafayette returned to his estates at Chavaniac, France, in 1782. He is still known today for his courage, integrity, and idealism, both in the United States and France. Lafayette and Washington share many of the qualities and character that made both men great figures in history. As with all great men, there are stories reflective of their fine character. One such story describes an incident in 1783, when the wheat harvests were poor, but Lafayette's barns were full. A foreman on the estate advised, "The bad harvest has raised the price of wheat. This is the time to sell." Lafayette knew the peasants in the surrounding villages were hungry and responded, "No, this is the time to give."

It was once said that the moral test of government is how that government treats those who are in the dawn of life, the children; those who are in the twilight of life, the elderly; and those who are in the shadows of life —the sick, the needy and the handicapped.

> *Hubert Humphrey*
> *(1911–78)*
> *vice president of the United States*

Humanity is composed but of two categories, the invalids and the nurses.

> *Walter Sickert (1860–1942)*
> *British painter and engraver*

You can't hold a man down without staying down with him.

> *Booker T. Washington*
> *(1856–1915)*
> *American educator*

The public be damned!

> *W. H. Vanderbilt (1821–85)*
> *American financier*

There are more hustlers in business than on street corners.

> *Malcolm Forbes (1919–90)*
> *American publisher*

My father always told me that all businessmen were sons-of-bitches, but I never believed it till now.

> *John F. Kennedy (1917–63)*
> *35th president of the United States*

The worst crime against working people is a company which fails to operate at a profit.

> *Samuel Gompers (1850–1924)*
> *American labor leader*

An idealist is a person who helps other people to be prosperous.

> *Henry Ford (1863–1947)*
> *American automobile*
> *manufacturer*

Air pollution is turning mother nature prematurely gray.

> *Irv Kupcinet (1912–)*
> *American newspaper*
> *columnist*

Give a man a fish, and he can eat for a day. But teach a man how to fish, and he'll be dead of mercury poisoning inside of three years.

> *Charlie Haas (1952–)*
> *American writer*

We are a cancer on nature.

> *Dave E. Foreman (1946–)*
> *American environmentalist*

We have learned that more is not necessarily better, that even our great nation has its recognized limits, and that we can neither answer all questions nor solve all problems. We cannot afford to do everything.

> *Jimmy Carter (1924–)*
> *39th president of the United States*

Man is a complex being; he makes deserts bloom and lakes die.

> *Gil Stern (1890–1973)*
> *American author*

I am not quite sure what the advantage is in having a few more dollars to spend if the air is too dirty to breathe, the water too polluted to drink, the commuters are losing out in the struggle to get in and out of the city, the streets are filthy, and the schools so bad that the young perhaps stay away, and the hoodlums roll citizens for some of the dollars they saved in the tax cut.

> *John Kenneth Galbraith (1908–)*
> *American economist*

Not one cent for scenery.

> *Joseph G. Cannon (1836–1926)*
> *speaker of the U.S. House of Representatives*
> *(denying funds request for conservation project)*

The nation behaves well if it treats the natural resources as assets which it must turn over to the next generation increased, and not impaired, in value.

> *Theodore Roosevelt (1858–1919)*
> *26th president of the United States*

You can be social minded without being a socialist.

> *Charles E. Wilson (1890–1961)*
> *chairman, General Motors Corporation and U.S. secretary of defense*

It is easier to make certain things legal than to make them legitimate.

> Sébastien-Roch Nicolas
> Chamfort (1741–94)
> French writer

We have no more right to consumer happiness without producing it than to consumer wealth without producing it.

> George Bernard Shaw
> (1856–1950)
> British playwright and
> social reformer

WEALTH

WEALTH: *a profusion or abundance; a great quantity of valuable material resources or possessions.*

Given the doubt that any blood is bluer than that of the British nor pride of duty any greater, it is often pointless to gratify a British boast with a response. Nonetheless, U.S. president Calvin Coolidge had his day in court when approached by a

British diplomat, an aristocrat no doubt, who produced a coin from his pocket declaring, "The king on this shilling is the one who made my great-great-grandfather a lord."

Coolidge responded by pulling a nickel from his pocket, blandly explaining to the Englishman, "My great-great-grandfather was made an angel by the Indian on this coin."

People's wealth and worth are very rarely related.

> Malcolm Forbes (1919–90)
> American publisher

I have no complex about wealth. I have worked hard for my money, producing things that people need. I believe that the able business leader who creates wealth and employment is more worthy of historical notice than politicians or soldiers.

> Jean Paul Getty (1892–
> 1976)
> American oil magnate and
> philanthropist

I make my money by supplying a public demand. If I break the law, my customers, who number hundreds of the best people in Chicago, are as guilty as I am. The only difference between us is that I sell and they buy. Everybody calls me a racketeer. I call myself a businessman. When I sell liquor, it's bootlegging. When my patrons serve it on a silver tray on Lake Shore Drive, it's hospitality.

> Al Capone (1899–1947)
> American gangster

Wealth is not without its advantages, and the case to the contrary, although it has often been made, has never proved widely persuasive.

> *John Kenneth Galbraith*
> *(1908–)*
> *American economist*

God must love the rich or he wouldn't have divided so much among so few of them.

> *H. L. Mencken (1880–1956)*
> *American editor*

Another advantage of being rich is that all your faults are called eccentricities.

> *Anonymous*

I don't like money actually, but it quiets my nerves.

> *Joe Louis (1914–81)*
> *American boxing champion*

The fellow that owns his own home is always just coming out of a hardware store.

> *Frank McKinney (Kin)*
> *Hubbard (1868–1930)*
> *American humorist*

He who wishes to be rich in a day will be hanged in a year.

> *Leonardo da Vinci (1452–*
> *1519)*
> *Italian artist, inventor, and*
> *scientist*

Why shouldn't the American people take half my money from me? I took all of it from them.

> *Edward A. Filene (1860–*
> *1937)*
> *American merchant*

I am richer than Harriman. I have all the money I want and he hasn't.

> *John Muir (1838–1914)*
> *American photographer*

No man can be conservative until he has something to lose.

> *James P. Warburg (1896–*
> *1969)*
> *American publicist*

It is simple, although not easy, to become a millionaire. Get a part-time job on Saturdays and do it for 10 years. Then take that money and invest it at 12 percent, wait 10 years, and you're a millionaire. However, most people don't want to give up their free time for 10 years. I've been working Saturdays since I was 16.

> *Dr. Jerry Buss (1933–)*
> *owner of American pro-*
> *fessional sports teams*

He who's got the gold, makes the rules.

> *Anonymous*

The man who dies rich dies disgraced.

> *Andrew Carnegie (1835–*
> *1919)*
> *American industrialist and*
> *philanthropist*

The rich man and his daughter are soon parted.

> Frank McKinney (Kin)
> Hubbard (1868–1930)
> American humorist

Wealth has never been a sufficient source of honor in itself. It must be advertised, and the normal medium is obtrusively expensive goods.

> John Kenneth Galbraith
> (1908–   )
> American economist

I've known what it is to be hungry, but I always went right to a restaurant.

> Ring Lardner (1885–1933)
> American short-story writer

Most of the rich people I've known have been fairly miserable.

> Agatha Christie (1890–
> 1976)
> British mystery writer

You know, Ernest, the rich are different from us.

> F. Scott Fitzgerald (1896–
> 1940)
> American writer

Yes, they have more money.

> Ernest Hemingway
> (1899–1961)
> American writer
> and journalist

The more money an American accumulates, the less interesting he becomes.

> Gore Vidal (1925–   )
> American author and
> dramatist

I'm opposed to millionaires, but it would be dangerous to offer me the position.

> Mark Twain (1835–1910)
> American author

Better to be *nouveau* than never to have been *riche* at all.

> Anonymous

A man who has a million dollars is as well off as if he were rich.

> John Jacob Astor (1763–
> 1848)
> American financier

I'd like to be rich enough so that I could throw soap away after the letters are worn off.

> Andy Rooney (1919–   )
> American author and
> television commentator

I've been rich and I've been poor; rich is better.

> Sophie Tucker (1884–1966)
> American actress

All heiresses are beautiful.

> John Dryden (1631–1700)
> English poet and dramatist

Don't try to die rich but live rich.

> Thomas Bird Mosher (1852–
> 1923)
> American publisher

The prosperous man is never sure that he is loved for himself.

> Marcus Lucan (39–65 A.D.)
> Roman poet

Since I am known as a "rich" person, I feel I have to tip at least $5 each time I check my coat. On top of that, I would have to wear a very expensive coat, and it would have to be insured. Added up, without a top-coat, I save over $20,000 a year.

> Aristotle Onassis
> (1900?–75)
> Greek shipping magnate

If you are poor, though you dwell in the busy marketplace, no one will inquire about you; if you are rich, though you dwell in the heart of the mountains, you will have distant relatives.

> Chinese proverb

It is not easy to find the relatives of a poor man.

> Menander (342–292 B.C.)
> Greek dramatist

The miser and the pig are of no use till death.

> Antoine Laumet de La
> Mothe (1658–1730)
> French soldier and
> colonialist

Money brings everything to you, even your daughters.

> Honoré de Balzac (1799–
> 1850)
> French novelist

We desire nothing so much as what we ought not to have.

> Publilius Syrus (1st century
> B.C.)
> Latin writer of mimes

It is better to deserve without receiving, than to receive without deserving.

> Robert Ingersoll (1833–99)
> American lawyer and orator

Poor people have more fun than rich people, they say; but I notice it's the rich people who keep saying it.

> Jack Paar (1918–   )
> American author and
> television-show host

POVERTY

POVERTY: *lack of something necessary; insufficiency.*

French novelist Honoré de Balzac spent his entire life hiding from creditors. One night a thief broke into Balzac's single-room apartment and tried to pick the lock on the writer's desk. He was startled by a sardonic laugh from the bed, where Balzac, who he had supposed was asleep, lay watching him. Startled, the thief asked, "Why are you laughing?" "I am laughing to think what risks you take to try to find money in a desk by night where the legal owner can never find any by day," Balzac replied.

When a poor man eats a chicken, one or the other is sick.

> *Yiddish proverb*

The gods sent not corn for the rich men only.

> *William Shakespeare (1564–1616)*
> *English dramatist and poet*

The task is not to make the poor wealthy, but productive.

> *Peter Drucker (1909–   )*
> *American business*
> *philosopher and author*

There's no scandal like rags, nor any crime so shameful as poverty.

> *George Farquhar (1678–1707)*
> *British dramatist*

Poverty is no sin.

> *George Herbert (1593–1633)*
> *English clergyman and poet*

I am a gentleman; I live by robbing the poor.

> *George Bernard Shaw (1856–1950)*
> *British playwright and social reformer*

What a man in the street wants is not a big debate on fundamental issues; he wants a little medical care, a rug on the floor, a picture on the wall, a little music in the house, and a place to take Molly and the grandchildren when he retires.

> *Lyndon B. Johnson (1908–73)*
> *36th president of the United States*

The poor you always have with you.

> *Jesus of Nazareth in John 12:8*

The trouble with being poor is that it takes up all your time.

> *Willem De Kooning (1904–   )*
> *American painter*

I've never been poor, only broke. Being poor is a frame of mind. Being broke is only a temporary situation.

> *Mike Todd (1907–58)*
> *American theatrical*
> *producer*

The chief problem of the lower-income farmers is poverty.

> *Nelson Rockefeller*
> *(1908–79)*
> *vice president of the United*
> *States*

God has always been hard on the poor, and He always will be.

> *Jean-Paul Marat (1743–93)*
> *French revolutionist*

In a country well governed, poverty is something to be ashamed of.

> *Confucius (551–479 B.C.)*
> *Chinese philosopher*

Every country has peasants—ours have money.

> *Gloria Steinem (1934–)*
> *American feminist and*
> *journalist*

Generally speaking, the poorer person summers where he winters.

> *Fran Lebowitz (1950–)*
> *American author*

How much health care Americans get should depend not on how much they can afford but on how much they need.

> *Edward M. Kennedy*
> *(1932–)*
> *U.S. senator*

What a fine arrangement that permits a factory girl to sweat for twelve hours so that the employer can use a portion of her unpaid labor to hire her sister as a maid, her brother as a groom, and her cousin as a soldier or a policeman.

> *Karl Marx (1818–83)*
> *German philosopher*

We boast the highest standard of living when it's only the biggest.

> *Frank Lloyd Wright (1867–*
> *1959)*
> *American architect*

As a child my family's menu consisted of two choices: take it or leave it.

> *Buddy Hackett (1924–)*
> *American comedian*

There were times my pants were so thin that I could sit on a dime and tell if it were heads or tails.

> *Spencer Tracy (1900–67)*
> *American actor*

There's another advantage of being poor—a doctor will cure you faster.

> *Frank McKinney (Kin)*
> *Hubbard (1868–1930)*
> *American humorist*

HUMAN RIGHTS

HUMAN RIGHTS: *those valued things that all humans are thought to be entitled to as viewed by various political philosophies.*

In 1949, Jackie Robinson broke the color barrier in baseball making his first appearance with the National League's Brooklyn Dodgers. As he was leaving the hotel, he kissed his wife good-bye, and jokingly said, "If you come down to Ebbets Field today, you won't have any trouble recognizing me." Adding after a short pause, "My number's 42."

We didn't all come over on the same ship, but we're all in the same boat.

> *Bernard Baruch*
> *(1870–1965)*
> *American financier*
> *and statesman*

It doesn't matter if a cat is black or white, so long as it catches mice.

> *Deng Xiaoping (1904–   )*
> *Chinese premier*

Two men were killed in the construction work in Panama. One was English, the other a laborer.

> *George S. Kaufman (1889–*
> *1961)*
> *American dramatist*

I've read your Bill of Rights a hundred times and I'll probably read it a hundred more before I die. I'm not sure the American people have any idea how blessed they are to have the Bill of Rights. After all, who needs a document to guarantee rights that people already presume they have? Ask the people who tore down fences and jumped walls. Ask the people who were cut off from their families and deprived of their jobs. Ask my fellow workers at the Gdansk shipyard. Freedom may be the soul of humanity, but sometimes you have to struggle to prove it.

> *Lech Walesa (1943–   )*
> *Polish Nobel Peace*
> *Prize laureate*

This book is dedicated to Abraham Lincoln. If it wasn't for Abe, I'd still be on the open market.

> *Dick Gregory (1932–   )*
> *American comedian*

We hold these truths to be self-evident, that all men are created equal, that they are endowed by their Creator with certain unalienable rights, that among these are life, liberty, and the pursuit of happiness.

> *Thomas Jefferson (1743–*
> *1826)*
> *3rd president of the United*
> *States*

I didn't know I was a slave until I found out I couldn't do the things I wanted.

> *Frederick Douglass*
> *(1817–95)*
> *American orator and*
> *journalist*

Emperors, kings, artisans, peasants, big people, little people—at bottom we are all alike and all the same; all just alike on the inside, and when our clothes are off nobody can tell which of us is which.

> *Mark Twain (1835–1910)*
> *American author*

Prejudice saves a lot of time, because you can form an opinion without the facts.

> *Anonymous*

In Germany, they came first for the communists, and I didn't speak up because I wasn't a communist. Then they came for the Jews, and I didn't speak up because I wasn't a Jew. Then they came for the trade unionists, and I didn't speak up because I wasn't a trade unionist. Then they came for the Catholics, and I didn't speak up because I was a Protestant. Then they came for me, and by that time no one was left to speak up.

> *Martin Niemöller (1892–*
> *1984)*
> *German theologian*

A minority group has "arrived" only when it has the right to produce some fools and scoundrels without the entire group paying for it.

> *Carl T. Rowan (1925–   )*
> *American columnist and*
> *diplomat*

There is good evidence . . . that a disregard for social performance trans-

lates, sooner or later, into significant dollar costs.

> *Juanita M. Kreps (1921–   )*
> *American economist and*
> *U.S. secretary of*
> *commerce*

I want to be the white man's brother, not his brother-in-law.

> *Martin Luther King, Jr.*
> *(1929–68)*
> *American clergyman and*
> *civil-rights leader*

He who will not reason is a bigot; he who cannot is a fool; and he who dares not is a slave.

> *Sir William Drummond*
> *(1854–1907)*
> *Canadian Poet*

I have a dream that one day every valley shall be exalted, every hill and mountain shall be made low, the rough places will be made straight and the glory of the Lord shall be revealed and all flesh shall see it together.

"I have a dream that one day on the red hills of Georgia, the sons of former slaves and the sons of former slave owners will be able to sit together at the table of brotherhood.

"I have a dream that my four little children will one day live in a nation where they will not be judged by the color of their skin, but by the content of their character.

> *Martin Luther King, Jr.*
> *(1929–68)*
> *American clergyman and*
> *civil-rights leader*

I have fought white domination. I have fought black domination. I have cherished the ideal of a free society in which all people live in harmony.

Nelson Mandela (1918–   )
South African black
nationalist leader

From the religious hilltops of New Hampshire, let freedom ring. From the mighty mountains of New York, let freedom ring. From the heightening Alleghenies of Pennsylvania, let freedom ring. But not only that: Let freedom ring from every hill and molehill of Mississippi. When this happens, when we let it ring, we will speed the day when all of God's children, black men and white men, Jews and Gentiles, Protestants and Catholics, will be able to join hands and sing in the words of the old Negro spiritual: "Free at last, free at last, thank God Almighty, we're free at last."

Martin Luther King, Jr.
(1929–68)
American clergyman and
civil-rights leader

It's hard being black. You ever been black? I was black once—when I was poor.

Larry Holmes (1949–   )
American boxing champion

The test of our progress is not whether we add more to the abundance of those who have much; it is whether we provide enough for those who have too little.

Franklin D. Roosevelt
(1882–1945)
32nd president of the
United States

When the whites came, we had the land and they had the Bibles. Now they have the land and we have the Bibles.

Chief Dan George
(1899–1981)
Squamish Indian chief

For those who do not think, it is best at least to rearrange their prejudices once in a while.

Luther Burbank (1849–
1926)
American horticulturist

I'm interested in the fact that the less secure a man is, the more likely he is to have extreme prejudice.

Clint Eastwood (1930–   )
American actor

Chapter 19

Government-Business Obligations

GOVERNMENT: *established system of political administration in which authority is exercised to rule, direct, and control the affairs of a nation, state, or district.*

F ew American presidents have been as adept as Ronald Reagan at presenting an idea successfully to the American public. His long acting career proved an excellent training ground for honing his ability to communicate and subtly persuade people to accept his point of view. During his first televised budget speech following his 1980 election, Reagan reached into his pocket, extracted a few coins, and then used them to illustrate the current value of the dollar. Recalling the incident, a political rival pointed out, "It takes an actor to do that. Carter would have emphasized all the wrong words. Ford would have fumbled and dropped the cash. Nixon would have pocketed it."

The following is an excerpt from a directive issued by the U.S. government's Equal Employment Opportunity Commission:

REPORTING REQUIREMENTS: Federal agencies and designated major operating components (as described in MD-702) are required to submit their sexual harassment plans to the Office of Government Employment EEOC, 60 days after effective date of this directive.

The next step will presumably be a request for a listing of all employees broken down by sex.

A government which robs Peter to pay Paul can always depend on the support of Paul.

> George Bernard Shaw
> (1856–1950)
> British playwright and
> social reformer

The nine most terrifying words in the English language are: "I'm from the government and I'm here to help."

> Ronald Reagan (1911–)
> 40th president of the United
> States

I've had a tough time learning how to act like a Congressman. Today I accidentally spent some of my own money.

> Joseph P. Kennedy II
> (1952–)
> U.S. congressman

Success in running a business carries by itself no promise of success outside business.

> Peter Drucker (1909–)
> American business
> philosopher and
> author

Being in politics is like being a football coach. You have to be smart enough to understand the game and dumb enough to think it's important.

> Eugene McCarthy
> (1916–)
> U.S. senator

Government today sits as an invisible partner of every company, every family, and every individual in the country.

> William L. Wearly
> (1915–)
> CEO, Ingersoll-Rand
> Corporation, Inter-
> national Division

A billion seconds ago it was 1951.
A billion minutes ago Jesus was alive and walking in Galilee.
A billion hours ago no one walked on two feet on earth.
And a billion dollars ago was 10.3 hours in Washington, D.C.

> Alexander B. Trowbridge,
> Jr. (1929–)
> U.S. secretary of commerce

The point to remember is that what the government gives it must first take away.

> John Strider Coleman
> (1897–1958)
> American business
> executive

A government that is big enough to give you all you want is big enough to take it all away.

> Barry Goldwater (1909–)
> U.S. senator

When business accepts help from government, it can be like going to bed with a hippopotamus. It's warm and nice for a moment, but then your bedmate rolls over and crushes you.

> Donald Rumsfeld (1932–)
> American pharmaceutical
> executive and U.S.
> secretary of defense

I'd like to see the government get out of war altogether and leave the whole field to private industry.

> Joseph Heller (1923–)
> American author

The best minds are not in government. If any were, business would hire them away.

> Ronald Reagan (1911–)
> 40th president of the United
> States

The business of government is to keep government out of business— that is, unless business needs government aid.

> Will Rogers (1879–1935)
> American actor and
> humorist

I have said to the people we mean to have less government in business as well as more business in government.

> Warren G. Harding (1865– 1923)
> 29th president of the United
> States

The less government interferes with private business, the better for general prosperity.

> Martin Van Buren (1782– 1862)
> 8th president of the United
> States

Politics has got so expensive that it takes lots of money to even get beat with.

> Will Rogers (1879–1935)
> American actor and
> humorist

Politics is the gentle art of getting votes from the poor and campaign funds from the rich, by promising to protect each from the other.

> Oscar Ameringer (1870– 1943)
> American publisher, author,
> and socialist leader

Once there were two brothers. One ran away to sea, the other was elected vice-president, and nothing was ever heard of either of them again.

> Thomas R. Marshall (1854– 1925)
> vice president of the United
> States

Inflation is like sin; every government denounces it and every government practices it.

> Sir Fredrick Leith-Ross
> (1887–1968)
> English economist and
> financier

No man should be in public office who can't make more money in private life.

> Thomas E. Dewey
> (1902–71)
> American lawyer and
> politician

A politician should have three hats. One for throwing in the ring, one for talking through, and one for pulling rabbits out of if elected.

> Carl Sandburg (1878–1967)
> American poet

It has been said that democracy is the worst form of government except all the others that have been tried.

> Winston Churchill (1874–
> 1965)
> British statesman and
> prime minister

A cardinal rule of politics is never get caught in bed with a live man or a dead woman.

> Larry Hagman (1931–   )
> American actor (as J. R.
> Ewing in the television
> series "Dallas")

Diplomacy is the art of saying "Nice doggie" until you can find a rock.

> Will Rogers (1879–1935)
> American actor and
> humorist

It is dangerous to be right when the government is wrong.

> Voltaire (1694–1778)
> French writer

Have you ever seen a political candidate talking to a rich person on television?

> Art Buchwald (1925–   )
> American journalist

I get no respect. The way my luck is running, if I was a politician I'd be honest.

> Rodney Dangerfield
> (1921–   )
> American actor and
> comedian

Since a politician never believes what he says, he is surprised when others believe him.

> Charles de Gaulle (1890–
> 1970)
> French general and
> president of the Fifth
> Republic

There is no more independence in politics than there is in jail.

> Will Rogers (1879–1935)
> American actor and
> humorist

Too bad that all the people who know how to run the country are busy driving taxicabs and cutting hair.

> *George Burns (1896–)*
> *American actor and*
> *comedian*

Anything that the private sector can do, government can do it worse.

> *Dixie Lee Ray (1914–)*
> *American politician*

A diplomat is a man who always remembers a woman's birthday but never remembers her age.

> *Robert Frost (1874–1963)*
> *American poet*

Every man's life, liberty, and property are in danger when the Legislature is in session.

> *Daniel Webster (1782–1852)*
> *American statesman and*
> *orator*

The vice presidency is sort of like the last cookie on the plate. Everybody insists he won't take it, but somebody always does.

> *Bill Vaughan (1915–77)*
> *American writer and editor*

Now I know what a statesman is; he's a dead politician. We need more statesmen.

> *Robert C. (Bob) Edwards*
> *(1864–1922)*
> *Canadian educator and*
> *humorist*

I'm not a member of any organized party. I'm a Democrat.

> *Will Rogers (1879–1935)*
> *American actor and*
> *humorist*

Blessed are the young, for they shall inherit the national debt.

> *Herbert Hoover (1874–*
> *1964)*
> *31st president of the United*
> *States*

Reader, suppose you were an idiot. And suppose you were a member of Congress. But I repeat myself.

> *Mark Twain (1835–1910)*
> *American author*

I don't know jokes; I just watch the government and report the facts.

> *Will Rogers (1879–1935)*
> *American actor and*
> *humorist*

LAWYERS AND THE LAW

LAW: *principles and regulations established by a government in the form of either legislation or custom.*

Probably the most controversial case Clarence Seward Darrow ever defended concerned the legality of teaching the theory of evolution; however, he spent the latter part of his life opposing capital punishment and successfully defending the underdog in over one hundred murder cases. After one such case, an exuberant client asked, "How can I ever repay your troubles?"

"Madam," replied the attorney, "ever since the ancient Phoenicians invented money, there has been only one answer to that question."

Lawyers are like beavers: They get in the mainstream and dam it up.

> *John Naisbitt (1929–   )*
> *American business writer*
> *and social researcher*

Well, I don't know as I want a lawyer to tell me what I cannot do. I hire him to tell me how to do what I want to do.

> *John Pierpont Morgan*
> *(1837–1913)*
> *American financier*

Lawyers, I suppose, were children once.

> *Charles Lamb (1775–1834)*
> *English essayist and critic*

The first thing we do, let's kill all the lawyers.

> *William Shakespeare (1564–1616)*
> *English dramatist and poet*

The minute you read something that you can't understand, you can almost be sure it was drawn up by a lawyer.

> *Will Rogers (1879–1935)*
> *American actor and*
> *humorist*

Law cannot persuade where it cannot punish.

> *Thomas Fuller (1608–61)*
> *English clergyman and*
> *author*

If there were no bad people, there would be no good lawyers.

> *Charles Dickens (1812–70)*
> *English novelist*

A man who is his own lawyer has a fool for a client.

> *Anonymous*

Bulls do not win bull fights.
People do.
People do not win people fights.
Lawyers do.

> *Norman R. Augustine*
> *(1935–)*
> *American author and*
> *chairman, Martin*
> *Marietta Corporation*

A lawyer is a learned gentleman who rescues your estate from your enemies and keeps it for himself.

> *Lord (Henry Peter)*
> *Brougham (1778–1868)*
> *British statesman, author,*
> *and jurist*

I sometimes wish that people would put a little more emphasis upon the observance of the law than they do upon its enforcement.

> *Calvin Coolidge (1872–*
> *1933)*
> *30th president of the United*
> *States*

The illegal we do immediately, the unconstitutional takes a little longer.

> *Henry Kissinger (1923–)*
> *American scholar and U.S.*
> *secretary of state*

There are three reasons why lawyers are being used more and more in scientific experiments. First, every year there are more and more of them around. Second, lab assistants don't get attached to them. And, third, there are some things that rats just won't do.

> *Anonymous*

A lawyer and a wagon wheel must be well greased.

> *German proverb*

Bad laws are the worst sort of tyranny.

> *Edmund Burke (1729–97)*
> *British statesman and*
> *orator*

When men are pure, laws are useless; when men are corrupt, laws are broken.

> *Benjamin Disraeli*
> *(1804–81)*
> *British novelist and prime*
> *minister*

A peasant between two lawyers is a fish between two cats.

> *Spanish proverb*

When you go into court you are putting your fate into the hands of twelve people who weren't smart enough to get out of jury duty.

> *Norm Crosby (1927–)*
> *American comedian*

A jury consists of twelve persons chosen to decide who has the better lawyer.

> *Robert Frost (1874–1963)*
> *American poet*

LIBERALS AND CONSERVATIVES

LIBERAL: *favorable to progress or reform, as in political affairs.*

CONSERVATIVE: *disposed to preserve existing conditions and institutions and to resist change.*

Responding to almost any cue, President Ronald Reagan gave us many great one-liners. Immediately after being shot outside the Washington Hilton Hotel in 1981, Reagan was rushed to the hospital for emergency surgery. As the gurney was rolled into the operating room, he glanced at the attending doctors and nurses and smiling said, "Please assure me that you are all Republicans!"

A man who is not a liberal at sixteen has no heart; a man who is not a conservative at sixty has no head.

> *Benjamin Disraeli*
> *(1804–81)*
> *British novelist and prime minister*

A conservative is a man who is too cowardly to fight and too fat to run.

> *Elbert Hubbard (1856–1915)*
> *American writer*

I can remember way back when a liberal was one who was generous with his own money.

> *Will Rogers (1879–1935)*
> *American actor and humorist*

Conservatives are not necessarily stupid, but most stupid people are conservatives.

> *John Stuart Mill (1806–73)*
> *English philosopher and economist*

A conservative is a liberal who has been mugged.

> *Anonymous*

A conservative is a man who just sits and thinks, mostly sits.

> *Woodrow Wilson (1856–1924)*
> *28th president of the United States*

The Republican party is a friend of Social Security the way Colonel Sanders was a friend to chickens.

> *Charles T. Manatt*
> *(1936–   )*
> *American lawyer and banker*

TAXES

TAX: *payment made to a government agency at either the local, state, or federal level by individuals and organizations having income or property, or engaging in various types of activities.*

After his appointment in 1961 as U.S. postmaster general, James Edward Day was given a letter addressed to God. It was from a little boy whose father had died and whose mother was having financial problems. In the letter, he prayed that God would send her a hundred dollars to help out. Day was moved by the little boy's plea and put a twenty-dollar bill in an envelope and sent it to the boy. A couple of weeks later, Day received a second letter:
Dear God:
Much obliged for all you have done, but we need another hundred dollars. But please, when you send it to Mom, don't do it through Washington, because the last time they deducted eighty percent of it there.

America's cowboy philosopher, Will Rogers, is best remembered for his salty remarks about the government and politics. Having overpaid his income tax, Rogers tried in vain to recoup the money, writing numerous letters that were never answered. Months went by, and eventually it was time to file taxes again. Rogers received his tax form but still had no acknowledgment, much less settlement, of his claim. So, in the section marked "Deductions," he listed: "Bad debt, U.S. Government—$40,000."

There is one difference between a tax collector and a taxidermist—the taxidermist leaves the hide.

> *Mortimer Caplan (1916–)*
> *American lawyer and*
> *commissioner, Internal*
> *Revenue Service*

We don't pay taxes; the little people pay taxes.

> *Leona Helmsley (1920–)*
> *wife of American hotel-*
> *chain owner Harry*
> *Helmsley*

Her level of arrogance has grown steadily worse in recent years. The bottom line is I don't want to create another Leona Helmsley.

> *Donald M. Trump*
> *(1946–)*
> *American real estate*
> *executive*
> *(explaining his decision to*
> *divorce Ivana Trump, his*
> *wife of thirteen years)*

Taxes are what we pay for a civilized society.

> *Oliver Wendell Holmes, Jr.*
> *(1841–1935)*
> *American jurist*

You don't see me at Vegas or at the races throwing my money around. I've got a government to support.

> *Bob Hope (1903–　)*
> *American actor and*
> *comedian*

The United States is the only country where it takes more brains to figure your tax than to earn the money to pay it.

> *Edward J. Gurney*
> *(1914–　)*
> *U.S. senator*

High tax rates don't redistribute income. They redistribute taxpayers. Some go to their yachts, some to poor countries. Bjorn Borg doesn't live in Sweden of course. He lives in Malta.

> *George Gilder (1939–　)*
> *American writer*

I don't think meals have any business being deductible. I'm for separation of calories and corporations.

> *Ralph Nader (1934–　)*
> *American consumer*
> *advocate*

Tax revision is like making love to a gorilla. You may think it's over, but it's only over when the gorilla says it is.

> *David Berenson (1910–　)*
> *American public accounting*
> *company executive*

There is nothing sinister in so arranging one's affairs as to keep taxes as low as possible.

> *Judge Learned Hand (1872–*
> *1961)*
> *American jurist*

I have no use for bodyguards, but I have a very special use for two highly trained certified public accountants.

> *Elvis Presley (1935–77)*
> *American singer*

The art of taxation consists in so plucking the goose as to get the most feathers with the least hissing.

> *attributed to Jean-Baptiste*
> *Colbert (1619–83)*
> *French statesman and*
> *minister of finance to*
> *Louis XIV*

We are dedicated to the preservation and strengthening of small business and our tax policy is designated to destroy small business. Small businesses are selling out because of tax laws for ITT.

> *Peter Drucker (1909–　)*
> *American business*
> *philosopher and author*

In this world nothing can be said to be certain, except death and taxes.

> *Benjamin Franklin*
> *(1706–90)*
> *American statesman and*
> *philosopher*

They say there are only two certainties in life, taxes and death. The only difference is, death doesn't get worse every time Congress meets.

> Spark M. Matsunaga
> (1916–90)
> U.S. senator

The income tax has made more liars out of the American people than golf has. Even when you make a tax form out on the level, you don't know, when it's through, if you are a crook or a martyr.

> Will Rogers (1879–1935)
> American actor and
> humorist

The wages of sin are unreported.

> Anonymous

The taxpayer—that's someone who works for the federal government but doesn't have to take a civil service exam.

> Ronald Reagan (1911–   )
> 40th president of the United
> States

The only way to cut government spending is not to give them the money to spend in the first place.

> Howard Jarvis (1902–86)
> American newspaper
> publisher and political
> activist

An income tax form is like a laundry list—either way you lose your shirt.

> Fred Allen (1894–1956)
> American comedian

I'm proud to pay taxes in the United States. The only thing is, I could be just as proud for half the money.

> Arthur Godfrey (1903–83)
> American entertainer

Tax reform means: "Don't tax me. Don't tax thee. Tax that guy behind the tree."

> Russell Long (1918–   )
> U.S. senator

Government expands to absorb revenue and then some.

> Tom Wicker (1926–   )
> American journalist and
> author

Inflation is the one form of taxation that can be imposed without legislation.

> Milton Friedman (1912–   )
> American economist

The nation should have a tax system which looks like someone designed it on purpose.

> William E. Simon (1927–   )
> American business executive
> and U.S. secretary of the
> treasury

Why does a slight tax increase cost you $200 and a substantial tax cut save you 30 cents?

> Peg Bracken (1920–   )
> American radio writer

People hate taxes the way children hate brushing their teeth—and in the same shortsighted way.

> Paul A. Samuelson
> (1915–   )
> American economist

Collecting more taxes than is absolutely necessary is legalized robbery.

> Calvin Coolidge (1872–1933)
> 30th president of the United States

Income tax returns are the most imaginative fiction being written today.

> Herman Wouk (1915–   )
> American author

The hardest thing in the world to understand is the income tax.

> Albert Einstein (1879–1955)
> American physicist

PROFITS

PROFIT: *in* finance: *reward to the entrepreneur for the risks assumed in the creation and operation of a business venture;*

   in accounting: *excess remaining from revenues after all costs and expenses involved in operations have been paid.*

Most of us have profited greatly from those experiences in our lives that helped build our character and strengthen our moral fiber. In *Harrap's Book of Business Anecdotes*, Peter Hay recalls one such experience. Paul Hoffman, director of the European Recovery Program in the years following World War II, grew up in Chicago and at eighteen held a job as an automobile salesman. One day a veterinarian came in to test-drive a used 1905 Jackson automobile. He liked the car, and Hoffman was already mentally calculating his sales commission when he offered to drive the vet home. It turned out that the vet lived on a farm forty miles outside town, and Hoffman knew that the Jackson Automobile Company slogan, "No hill too steep; no sand too deep," was not a guarantee of any sort that the old car would make it. It sputtered, clanged, and banged its way to the farm.

But make it, they did. The veterinarian was quite impressed and was ready to sign the papers as soon as they walked in the house. Hoffman, on the other hand, was surprised they had made it at all. The vet took pen in hand, and then, looking up at Hoffman, asked, "One question, son. If you were me, would you buy this car?"

Hoffman could feel his breathing stop; his mind was clear, but it was difficult to speak. Thoughts were racing through his head when he saw an embroidered sign hanging on the wall: JESUS HEARS EVERY WORD YOU SAY.

There was no sale that day.

It is a socialist idea that making profits is a vice; I consider the real vice is making losses.

> *Winston Churchill (1874–*
> *1965)*
> *British statesman and*
> *prime minister*

You show me a capitalist, I'll show you a bloodsucker.

> *Malcolm X (1925–65)*
> *American black nationalist*
> *and religious leader*

The number one corporate responsibility is to make a profit . . . this sounds like you're not even thinking of society, your fellow man or anybody else. It sounds like you're selfish. But profit is like breathing. If you can't do that, you can forget about doing anything else. Once a corporation learns how to breathe, or make a profit, then it can turn to the other corporate responsibilities, like creating jobs and adding to GNP.

> *Robert Mercer (1924–   )*
> *president, Goodyear*
> *Corporation*

At the close of the first day [in 1861] the cash drawer revealed a total intake of $24.67. Of this sum, $24 was spent for advertising and 67 cents saved for making change next morning.

> *John Wanamaker (1838–*
> *1922)*
> *American merchant*

You can absolutely go broke being successful.

> *Jerry White (1941–   )*
> *American educator*

Any business arrangement that is not profitable to the other fellow will in the end prove unprofitable to you. The bargain that yields mutual satisfaction is the only one that is apt to be repeated.

> *B. C. Forbes (1880–1954)*
> *American publisher*

The fear of capitalism has compelled socialism to widen freedom, and the fear of socialism has compelled capitalism to increase equality.

> *Will (1885–1981) and Ariel*
> *(1898–1981) Durant*
> *American historians*

From each according to his ability, to each according to his needs.

> *Karl Marx (1818–83)*
> *German philosopher*

I believe that the power to make money is a gift from God.

> *John D. Rockefeller (1839–*
> *1937)*
> *American oil magnate and*
> *philanthropist*

Capitalism is humanitarianism.

> *Margaret Thatcher*
> *(1925–   )*
> *prime minister of Great*
> *Britain*

Money alone sets all the world in motion.

> *Publilius Syrus (1st century*
> *B.C.)*
> *Latin writer of mimes*

The highest use of capital is not to make more money, but to make money do more for the betterment of life.

> Henry Ford (1863–1947)
> American automobile
> manufacturer

Do you know the only thing that gives me pleasure? It's to see my dividends coming in.

> John D. Rockefeller (1839–1937)
> American oil magnate and
> philanthropist

The only way to keep score in business is to add up how much money you make.

> Harry B. Helmsley
> (1909–)
> American hotel-chain owner

Little by little, the pimps have taken over the world. They don't do anything, they don't make anything—they just stand there and take their cut.

> Jean Giraudoux (1882–1944)
> French writer

Capital as such is not evil; it is its wrong use that is evil.

> Mohandas K. Gandhi
> (1869–1948)
> Indian nationalist leader

I use the words "profit" and "capitalism" proudly. Because when business is healthy, all of society is healthy.

> Harry Jack Gray (1919–)
> chairman, United Technologies Corporation

Don't get the idea that I'm knocking the American system.

> Al Capone (1899–1947)
> American gangster

Business without profit is not business any more than a pickle is candy.

> Charles F. Abbott (1937–)
> American lawyer

That's the American way. If little kids don't aspire to make money like I did, what the hell good is this country?

> Lee Iacocca (1924–)
> chairman, Chrysler
> Corporation

It is better to sell a large number of cars at a reasonably small margin than to sell fewer at a large margin of profit . . . it enables a large number of people to buy and enjoy [the car] and it gives a large number of men employment at good wages. Those are two aims I have in life.

> Henry Ford (1863–1947)
> American automobile
> manufacturer

Some see private enterprise as a predatory target to be shot, others as a cow to be milked, but few are those who see it as a sturdy horse pulling the wagon.

> Winston Churchill (1874–1965)
> British statesman and prime minister

Social responsibility is tied directly to making a profit.

> John D. Harper (1910–)
> chairman, Aluminum Company of America

It is no secret that organized crime in America takes in over forty billion dollars a year. This is quite a profitable sum especially when one considers that the Mafia spends very little for office supplies.

> Woody Allen (1935–)
> American actor, film director, and comedian

SCOPE OF BUSINESS

SCOPE OF BUSINESS: *individuals, organizations, and activities affected by the operations of a firm.*

In spite of his unwavering determination to crush Hitler and his success as a leader among the Allied nations, Sir Winston Churchill was defeated in 1945 by Clement Attlee and the Labour party's platform of rapid social and political reform. While Churchill led the Conservative party, he was ineffective in preventing the Labour party from rapidly nationalizing business and industry in Great Britain. It happened one day that these two great opposing leaders ran into each other in the men's room of the House of Commons. Doing his best to avoid Attlee, Churchill went to the urinal farthest from the one the prime minister was addressing.

"A bit standoffish today, Winston?" remarked Attlee.

"That's right," Churchill shot back, "because every time you see something big, you want to nationalize it."

I like business because it is competitive, because it rewards deeds rather than words.

I like business because it compels earnestness and does not permit me to neglect today's task while thinking about tomorrow.

I like business because it undertakes to please, not reform; because it is honestly selfish, thereby avoiding hypocrisy and sentimentality.

I like business because it promptly penalizes mistakes, shiftlessness, and inefficiency, while rewarding well those who give it the best they have in them.

Last, I like business because each day is a fresh adventure.

> Robert Hervey Cabell (1865–1947)
> president, Armour & Company

Business is like riding a bicycle. Either you keep moving or you fall down.

American business saying

You never expected justice from a company, did you? They have neither a soul to lose, nor a body to kick.

Sydney Smith (1771–1845)
English essayist

A business, like an automobile, has to be driven in order to get results.

B. C. Forbes (1880–1954)
American publisher

Corporation: an ingenious device for obtaining individual profit without individual responsibility.

Ambrose Bierce (1842–
ca. 1914)
American author

Three things happen in every merger: first, a cloud of ambiguity; second, a drop in trust level; third, self-preservation. Then a fifteen per cent drop in middle management productivity.

Price Pritchett (1941–   )
American business
consultant

The business of America is business.

Calvin Coolidge (1872–
1933)
30th president of the United
States

Business underlies everything in our national life, including our spiritual life. Witness the fact that in the Lord's Prayer, the first petition is for daily bread. No one can worship God or love his neighbor on an empty stomach.

Woodrow Wilson (1856–
1924)
28th president of the United
States

Being good in business is the most fascinating kind of art.

Andy Warhol (1927?–87)
American painter and
motion-picture producer

Part V

THE
TWENTY-FIRST
CENTURY
MANAGER

Chapter 20

Education and
the Manager

EDUCATION: *knowledge and development resulting
from a learning process.*

Americans have proved themselves to be the worst spellers
in the English-speaking world. A 1989 Gallup spelling quiz
found the best spellers to be in Australia, followed by Canada,
the United Kingdom, and then the United States. Americans
misspelled an average of more than six out of the ten words on
the quiz, and America's best turned out to be between the ages
of thirty-five and forty-four. But, if it's any consolation, in the top
four countries only one in twenty adults could spell all ten words
correctly. Great Britain was the only country in which women
did not excel men—their spellers being of equal ability regardless of sex. The ten words on the quiz were *magazine, sandwich,
kerosene, calamity, penitentiary, picnicking, deceive, accelera-
tor, cauliflower,* and *parallel.*

Alex Karras, American actor and one of the more humorous members of the National Football League's Detroit Lions, frequently
jokes about his education. A University of Iowa alumnus, Karras
once confided, "I never graduated. I was there for only two
terms—Truman's and Eisenhower's."

Those who know not, and know that they know not, these are foolish.
Those who know not, and know not that they know not, these are the simple and should be instructed.
Those who know, and know not that they know, these are asleep; wake them.
Those who know and know they know, these are the wise; listen to them.

>   *Arab proverb*

Knowledge is a process of piling up facts; wisdom lies in their simplification.

>   *Martin H. Fischer (1879–1962)*
>   *American scientist, author, and educator*

Education is what survives when what has been learnt has been forgotten.

>   *B. F. Skinner (1904–90)*
>   *American psychologist*

Maybe work should be redefined to some extent. . . . Maybe going to school and learning should be considered work and the students that are paying tuition should be paid.

>   *Studs Terkel (1912–   )*
>   *American writer*

I think the world is run by C students.

>   *Al McGuire (1928–   )*
>   *American basketball coach*

You can always tell a Harvard man, but you can't tell him much.

>   *attributed to James Barnes (1866–1936)*
>   *American author*

I never let my schooling interfere with my education.

>   *Mark Twain (1835–1910)*
>   *American writer*

In the space age the most important space is between the ears.

>   *Thomas J. Barlow (1922–   )*
>   *CEO, Anderson, Clayton & Company*

Any intelligent fool can make things bigger, more complex, and more violent. It takes a touch of genius—and a lot of courage—to move in the opposite direction.

>   *Ernst F. Schumacher (1911–77)*
>   *English economist*

There is no crisis to which academics will not respond with a seminar.

>   *Anonymous*

I oppose federal aid to education because no one has been able to prove the need for it.

>   *Ronald Reagan (1911–   )*
>   *40th president of the United States*

The more we study, the more we discover our ignorance.

> *Percy Bysshe Shelley (1792–1822)*
> *English poet*

A professor is one who talks in someone else's sleep.

> *Wystan Hugh Auden (1907–73)*
> *American poet*

Who dares to teach must never cease to learn.

> *John Cotton Dana (1856–1929)*
> *American librarian (motto of Kean College of New Jersey)*

He that teaches himself hath a fool for a master.

> *Benjamin Franklin (1706–90)*
> *American statesman and philosopher*

He who can, does; he who cannot, teaches.

> *George Bernard Shaw (1856–1950)*
> *British playwright and social reformer*

Universities are full of knowledge; the freshmen bring a little in and the seniors take none away, and knowledge accumulates.

> *Abbott L. Lowell (1856–1943)*
> *American political scientist and educator*

Everyone is ignorant, only on different subjects.

> *Will Rogers (1879–1935)*
> *American actor and humorist*

Every man is a damn fool for at least five minutes every day; wisdom consists in not exceeding the limit.

> *Elbert Hubbard (1856–1915)*
> *American writer*

The brighter you are, the more you have to learn.

> *Don Herold (1927–   )*
> *American author*

The school is not the end but only the beginning of an education.

> *Calvin Coolidge (1872–1933)*
> *30th president of the United States*

One pound of learning requires ten pounds of common sense to apply it.

> *Anonymous*

Don't try to fix the students, fix ourselves first. The good teacher makes the poor student good and the good student superior. When our students fail, we, as teachers, too, have failed.

> *Marva Collins (1936–   )*
> *American educator*

Education is only a ladder to gather fruit from the tree of knowledge, not the fruit itself.

> *Anonymous*

You can lead a boy to college, but you cannot make him think.

> Elbert Hubbard (1856–1915)
> American writer

To be conscious that you are ignorant of the facts is a great step to knowledge.

> Benjamin Disraeli (1804–81)
> British novelist and prime minister

Technology, especially electronics, is not what you might call my strong point . . . I mean all I know about computers wouldn't cover a silicon chip.

> George Bush (1924–   )
> 41st president of the United States

The man who is too old to learn was probably always too old to learn.

> Henry S. Hasskins
> American economist

When a subject becomes totally obsolete we make it a required course.

> Peter Drucker (1909–   )
> American business philosopher and author

Studying literature at Harvard is like learning about women at the Mayo Clinic.

> Roy Blount, Jr. (1941–   )
> American author

Harvard, to me, combines the worst of German academic arrogance with bad American theological seminary habits.

> Peter Drucker (1909–   )
> American business philosopher and author

If you give a person a fish, he will eat once; if you teach him how to fish, he will eat the rest of his life.

> Chinese proverb

If you think education is expensive, try ignorance.

> Derek Bok (1930–   )
> president, Harvard University

The schools ain't what they used to be and never was.

> Will Rogers (1879–1935)
> American actor and humorist

[The] real villain of the oil crisis is the Harvard Business School . . . almost every Arab sheik now in charge of his country's oil policy was trained at Harvard.

> Art Buchwald (1925–   )
> American journalist

The chief object of education is not to learn things but to unlearn things.

> G. K. Chesterton (1874–1936)
> English journalist and author

In business school classrooms they construct wonderful models of a non-world.

> *Peter Drucker (1909–   )*
> *American business*
> *philosopher and author*

A child miseducated is a child lost.

> *John F. Kennedy (1917–63)*
> *35th president of the United*
> *States*

Nothing in life is to be feared. It is only to be understood.

> *Marie Curie (1867–1934)*
> *French chemist*

The man who does not read good books has no advantage over the man who can't read them.

> *Mark Twain (1835–1910)*
> *American author*

Management is now where the medical profession was when it decided that working in a drug store was not sufficient training to become a doctor.

> *Lawrence Appley (1904–   )*
> *president, American*
> *Management Association*

If you wish to be happy for an hour, get intoxicated.
If you wish to be happy for three days, get married.

If you wish to be happy for eight days, kill your pig and eat it.
If you wish to be happy forever, learn to fish.

> *Chinese proverb*

Our progress as a nation can be no swifter than our progress in education. . . . The human mind is our fundamental resource.

> *John F. Kennedy (1917–63)*
> *35th president of the United*
> *States*

Records of old wars mean nothing to me. History is more or less bunk. It's tradition.

> *Henry Ford (1863–1947)*
> *American automobile*
> *manufacturer*

There are three ingredients in the good life: learning, earning, and yearning.

> *Christopher Morley (1890–*
> *1957)*
> *American writer*

Native ability without education is like a tree without fruit.

> *Samuel Johnson (1709–84)*
> *English lexicographer and*
> *author*

Never learn to do anything: if you don't learn, you'll always find someone else to do it for you.

> *Mark Twain (1835–1910)*
> *American author*

It doesn't make much difference what you study, as long as you don't like it.

> Finley Peter Dunne (1867–1936)
> American humorist

When you stop learning, stop listening, stop looking and asking questions, always new questions, then it is time to die.

> Lillian Smith (1897–1966)
> American author

EXPERIENCE

EXPERIENCE: *the accumulation of knowledge or skill resulting from participation in activities or events.*

Paul "Bear" Bryant was one of college football's all-time greats. In addition to being voted coach of the year on three separate occasions and coaching the University of Alabama Crimson Tide to five national championships, his teams amassed an amazing total of 323 victories during his tenure at Kentucky, Texas A&M, and Alabama. Over the years, he coached a number of star players, perhaps the most famous being Joe Namath, who would later lead the New York Jets to victory in the 1969 Super Bowl.

At one of the Bear's squad meetings, he told his players, "This is a class operation. I want your shoes to be shined. I want you to have a tie on, get your hair cut, and keep a crease in your pants. I also want you to go to class. I don't want no dumbbells on this team. If there is a dumbbell in the room, I wish he would stand up.

Namath immediately rose to his feet. The Bear looked over at him, puzzled. "Joe, how come you're standing up? You ain't dumb."

With a crooked little grin, Joe replied, "Coach, I just hate like the devil for you to be standing up there by yourself."

When I was a boy of fourteen, my father was so ignorant I could hardly stand to have the old man around. But when I got to be twenty-one, I was astonished at how much he had learned in seven years.

> attributed to Mark Twain (1835–1910)
> American author

Does he have 17 years of experience or one year of experience 17 times?

> Paul R. Wiesenfeld (1914–58)
> American lawyer

Never insult an alligator until you've crossed the river.

> Cordell Hull (1871–1955)
> U.S. secretary of state

The man who makes no mistakes does not usually make anything.

> William Connor Magee
> (1821–91)
> bishop of Peterborough

It's not the crook in modern business that we fear, but the honest man who doesn't know what he is doing.

> Owen D. Young (1874–
> 1962)
> American lawyer and vice
> president, General
> Electric

Experience taught me a few things. One is to listen to your gut, no matter how good something sounds on paper. The second is that you're generally better off sticking with what you know. And the third is that sometimes your best investments are the ones you don't make.

> Donald Trump (1946–   )
> American real estate
> executive

The unexamined life is not worth living.

> Socrates (ca. 470–399 B.C.)
> Greek philosopher

Experience is the name everyone gives to their mistakes.

> Oscar Wilde (1854–1900)
> Irish poet, playwright, and
> novelist

Failure is success if we learn from it.

> Malcolm Forbes (1919–90)
> American publisher

Experience is what enables you to recognize a mistake when you make it again.

> Earl Wilson (1907–87)
> American newspaper
> columnist

I don't want men of experience working for me. The experienced man is always telling me why something can't be done. He is smart; he is intelligent; he thinks he knows the answers. The fellow who has not had any experience is so dumb he doesn't know a thing can't be done—and he goes ahead and does it.

> Charles F. Kettering (1876–
> 1958)
> American electrical
> engineer and inventor

a optimist is a guy
that has never had
much experience

> Don Marquis (1878–1937)
> American newspaperman
> and humorist

He who has once burnt his mouth always blows his soup.

> German proverb

Experience is not what happens to you; it is what you do with what happens to you.

> Aldous Huxley (1894–1963)
> English author and critic

Intelligence is not to make no mistakes, but quickly to see how to make them good.

> Bertolt Brecht (1898–1956)
> German dramatist

He who would learn to fly one day must first learn to stand and walk and run and climb and dance; one cannot fly into flying.

> *Friederich W. Nietzsche (1844–1900)*
> *German philosopher*

The worse the carpenter, the more the chips.

> *Dutch proverb*

A bad workman never gets a good tool.

> *Thomas Fuller (1608–61)*
> *English clergyman and author*

Every invalid is a physician.

> *Irish proverb*

It is time I stepped aside for a less experienced and less able man.

> *Professor Scott Elledge (1914–   )*
> *on his retirement from Cornell University*

I hear and I forget.
I see and I remember.
I do and I understand.

> *Confucius (551–479 B.C.)*
> *Chinese philosopher and teacher*

Experience is the worst teacher; it gives the test before presenting the lesson.

> *Vernon Law (1930–   )*
> *American professional baseball player*

Man is the only animal that can be skinned more than once.

> *Jimmy Durante (1893–1980)*
> *American actor*

One of these days in your travels a guy is going to come up to you and show you a nice brand-new deck of cards on which the seal is not yet broken, and this guy is going to offer to bet you that he can make the jack of spades jump out of the deck and squirt cider in your ear. But, son, do not bet this man, for as sure as you stand there, you are going to wind up with an earful of cider.

> *Damon Runyon (1884–1946)*
> *American author*

An MBA's first shock could be the realization that companies require experience before they hire a chief executive officer.

> *Robert Half (1918–   )*
> *American personnel-agency executive*

The scalded cat fears even cold water.

> *Thomas Fuller (1608–61)*
> *English clergyman and author*

Experience is a great advantage. The problem is that when you get the experience, you're too damned old to do anything about it.

> *Jimmy Connors (1952–   )*
> *American tennis champion*

I've had a lot of experience with people smarter than I am.

> Gerald Ford (1913–)
> 38th president of the United
> States

All that I know I learned after I was thirty.

> Georges Clemenceau (1841–
> 1929)
> French statesman

A failure is a man who has blundered but is not capable of cashing in on the experience.

> Elbert Hubbard (1856–
> 1915)
> American writer

Don't brood on what's past, but never forget it either.

> Thomas H. Raddall
> (1903–)
> Canadian author

Those who cannot remember the past are condemned to repeat it.

> George Santayana (1863–
> 1952)
> American poet and
> philosopher

If money is your hope for independence, you will never have it. The only real security that a man can have in this world is a reserve of knowledge, experience, and ability.

> Henry Ford (1863–1947)
> American automobile
> manufacturer

I have learned silence from the talkative, toleration from the intolerant, and kindness from the unkind; yet strange, I am ungrateful to these teachers.

> Kahlil Gibran (1883–1931)
> Lebanese novelist, poet, and
> artist

Our deeds follow us, and what we have been makes us what we are.

> John Dykes (1832–76)
> English clergyman and
> religious composer

People are not remembered by how few times they fail, but by how often they succeed. Every wrong step is another step forward.

> Thomas Edison (1847–1931)
> American inventor

Difficulties are things that show what men are.

> Epictetus (ca. A.D. 55–
> ca. 135)
> Greek philosopher

Lord, deliver me from the man who never makes a mistake, and also from the man who makes the same mistake twice.

> Dr. William J. Mayo (1861–
> 1939)
> founder, Mayo Clinic

You can observe a lot by just watching.

> Yogi Berra (1925–)
> American baseball player
> and manager

This is as true in everyday life as it is in battle. We are given one life and the decision is ours whether to wait for circumstances to make up our mind or whether to act, and in acting, to live.

Omar Bradley (1893–1981)
general, U.S. Army

An old poacher makes a good game-keeper.

Anonymous

The grass is not, in fact, always green-er on the other side of the fence. No, not at all. Fences have nothing to do with it. The grass is greenest where it is watered. When crossing over fences, carry water with you and tend the grass wherever you may be.

Robert Fulghum (1937–   )
American author

It's what you learn after you know it all that counts.

John Wooden (1910–   )
American college basketball coach

The hardest thing to learn in life is which bridge to cross and which to burn.

David L. Russell (1921–   )
American educator

Education is when you read the fine print. Experience is what you get if you don't.

Pete Seeger (1919–   )
American folksinger and songwriter

It is hard to convince a high school student that he will encounter a lot of problems more difficult than those of algebra and geometry.

Ed Howe (1853–1937)
American journalist

A man who carries a cat by the tail learns something he can learn in no other way.

Mark Twain (1835–1910)
American author

Chapter 21

Personal Characteristics of Managers

PERSONAL CHARACTERISTICS: *physical, mental, and emotional features that combine to make each manager unique.*

Max Hart, the hard-driving American clothing tycoon, is said to have been dissatisfied with his firm's latest advertising campaign. He called in his advertising manager to tell him what was wrong with the ad. "Nobody reads that much copy," Hart complained.

Standing his ground, the manager challenged, "I'll bet you ten dollars, Mr. Hart, that I can write a whole newspaper page of solid type and you will read every word of it." Confident he was right, Hart quickly accepted the bet.

Playing it for all it was worth, the adman continued, "I won't have to write even a paragraph to prove my point. I'll just give you the headline: THIS PAGE IS ALL ABOUT MAX HART."

Success has gone to my hips.

> *Dolly Parton (1946–   )*
> *American singer*

Never get into fights with ugly people because they have nothing to lose.

> *Anonymous*

If I were two-faced, would I be wearing this one?

> *Abraham Lincoln (1809–65)*
> *16th president of the United States*

To be good-looking is a handicap, it's often said—usually by those who aren't.

> *Malcolm Forbes (1919–90)*
> *American publisher*

When the candles are out, all women are fair.

> *Plutarch (ca. 46–120 A.D.)*
> *Greek biographer and moralist*

I never expected to see the day when girls would get sunburned in the places they do today.

> *Will Rogers (1879–1935)*
> *American actor and humorist*

Beauty is only skin deep, but ugly goes clear to the bone.

> *Anonymous*

We are all more average than we think.

> *Gorham Munson (1896–1969)*
> *American publisher and critic*

Whenever you're sitting across from some important person, always picture him sitting there in a suit of long red underwear. That's the way I always operated in business.

> *Joseph P. Kennedy (1888–1969)*
> *American businessman and diplomat*

If you look like your passport photo, then in all probability you need the journey.

> *Earl Wilson (1907–87)*
> *American newspaper columnist*

No rich man is ugly.

> *Zsa Zsa Gabor (1919–   )*
> *American actress*

Personal beauty requires that one should be tall; little people may have charm and elegance, but beauty—no.

> *Aristotle (384–322 B.C.)*
> *Greek philosopher*

If you're small, you better be a winner.

> *Billie Jean King (1943–   )*
> *American tennis champion*

Nobody roots for Goliath.

> *Wilt Chamberlain (1936–   )*
> *American professional basketball player*

I base my fashion taste on what doesn't itch.

> *Gilda Radner (1946–89)*
> *American comedienne*

Fashion is a form of ugliness so intolerable that we have to alter it every six months.

Oscar Wilde (1854–1900)
Irish poet, playwright, and
novelist

Every generation laughs at the old fashions but religiously follows the new.

Henry David Thoreau
(1817–62)
American naturalist and
writer

HEALTH AND DIET

HEALTH: *personal fitness and well-being, with freedom from disease.*

DIET: *a regulated selection of foods, especially as prescribed by a physician.*

Even though millions of people have joined the fitness era of the

1990s, a substantial number of adults applaud the sentiments of the great American author Mark Twain. Twain reveled in his sedentary existence. "I have never taken any exercise, except for sleeping and resting, and I never intend to take any," he explained. "Exercise is loathsome."

Never go to a doctor whose office plants have died.

Erma Bombeck (1927–   )
American writer and
humorist

A really busy person never knows how much he weighs.

Ed Howe (1853–1937)
American journalist

I will not eat oysters. I want my food dead—not sick, not wounded—dead.

Woody Allen (1935–   )
American actor, film
director, and comedian

I am disturbed when I see a cigarette between the lips or fingers of some important person upon whose intelligence and judgment the welfare of the world in part depends.

Linus Pauling (1901–   )
American scientist

In Mexico we have a word for sushi: *bait!*

José Simon (1920–   )
American scholar

It has always been my rule never to smoke when asleep, and never to refrain when awake.

Mark Twain (1835–1910)
American author

I won't say I'm out of condition now —but I even puff going down stairs.

> Dick Gregory (1932–)
> American comedian

I have never yet met a healthy person who worried very much about his health, or a really good person who worried much about his own soul.

> J. B. S. Haldane (1892–1964)
> British scientist

Cocaine is God's way of saying you're making too much money.

> Robin Williams (1952–)
> American actor and
> comedian

Roses are red, violets are blue, I'm a schizophrenic, and so am I.

> Anonymous

Those obsessed with health are not healthy; the first requisite of good health is a certain calculated carelessness about oneself.

> Sydney J. Harris (1917–86)
> American newspaper
> columnist

I was alarmed at my doctor's report: He said I was sound as a dollar.

> William J. Proxmire (1915–)
> U.S. senator

A neurotic is the person who builds a castle in the air. A psychotic is the person who lives in it. And a psychiatrist is the person who collects the rent.

> Anonymous

The desire to take medicine is perhaps the greatest feature which distinguishes man from animals.

> Sir William Osler (1849–1919)
> Canadian physician

People who cannot find time for recreation are obliged sooner or later to find time for illness.

> John Wanamaker (1838–1922)
> American merchant

The only reason I would take up jogging is so that I could hear heavy breathing again.

> Erma Bombeck (1927–)
> American writer and
> humorist

I don't jog. If I die, I want to be sick.

> Abe Lemons (1922–)
> American basketball coach

No man is lonely while eating spaghetti.

> Robert Morley (1908–)
> British actor and
> playwright

Everything you see I owe to spaghetti.

> Sophia Loren (1934–)
> American actress

The only way to keep your health is to eat what you don't want, drink what you don't like, and do what you'd rather not.

> *Mark Twain (1835–1910)*
> *American author*

To reduce stress, avoid excitement; spend more time with your spouse.

> *Robert Orben (1927–   )*
> *American humorist*

Thanks to jogging, today more people collapse in perfect health than ever before.

> *Anonymous*

I get my exercise acting as a pall-bearer to my friends who exercise.

> *Chauncey Depew (1834–1928)*
> *American lawyer and speaker*

Be careful about reading health books. You may die of a misprint.

> *Mark Twain (1835–1910)*
> *American author*

If you resolve to give up smoking, drinking, and loving, you don't actually live longer; it just seems longer.

> *Clement Freud (1924–   )*
> *English author*

Part of the secret of success in life is to eat what you like and let the food fight it out inside.

> *Mark Twain (1835–1910)*
> *American author*

If American men are obsessed with money, American women are obsessed with weight. The men talk of gain, the women talk of loss, and I do not know which talk is the more boring.

> *Marya Mannes (1904–   )*
> *American writer*

Imprisoned in every fat man, a thin one is wildly signaling to be let out.

> *Cyril Connolly (1903–74)*
> *English critic and writer*

I'm on a seafood diet. I see food and I eat it.

> *Anonymous*

Eat, drink, and be merry, for tomorrow ye diet.

> *Lewis C. Henry (1885–1941)*
> *U.S. congressman*

DRINKING

DRINKING: *imbibing alcoholic liquors, especially excessively or habitually.*

Once on a motion-picture studio set, American actor and notorious liquor fancier W. C. Fields spotted a beautiful Saint Bernard, complete with a keg hanging around his neck. "Ah yes, man's best friend," called out Fields. "And a dog, too."

There are more old drunkards than old physicians.

> *François Rabelais (1483–1553)*
> *French satirist and humorist*

I distrust camels, and anyone else who can go a week without a drink.

> *Joe E. Lewis (1902–71)*
> *American comedian*

If you drink, don't drive. Don't even putt.

> *Dean Martin (1917–   )*
> *American actor and comedian*

I drink to make other people more interesting.

> *George Jean Nathan (1882–1958)*
> *American editor and drama critic*

Practically anything you say will seem amusing if you're on all fours.

> *P. J. O'Rourke (1945–   )*
> *American writer*

'Twas a woman who drove me to drink, and I never had the courtesy to thank her for it.

> *W. C. Fields (1880–1946)*
> *American actor and comedian*

Everybody should believe in something; I believe I'll have another drink.

> *Anonymous*

I have to think hard to name an interesting man who does not drink.

> *Richard Burton (1925–84)*
> *Welsh actor*

My only regret in life is that I did not drink more champagne.

> *John Maynard Keynes (1883–1946)*
> *English economist*

A man is never drunk if he can lie on the floor without holding on.

> *Joe E. Lewis (1902–71)*
> *American comedian*

The innkeeper loves the drunkard, but not for a son-in-law.

Yiddish proverb

My uncle was the town drunk—and we lived in Chicago.

George Gobel (1919–   )
American actor and
comedian

A prohibitionist is the sort of man one wouldn't care to drink with—even if he drank.

H. L. Mencken (1880–1956)
American editor

HAPPINESS

HAPPINESS: *a state of satisfaction, well-being, and contentment.*

Herbert Hoover's presidency was dominated by the effects of the stock-market crash in 1929 and the Depression that followed. Hard-pressed on the homefront to alleviate not only the economic Depression but the mental depression experienced by the American people, Hoover appealed to the very popular singer Rudy Vallee. "If you can sing a song that would make people forget their troubles and the Depression, I'll give you a medal."

When a man is happy, he does not hear the clock strike.

German proverb

He who laughs, lasts.

Robert Fulghum (1937–   )
American author

Happy people rarely correct their faults.

François Duc de La
Rochefoucauld
(1613–50)
French writer and
moralist

When what we are is what we want to be, that's happiness.

Malcolm Forbes (1919–90)
American publisher

Success is getting what you want; happiness is wanting what you get.

Anonymous

Everything is funny as long as it is happening to somebody else.

Will Rogers (1879–1935)
American actor and
humorist

To carry care to bed is to sleep with a pack on your back.

Thomas C. Haliburton
(1796–1865)
English writer

The best way to cheer yourself up is to cheer everybody else up.

Mark Twain (1835–1910)
American author

You cannot prevent the birds of sorrow from flying over your head, but you can prevent them from building nests in your hair.

Chinese proverb

The day most wholly missed is the one on which one does not laugh.

Sébastien-Roch Nicolas
Chamfort (1741–94)
French writer

Laughing is the sensation of feeling good all over and showing it principally in one spot.

Josh Billings (1818–85)
American humorist

Happiness doesn't depend on what we have but it does depend on how we feel towards what we have. We can be happy with little and miserable with much.

William Dempster Hoard
(1836–1918)
American publisher and
agriculturist

Let us all be happy, and live within our means, even if we have to borrow the money to do it with.

Artemus Ward (1834–67)
American humorist

Most of us are just about as happy as we make up our minds to be.

Abraham Lincoln (1809–65)
16th president of the United
States

The secret of happiness is not in doing what one likes, but in liking what one does.

James Matthew Barrie
(1860–1937)
Scottish novelist and
dramatist

Happiness Is Lubbock, Texas, in my Rearview Mirror

song title by American
singer Mac Davis
(1942–   )

Happiness? A good cigar, a good meal, a good woman—or a bad woman; it depends on how much happiness you can handle.

George Burns (1896–   )
American actor and
comedian

GAMES MANAGERS PLAY

LEISURE: *free, unoccupied time during which a person may engage in relaxation, travel, or other pleasurable activities*

Spectators often express their expertise of a game or a particular play to the bewilderment of those on the field. Former Wake Forest football coach Chuck Mills likes to describe a spectator as a person "who sits forty rows up in the stands and wonders why a seventeen-year-old kid can't hit another seventeen-year-old kid with a ball from forty yards away . . . and then he goes out to the parking lot and can't find his car."

Baltimore Orioles outfielder and team comedian John Lowenstein was asked for his suggestions on ways to improve the game of baseball. "They should move first base back a step to eliminate all the close plays."

Recent history has evidenced drastic changes in the time spent working and playing. Most of us remember vivid Depression-era pictures of tired, dirty children spending fifteen hours and more in deplorable factory conditions. By contrast, today we think of four-day workweeks and flextime plans that are becoming an established part of the working world during the close of the twentieth century. Even though it appears that today's work force has become obsessed with time off, Ralph Barsodi points out that there is less leisure now than in the Middle Ages, when one third of the year consisted of holidays and festivals.

A day out-of-doors, someone I loved to talk with, a good book and some simple food and music—that would be rest.

> Eleanor Roosevelt (1884–1962)
> American humanitarian and writer

A race track is a place where windows clean people.

> Danny Thomas (1914–91)
> American actor

The deer season just opened. A deer hunter in Ventura County brought in his first man yesterday.

> Will Rogers (1879–1935)
> American actor and humorist

An atheist is a guy who watches a Notre Dame–SMU football game and doesn't care who wins.

> Dwight D. Eisenhower (1890–1969)
> 34th president of the United States

The urge to gamble is so universal and its practice so pleasurable that I assume it must be evil.

> Heywood Broun (1888–1939)
> American journalist

Fishermen don't lie. They just tell beautiful stories.

> Syngman Rhee (1875–1965)
> first president of the
> Republic of Korea

One day in the country is worth a month in town.

> Christina Rosetti (1830–94)
> English poet

The typical successful American businessman was born in the country where he worked like hell so he could live in the city where he worked like hell so he could live in the country.

> Don Marquis (1878–1937)
> American humorist

No wonder nobody comes here—it's too crowded.

> Yogi Berra (1925–   )
> American baseball player
> and manager

Thanks to the Interstate Highway System, it is now possible to travel from coast to coast without seeing anything.

> Charles Kuralt (1934–   )
> American news reporter
> and journalist

The world is a book, and those who do not travel read only a page.

> Saint Augustine
> (A.D. 354–430)
> bishop of Hippo

I hate small towns because once you've seen the cannon in the park there's nothing else to do.

> Lenny Bruce (1925–66)
> American social satirist

I always turn to the sports pages first, which record people's accomplishments. The front page has nothing but man's failures.

> Earl Warren (1891–1974)
> Chief Justice of the U.S.
> Supreme Court

One ought, every day at least, to hear a little song, read a good poem, see a fine picture and if it were possible to speak a few reasonable words.

> Johann Wolfgang von Goethe
> (1749–1832)
> German poet and dramatist

Early to rise and early to bed makes a man healthy and wealthy and dead.

> James Thurber (1894–1961)
> American writer

Vacation is time off to remind employees that the business can get along without them.

> Earl Wilson (1907–87)
> American newspaper
> columnist

A good vacation is over when you begin to yearn for your work.

> *Dr. Morris Fishbein (1889–1976)*
> *American physician and editor*

It is "better than it sounds."

> *Mark Twain (1835–1910)*
> *American author*
> *(commenting on the music of German composer Richard Wagner)*

I do much of my creative thinking while golfing. If people know you are working at home they think nothing of walking in for a coffee. But they wouldn't dream of interrupting you on the golf course.

> *Harper Lee (1926–)*
> *American author*

Golf is a good walk spoiled.

> *Mark Twain (1835–1910)*
> *American author*

I play in the low 80s. If it's any hotter than that, I won't play.

> *Joe E. Lewis (1902–71)*
> *American comedian*

Very few blacks will take up golf until the requirement for plaid pants is dropped.

> *Franklin Ajaye (1949–)*
> *American actor*

I went to a fight the other night and a hockey game broke out.

> *Rodney Dangerfield (1921–)*
> *American actor and comedian*

Most people spend most of their days doing what they do not want to do in order to earn the right, at times, to do what they may desire.

> *John M. Brown (1900–69)*
> *American literary critic*

I know only two tunes. One is "Yankee Doodle" and the other isn't.

> *Ulysses S. Grant (1822–85)*
> *17th president of the United States*

An intellectual is a person who can listen to the *William Tell* overture and not think of the Lone Ranger.

> *Anonymous*

Leisure only means a chance to do other jobs that demand attention.

> *Oliver Wendell Holmes, Jr. (1841–1935)*
> *American jurist*

A perpetual holiday is a good working definition of hell.

> *George Bernard Shaw (1856–1950)*
> *British playwright and social reformer*

The sport of skiing consists of wearing three thousand dollars' worth of clothes and equipment and driving two hundred miles in the snow in order to stand around at a bar and get drunk.

> P. J. O'Rourke (1945–   )
> American author

If a man watches three football games in a row, he should be declared legally dead.

> Erma Bombeck (1927–   )
> American writer and
> humorist

If all the year were playing holidays, to sport would be as tedious as to work.

> William Shakespeare (1564–
> 1616)
> English dramatist and poet

I love sport because I love life, and sport is one of the basic joys of life.

> Yevgeny Yevtushenko
> (1933–   )
> Russian author and poet

In America, it is sport that is the opiate of the masses.

> Russell Baker (1925–   )
> American journalist and
> humorist

Sports do not build character. They reveal it.

> Heywood Broun (1888–
> 1939)
> American journalist

I hate television. I hate it as much as peanuts. But I can't stop eating peanuts.

> Orson Welles (1915–85)
> American actor and motion-
> picture producer

If you watch a game, it's fun. If you play it, it's recreation. If you work at it, it's golf.

> Bob Hope (1903–   )
> American actor and
> comedian

If I miss one day's practice, I notice it. If I miss two days, the critics notice it. If I miss three days, the audience notices it.

> Ignace Paderewski (1860–
> 1941)
> Polish concert pianist and
> patriot

Football features two of the worst parts of American life—violence punctuated by committee meetings.

> George F. Will (1941–   )
> American news
> commentator and author

Almost any game with any ball is a good game

> Robert Lynd (1892–1970)
> American sociologist

It has always been my private conviction that any man who pits his intelligence against a fish and loses has it coming.

> John Steinbeck (1902–68)
> American novelist

SELF-ESTEEM

SELF-ESTEEM: *the image a person has of who he or she is; respect for oneself.*

Henry Labouchère, a British politician and journalist, always treated his contemporary, William Gladstone, with respect in public but in private attacked his political methods and style. He once said that he did not object that Gladstone always seemed to have the ace of trumps up his sleeve; what he did object to was Gladstone's pretense that God had put it there.

After I am dead, I would rather have men ask why Cato has no monument than why he had one.

> *Cato the Elder*
> *(234–149 B.C.)*
> *Roman statesman*

The man who has cured himself of B.O. and halitosis, has learned French to surprise the waiter, and the saxophone to amuse the company, may find that people still avoid him because they do not like him.

> *Heywood Broun (1888–*
> *1939)*
> *American journalist*

I made a disastrous choice of profession. Business has become respectable and stockbroking almost *chic*. But I became a ballet critic, which is barely legal in this country between consenting adults.

> *Richard Buckle (1916–   )*
> *British author and critic*

Self-made men are always apt to be a little too proud of the job.

> *Josh Billings (1818–85)*
> *American humorist*

I've made it a point never to learn my Social Security number because I'm a person, not a number.

> *H. Ross Perot (1930–   )*
> *American computer*
> *millionaire and*
> *philanthropist*

Socrates, the point is not to know oneself, but to forget.

> *Jean Dubuffet (1901–85)*
> *French artist*

We are what we pretend to be, so we must be careful what we pretend to be.

> *Kurt Vonnegut, Jr.*
> *(1922–   )*
> *American author*

Only the shallow know themselves.

> *Oscar Wilde (1854–1900)*
> *Irish poet, playwright,*
> *and novelist*

The man who insists he is as good as anybody believes he is better.

> *Ed Howe (1853–1937)*
> *American journalist*

Who steals my purse steals trash; 'tis
   something, nothing; . . .
But he that filches from me my good
   name
Robs me of that which not enriches
   him,
And makes me poor indeed.

> *William Shakespeare (1564–*
> *1616)*
> *English dramatist and*
> *writer*

Character is what you are in the dark.

> *Dwight L. Moody (1837–99)*
> *American evangelist*

The best index to a person's character is (a) how he treats people who
can't do him any good, and (b) how
he treats people who can't fight back.

> *Abigail Van Buren*
> *(1918–   )*
> *American advice columnist*

The only thing worse than being
talked about is not being talked
about.

> *Oscar Wilde (1854–1900)*
> *Irish poet, playwright,*
> *and novelist*

Anger makes dull men witty, but it
keeps them poor.

> *Francis Bacon (1561–1626)*
> *English philosopher*

It's good to have money and the
things money can buy, but it's good,
too, to check up once in a while and
make sure that you haven't lost the
things that money can't buy.

> *George Horace Lormier*
> *(1867–1937)*
> *American editor*

There are many who dare not kill
themselves for fear of what the
neighbors will say.

> *Cyril Connolly (1903–74)*
> *English literary critic*

The trouble with most of us is that
we would rather be ruined by praise
than saved by criticism.

> *Norman Vincent Peale*
> *(1898–   )*
> *American clergyman and*
> *author*

He who knows others is clever; he
who knows himself is enlightened.

> *Lao-tzu (6th century B.C.)*
> *Chinese philosopher and*
> *founder of Taoism*

He travels the fastest who travels
alone.

> *Rudyard Kipling (1865–*
> *1936)*
> *English author*

Worry a little bit every day and in a
lifetime you will lose a couple of
years. If something is wrong, fix it if
you can. But train yourself not to
worry. Worry never fixes anything.

> *Mary Hemingway (1908–86)*
> *American journalist*

One of the great disadvantages of being a coward is that one is constantly having to eat things that one does not wish to eat.

> *Robert Lynd (1892–1970)*
> *American sociologist*

·Don't compromise yourself. You are all you've got.

> *Janis Joplin (1943–70)*
> *American singer*

When you are right you cannot be too radical; when you are wrong, you cannot be too conservative.

> *Martin Luther King, Jr.*
> *(1929–68)*
> *American clergyman and*
> *civil-rights leader*

We always admire the other fellow more after we have tried to do his job.

> *William Feather (1889–*
> *1981)*
> *American author and*
> *publisher*

When people begin to ignore human dignity, it will not be long before they begin to ignore human rights.

> *G. K. Chesterton (1874–*
> *1936)*
> *English journalist and*
> *author*

Have you considered that if you "don't make waves" nobody includ-

ing yourself will know that you are alive?

> *Theodore Isaac Rubin*
> *(1923–   )*
> *American psychiatrist and*
> *author*

An appeaser is one who feeds a crocodile hoping it will eat him last.

> *Winston Churchill (1874–*
> *1965)*
> *British statesman and*
> *prime minister*

These then are my last words to you. Be not afraid of life. Believe that life is worth living and your belief will help create the fact.

> *William James (1842–1910)*
> *American psychologist and*
> *philosopher*

The first and great commandment is "Don't let them scare you."

> *Elmer Davis (1890–1958)*
> *American radio*
> *broadcaster and news*
> *commentator*

It is impossible for a man to be cheated by anyone but himself.

> *Ralph Waldo Emerson*
> *(1803–82)*
> *American essayist and poet*

When angry, count four; when very angry, swear.

> *Mark Twain (1835–1910)*
> *American author*

Your own mind is a sacred enclosure into which nothing harmful can enter except by your permission.

> Ralph Waldo Emerson
> (1803–82)
> American essayist and poet

In his private heart no man much respects himself.

> Mark Twain (1835–1910)
> American author

Nothing is so silly as the expression of a man who is being complimented.

> André Gide (1869–1951)
> French novelist, essayist,
> and critic

People only see what they are prepared to see.

> Ralph Waldo Emerson
> (1803–82)
> American essayist and poet

What one sees depends upon where one sits.

> James R. Schlesinger (1929–   )
> U.S. secretary of defense

Though familiarity may not breed contempt, it takes the edge off admiration.

> William Hazlitt (1778–1830)
> English essayist and critic

A man who trims himself to suit everybody will soon whittle himself away.

> Charles Schwab (1862–1939)
> American industrialist

The easiest thing to be in the world is you. The most difficult thing to be is what other people want you to be. Don't let them put you in that position.

> Leo Buscaglia (1925–   )
> American educator and
> author

Man is what he believes.

> Anton Chekhov (1860–1904)
> Russian author

People who bite the hand that feeds them usually lick the boot that kicks them.

> Eric Hoffer (1902–83)
> American longshoreman
> and philosopher

I'm a deeply superficial person.

> Andy Warhol (1930?–87)
> American painter and motion-
> picture producer

In the hope of bettering themselves, men willingly change masters.

> Niccolò Machiavelli (1469–1527)
> Italian political philosopher

In modern society the opposite of courage is not cowardice; it is conformity.

Rollo May (1909–   )
American psychologist and
therapist

When a stupid man is doing something he is ashamed of, he always declares that it is his duty.

George Bernard Shaw
(1856–1950)
British playwright and
social reformer

Chapter 22

The Manager's Family

FAMILY: *group of people related by blood or marriage; relatives.*

William Gladstone, four times prime minister to Queen Victoria and the dominant figure of the Liberal party for the last half of the nineteenth century, was known as a deeply religious man who emphasized the moral tone of politics during his time. Gladstone found an old portrait of an aristocrat in sixteenth-century attire in an antique shop one day. He inquired the price since he rather liked the painting, but found it too high. A short time later, Gladstone noticed the same painting hanging in the house of a rich merchant he was visiting. As he stood admiring the portrait once again, Gladstone's host approached him and said, "I'm glad you like him. He is one of my Elizabethan ancestors. Actually, he was a minister to the queen."

Gladstone dryly responded, "Three guineas less and he would have been my ancestor."

Until Eve arrived, this was a man's world.

> *Richard Armour (1906–89)*
> *American artist*

I have already given two cousins to the war and I stand ready to sacrifice my wife's brother.

> *Artemus Ward (1834–67)*
> *American humorist*

The Manager's Family   259

The man who has nothing to boast of but his illustrious ancestors is like a potato—the only good belonging to him is underground.

> *Thomas Overbury (1581–1613)*
> *English poet*

A man can't get rich if he takes proper care of his family.

> *Navajo proverb*

I learned about the strength you can get from a close family life. I learned to keep going, even in bad times. I learned not to despair, even when my world was falling apart. I learned that there are no free lunches. And I learned the value of hard work. In the end you've got to be productive. That's what made this country great —and that's what's going to make us great again.

> *Lee Iacocca (1924–   )*
> *chairman, Chrysler Corporation*

PARENTS AND GRANDPARENTS

PARENTS: *individuals that bring forth offspring.*

GRANDPARENTS: *parents of one's father or mother.*

Joseph Kennedy once jokingly compared his granddaughter Caroline to her father, the thirty-fifth president of the United States. "Caroline's very bright, smarter than you were, Jack, at that age," he remarked. "Yes, she is," admitted President Kennedy. "But look who *she* has for a father!"

I don't know who my grandfather was; I am much more concerned to know what his grandson will be.

> *Abraham Lincoln (1809–65)*
> *16th president of the United States*

There's nothing wrong with teenagers that reasoning with them won't aggravate.

> *Anonymous*

I have found the best way to give advice to your children is to find out what they want and then advise them to do it.

> *Harry S Truman (1884–1972)*
> *33rd president of the United States*

Children become adults when they stop asking their parents for an allowance and request a loan.

> *Anonymous*

Every generation revolts against its fathers and makes friends with its grandfathers.

> Lewis Mumford (1895–1990)
> American writer

Nearly every man is a firm believer in heredity, until his son makes a fool of himself.

> Anonymous

Parents were invented to make children happy by giving them something to ignore.

> Ogden Nash (1902–71)
> American writer of humorous verse

Even very young children need to be informed about dying. Explain the concept of death very carefully to your child. This will make threatening him with it much more effective.

> P. J. O'Rourke (1945–   )
> American writer

There are two classes of travel—first class and with children.

> Robert Benchley (1889–1945)
> American humorist

A father is a banker provided by nature.

> French proverb

If you have never been hated by your child, you have never been a parent.

> Bette Davis (1908–89)
> American actress

There's not a man in America who at one time or another hasn't had a secret desire to boot a child in the ass.

> attributed to W. C. Fields (1880–1946)
> American actor and comedian

We learn from experience. A man never wakes up his second baby just to see it smile.

> Grace Williams (1917–   )
> American public official

CHILDREN

CHILDREN: *sons or daughters between infancy and youth; the first generation of offspring.*

Notorious for frolicking and cavorting through the halls of the White House, President Theodore Roosevelt's daughter Alice burst into a room one day where the president was discussing important business. The visitor interrupted their conversation, complaining about the little girl's intrusion, to which Roosevelt asserted, "I can be president of the United States or I can control Alice. I cannot possibly do both."

Whenever I hear people discussing birth control, I always remember that I was the fifth.

> *Clarence Darrow (1857–1938)*
> *American lawyer and author*

Contraceptives should be used on every conceivable occasion.

> *Spike Milligan (1918–)*
> *British actor and motion-picture director*

We have not passed that subtle line between childhood and adulthood until we move from the passive voice to the active voice—that is, until we have stopped saying "It got lost," and say, "I lost it."

> *Sydney J. Harris (1917–86)*
> *American newspaper columnist*

There's no such thing as a tough child—if you parboil them first for seven hours, they always come out tender.

> *W. C. Fields (1880–1946)*
> *American actor and comedian*

When I was a child, I spake as a child, I understood as a child, I thought as a child; but when I became a man, I put away childish things.

> *1 Corinthians 13:11*

If you want to see what children can do, you must stop giving them things.

> *Norman Douglas (1868–1952)*
> *English author*

The worst misfortune that can happen to an ordinary man is to have an extraordinary father.

> *Anonymous*

I didn't have a normal teenage life. A few girlfriends, a few dances, but mostly I was fighting, burning cars.

> *Daniel Ortega (1945–)*
> *president of Nicaragua*

When I look at my children, I often wish I had remained a virgin.

> *Lillian Carter (1898–1983)*
> *mother of U.S. president Jimmy Carter*

Insanity is hereditary; you can get it from your children.

> *Sam Levenson (1911–80)*
> *American humorist*

The first half of our lives is ruined by our parents and the second half by our children.

> *Clarence Darrow (1857–1938)*
> *American lawyer and author*

I never met a kid I liked.

> *W. C. Fields (1880–1946)*
> *American actor and comedian*

Don't take up a man's time talking about the smartness of your children; he wants to talk to you about the smartness of his children.

> *Ed Howe (1853–1937)*
> *American journalist*

Children begin by loving their parents. After a time they judge them. Rarely, if ever, do they forgive them.

> *Oscar Wilde (1854–1900)*
> *Irish poet, playwright, and*
> *novelist*

A spoiled child never loves its mother.

> *Sir Henry Taylor (1800–86)*
> *English playwright*

Happy is the child whose father died rich.

> *Anonymous*

When I grow up I want to be a little boy.

> *Joseph Heller (1923–   )*
> *American author*

MARRIAGE AND DIVORCE

MARRIAGE: *institution whereby men and women are joined in a special kind of legal and social dependence for the purpose of founding and maintaining a family.*

DIVORCE: *legal dissolution of a marriage; severance.*

Winston Churchill is the prototypical example of English dry wit and humor, and he spared it on no one. In a conversation with Churchill at

his family home, Blenheim Place, Lady Nancy Astor, Britain's first woman member of Parliament, was espousing women's rights to an ungrateful ear. Churchill repeatedly opposed her on one issue after another until, finally exasperated, Lady Astor threatened, "Winston, if I were married to you, I'd put poison in your coffee!"

Churchill calmly responded, "And if you were my wife, I'd drink it."

Men marry because they are tired; women because they are curious. Both are disappointed.

> *Oscar Wilde (1854–1900)*
> *Irish poet, playwright, and*
> *novelist*

To succeed with the opposite sex, tell her you're impotent. She can't wait to disprove it.

> *Cary Grant (1904–86)*
> *American actor*

I never felt I could give up my life of freedom to become a man's housekeeper.

> *Susan B. Anthony (1820–*
> *1906)*
> *American suffragette*

What ought to be done to the man who invented the celebrating of anniversaries? Mere killing would be too light.

> *Mark Twain (1835–1910)*
> *American author*

A man should be taller, older, heavier, uglier, and hoarser than his wife.

> *Ed Howe (1853–1937)*
> *American journalist*

Jesus was a bachelor.

> *Don Herold (1927–   )*
> *American author*

A man may be a fool and not know it, but not if he is married.

> *H. L. Mencken (1880–1956)*
> *American editor*

The poor wish to be rich, the rich wish to be happy, the single wish to be married, and the married wish to be dead.

> *Ann Landers (1918–   )*
> *American advice columnist*

I married beneath me—all women do.

> *Lady Nancy Astor (1879–*
> *1964)*
> *English political leader*

My toughest fight was with my first wife.

> *Muhammad Ali (1942–   )*
> *American boxing champion*

I'm very old-fashioned. I believe that people should marry for life, like pigeons and Catholics.

> *Woody Allen (1935–   )*
> *American actor, film*
> *director, and comedian*

Husbands are like fires. They go out if unattended.

> *Zsa Zsa Gabor (1919–   )*
> *American actress*

Never get married in the morning, because you never know who you'll meet that night.

> *Paul Hornung (1935–   )*
> *American professional*
> *football player*

Any young man who is unmarried at the age of twenty-one is a menace to the community.

> *Brigham Young (1801–77)*
> *American religious leader*

American women expect to find in their husbands a perfection that English women only hope to find in their butlers.

> Somerset Maugham (1874–1965)
> English novelist and dramatist

Husbands think we should know where everything is: like the uterus is a tracking device. He asks me, "Roseanne, do we have any Cheetos left?" Like he can't go over to that sofa cushion and lift it himself.

> Roseanne Barr (1952–   )
> American actress and comedienne

Women seem to be all right on bargains till it comes to picking out a husband.

> Frank McKinney (Kin) Hubbard (1868–1930)
> American humorist

A husband is one who stands by you in troubles you wouldn't have had if you hadn't married him.

> Anonymous

When you see what some girls marry, you realize how they must hate to work for a living.

> Helen Rowland (1876–?)
> English author

Nothing ages man like living always with the same woman.

> Norman Douglas (1868–1952)
> English author

All work and no play makes Jack a dull boy—and Jill a rich widow.

> Evan Esar (1899–   )
> American author

Back of every achievement is a proud wife and a surprised mother-in-law.

> Brooks Hays (1898–1981)
> American author and Arkansas congressman

Errol Flynn died on a 70-foot boat with a 17-year-old girl. Walter has always wanted to go that way, but he's going to settle for a 17-footer with a 70-year-old.

> Betty Cronkite (1940–   )
> wife of American news commentator Walter Cronkite

If you haven't seen your wife smile at a traffic cop, you haven't seen her smile her prettiest.

> Frank McKinney (Kin) Hubbard (1868–1930)
> American humorist

Married and unmarried women waste a great deal of time in feeling sorry for each other.

> Anonymous

Marriage is a great institution, but I'm not ready for an institution.

> Mae West (1892–1980)
> American actress

An archeologist is the best husband a woman can have; the older she gets, the more interested he is in her.

Agatha Christie (1890–1976)
British mystery writer

Before I got married, I had six theories about bringing up children; now, I have six children and no theories.

John Wilmot, Lord Rochester (1647–80)
English poet

The most dangerous food is wedding cake.

American proverb

A husband should not insult his wife publicly, at parties. He should insult her in the privacy of the home.

James Thurber (1894–1961)
American writer

Before marriage, a man declares that he would lay down his life to serve you; after marriage, he won't even lay down his newspaper to talk to you.

Helen Rowland (1876–?)
English author

Marriage is the only adventure open to the cowardly.

Voltaire (1694–1778)
French writer

Who of us is mature enough for offspring before the offspring themselves arrive? The value of marriage is not that adults produce children, but that children produce adults.

Peter DeVries (1910–   )
American author

A bachelor is a man who never makes the same mistake once.

Ed Wynn (1886–1966)
American actor and comedian

She Got the Gold Mine, I Got the Shaft

song title by American singer Jerry Reed (1937–   )

All any woman asks of her husband is that he love her and obey her commandments.

John W. Raper (1870–1950)
American author

Many a man has fallen in love with a girl in a light so dim he would not have chosen a suit by it.

Maurice Chevalier (1888–1972)
French singer and actor

It's a funny thing that when a man hasn't anything on earth to worry about, he goes off and gets married.

Robert Frost (1874–1963)
American poet

Never confuse "I love you" with "I want to marry you."

> *Cleveland Amory (1917–)*
> *American writer and social*
> *critic*

Marriage is a covered dish.

> *Swiss proverb*

It wasn't exactly a divorce—I was traded.

> *Tim Conway (1933–)*
> *American actor and*
> *comedian*

The honeymoon is over when he phones that he'll be late for supper—and she has already left a note that it's in the refrigerator.

> *Bill Lawrence (1916–72)*
> *American radio-TV*
> *producer and director*

When I was born, my mother was terribly disappointed. Not that she wanted a girl—she wanted a divorce.

> *Woody Allen (1935–)*
> *American actor, film*
> *director, and comedian*

Why do Jewish divorces cost so much? Because they're worth it.

> *Henny Youngman (1906–)*
> *American comedian*

A psychiatrist is a fellow who asks you a lot of expensive questions your wife asks for nothing.

> *Joey Adams (1911–)*
> *American comedian*

I told my wife the truth. I told her I was seeing a psychiatrist. Then she told *me* the truth: that she was seeing a psychiatrist, two plumbers, and a bartender.

> *Rodney Dangerfield*
> *(1921–)*
> *American actor and*
> *comedian*

Marriage is a good deal like taking a bath—not so hot once you get accustomed to it.

> *Bill Lawrence (1916–72)*
> *American radio-TV*
> *producer and director*

She's descended from a long line her mother listened to.

> *Gypsy Rose Lee (1914–70)*
> *American entertainer*

Be not hasty to marry; it's better to have one plow going than two cradles, and more profit to have barn filled than a bed.

> *Thomas Fuller (1608–61)*
> *English clergyman and*
> *author*

You don't know a woman till you've met her in court.

> *Norman Mailer (1925–)*
> *American writer*

The wages of sin is alimony.

> *Carolyn Wells (1862–1942)*
> *American writer*

You never realize how short a month is until you pay alimony.

> *John Barrymore (1882–1942)*
> *American actor*

She cried, and the judge wiped her tears with my checkbook.

> *Tommy Manville (1894–1967)*
> *oft-married American asbestos manufacturer*

I don't think I'll get married again. I'll just find a woman I don't like and give her a house.

> *Lewis Grizzard (1946–   )*
> *American humorist*

LOVE AND FRIENDSHIP

LOVE: *strong affection for another arising out of kinship or personal ties.*

FRIENDSHIP: *state of being attached to another by affection or esteem.*

The marriage of Lady Caroline of Brunswick to Great Britain's king, George IV, in 1795 was a troubled one. After the birth of their only child the following year, they separated and remained apart until George's accession to the British throne in 1820, at which time the popular Caroline returned to claim her place as queen. A heated battle between the two ensued, and George petitioned for divorce. In May of 1821, the king's groom burst into the royal bedchamber and announced, "Sir, your bitterest enemy is dead."

Thrilled, George IV exclaimed, "Is she, by God!" Somewhat taken aback, the groom explained that it was Napoleon who had died. A few months later Caroline died.

Instead of loving your enemies, treat your friends a little better.

> *Ed Howe (1853–1937)*
> *American journalist*

You learn in this business: If you want a friend, get a dog.

> *Carl Icahn (1936–   )*
> *CEO, Trans World Airlines*

Never explain. Your friends do not need it and your enemies will not believe you anyway.

> Elbert Hubbard (1856–1915)
> American writer

Tell me whom you love, and I will tell you what you are.

> Arsène Houssaye (1815–96)
> French writer

Fate makes our relatives, choice makes our friends.

> Jacques Delille (1738–1813)
> French abbé and poet

Old friends are best. King James used to call for his old shoes; they were easiest for his feet.

> John Selden (1584–1654)
> English jurist and antiquarian

You like me! You really like me!

> Sally Field (1946–   )
> American actress
> (on receiving an Academy Award)

After the verb "to love," "to help" is the most beautiful verb in the world!

> Bertha von Suttner (1843–1914)
> Austrian novelist

A dog is the only thing on earth that loves you more than you love yourself.

> Josh Billings (1818–85)
> American humorist

A lover . . . tries to stand in well with the pet dog of the house.

> Molière (1622–73)
> French actor and dramatist

Getting people to like you is merely the other side of liking them.

> Norman Vincent Peale (1898–   )
> American clergyman and author

We owe to the Middle Ages the two worst inventions of humanity—romantic love and gunpowder.

> André Maurois (1885–1967)
> French writer

Those who hate you don't win unless you hate them, and then you destroy yourself.

> Richard Nixon (1913–   )
> 37th president of the United States

Your friend is the man who knows all about you, and still likes you.

> Elbert Hubbard (1856–1915)
> American writer

Show me a friend in need and I'll show you a pest.

> Joe E. Lewis (1902–71)
> American comedian

My idea of an agreeable person is a person who agrees with me.

> Benjamin Disraeli
> (1804–81)
> British novelist and prime
> minister

He who cannot love must learn to flatter.

> Johann Wolfgang von Goethe
> (1749–1832)
> German poet and dramatist

You can make more friends in two months by becoming interested in other people than you can in two years by trying to get people interested in you.

> Dale Carnegie (1888–1955)
> American writer and
> speaker

Only little boys and old men sneer at love.

> Louis Auchincloss
> (1917–   )
> American writer

The most romantic thing any woman ever said to me in bed was "Are you sure you're not a cop?"

> Larry Brown (1940–   )
> American professional
> basketball coach

The greatest love is a mother's, then a dog's, then a sweetheart's.

> Polish proverb

Most people enjoy the inferiority of their best friends.

> Philip Dormer Stanhope
> (1694–1773)
> Earl of Chesterfield
> English statesman and
> author

In love, there is always one who kisses and one who offers the cheek.

> French proverb

WOMEN AND FEMINISM

FEMINISM: *doctrine that advocates the rights of women; a social movement of and for women.*

Understanding women is probably one of the best assets a salesperson could ever have. Peddlers in the late 1700s found that they had to create a demand then just as major corporations do today. Jim "Jubilee" Fisk and his partner, Volney Haskell, figured out a scheme that ensured sales of their goods before they actually drove their wagon into a town. One of them would go into a town alone, find one of the prettiest girls in town, and give her a shawl, thereby guaranteeing every other fashion-conscious lady in the town would see it and want one of her own. The following

week, the other partner, driving the wagonload of shawls into town, would be overtaken by women anxious to purchase a shawl of their own.

A woman without a man is like a fish without a bicycle.

> Gloria Steinem (1934–   )
> American feminist and
> journalist

The supply of good women far exceeds that of the men who deserve them.

> Robert Graves (1895–1985)
> British author

I have an idea that the phrase "weaker sex" was coined by some woman to disarm the man she was preparing to overwhelm.

> Ogden Nash (1902–71)
> American writer of
> humorous verse

Most hierarchies were established by men who now monopolize the upper levels, thus depriving women of their rightful share of opportunities for incompetence.

> Laurence J. Peter (1919–90)
> American author

All the books extolling the simple life are written by men.

> William Feather (1889–
> 1981)
> American author and
> publisher

If you want something said, ask a man.
If you want something done, ask a woman.

> Margaret Thatcher
> (1925–   )
> prime minister of Great
> Britain

The only place men want depth in a woman is in her décolletage.

> Zsa Zsa Gabor (1917–   )
> American actress

Doctors and lawyers must go to school for years and years, often with little sleep and with great sacrifice to their first wives.

> Roy G. Blount, Jr. (1941–   )
> American author

I don't mind living in a man's world as long as I can be a woman in it.

> Marilyn Monroe (1926–62)
> American actress

The woman is hard upon the woman.

> Alfred, Lord Tennyson
> (1809–92)
> English poet

When women kiss it always reminds one of prizefighters shaking hands.

> *H. L. Mencken (1880–1956)*
> *American editor*

Women give us solace, but if it weren't for women we should never need solace.

> *Don Herold (1927–)*
> *American author*

My advice to the women's clubs of America is raise more hell and fewer dahlias.

> *William Allen White (1868–*
> *1944)*
> *American journalist and*
> *writer*

I'm furious about the Women's Liberationists. They keep getting up on soapboxes and proclaiming that women are brighter than men. That's true, but it should be kept very quiet or it ruins the whole racket.

> *Anita Loos (1893–1981)*
> *American author and*
> *playwright*

No one should have to dance backward all their lives.

> *Jill Ruckelshaus (1937–)*
> *U.S. Commission on Civil*
> *Rights officer*

Some of us are becoming the men we wanted to marry.

> *Gloria Steinem (1934–)*
> *American feminist and*
> *journalist*

Buy old masters. They fetch a much better price than old mistresses.

> *William Maxwell Aitken,*
> *Lord Beaverbrook (1879–1964)*
> *British newspaper publisher*

A man can sleep around, no questions asked; but if a woman makes nineteen or twenty mistakes she's a tramp.

> *Joan Rivers (1933–)*
> *American comedienne*

Men are creatures with two legs and eight hands.

> *Jayne Mansfield (1934–67)*
> *American actress*

She's the original good time that was had by all.

> *Bette Davis (1907–89)*
> *American actress*
> *(referring to a starlet)*

Generally women are better than men—they have more character. I prefer men for some things, obviously, but women have a greater sense of honor and are more willing to take a chance with their lives. They are more open and decent in their relationship with a man. Men run all the time. I don't know how they live with themselves, they are so preoccupied with being studs.

> *Lauren Bacall (1924–)*
> *American actress*

If women didn't exist, all the money in the world would have no meaning.

> *Aristotle Onassis*
> *(1900?–75)*
> *Greek shipping magnate*

There are very few jobs that actually require a penis or vagina. All other jobs should be open to everybody.

> *Florynce B. Kennedy*
> *(1916–   )*
> *American feminist*

They have a right to work wherever they want—as long as they have dinner ready when you get home.

> *John Wayne (1907–79)*
> *American actor*

There is a new minority in the American work force: white males. . . . In 1954, white males were in the majority, 62.5 percent of the work force. By June 1984, they had become the minority, 49.3 percent. . . . Increasingly, that "average worker" is a woman.

> *John Naisbitt (1929–   )*
> *and Patricia Aburdene*
> *(1947–   )*
> *American business writers*
> *and social researchers*

I don't in a day at my desk ever once think about what my sex is. I'm thinking about my job.

> *Karen N. Horn (1943–   )*
> *American financial*
> *executive*

I have yet to hear a man ask for advice on how to combine marriage and a career.

> *Gloria Steinem (1934–   )*
> *American feminist and*
> *journalist*

The only jobs for which no man is qualified are human incubator and wet nurse. Likewise, the only job for which no woman is or can be qualified is sperm donor.

> *Wilma Scott Heide*
> *(1926–   )*
> *American feminist*

To be successful, a woman has to be much better at her job than a man.

> *Golda Meir (1898–1978)*
> *prime minister of Israel*

Whatever women do they must do twice as well as men to be thought half as good. Luckily, this is not difficult.

> *Charlotte Whitton (1896–*
> *1975)*
> *mayor of Ottawa*

Being a woman is a terribly difficult task, since it consists principally in dealing with men.

> *Joseph Conrad (1857–1924)*
> *British novelist*

Women's work! Housework's the hardest work in the world. That's why men won't do it.

> *Edna Ferber (1887–1968)*
> *American writer*

Men get their pictures on money, but women get their hands on it.

> *Ruth Sherrill (1900–52)*
> *American banker*

I kissed my first girl and smoked my first cigarette on the same day. I haven't had time for tobacco since.

> *Arturo Toscanini (1867–1957)*
> *Italian conductor*

I married the first man I ever kissed. When I tell my children that, they just about throw up.

> *Barbara Bush (1925–   )*
> *wife of U.S. president*
> *George Bush*

A pessimist is a man who thinks all women are bad. An optimist is one who hopes they are.

> *Chauncey Depew (1834–1928)*
> *American lawyer and*
> *politician*

The mirror over my bed reads, "Objects appear larger than they are."

> *Garry Shandling (1949–   )*
> *American comedian*

If it weren't for pickpockets, I'd have no sex life at all.

> *Rodney Dangerfield*
> *(1921–   )*
> *American actor and*
> *comedian*

When women go wrong, men go right after them.

> *Mae West (1892–1980)*
> *American actress*

Whether women are better than men I cannot say—but I can say they are certainly no worse.

> *Golda Meir (1898–1978)*
> *prime minister of Israel*

The quickest way to get to know most people is to go shopping with them.

> *Anonymous*

I hate women because they always know where things are.

> *James Thurber (1894–1961)*
> *American author*

There's no reason why a woman shouldn't be in the White House as President, if she wants to be. But she'll be sorry when she gets there.

> *Harry S Truman (1884–1972)*
> *33rd president of the United*
> *States*

Behind every great man is a woman with nothing to wear.

> *L. Grant Glickman*

High heels were invented by a woman who had been kissed on the forehead.

> *Christopher Morley (1890–1957)*
> *American writer*

Where all the women are strong, all the men are good-looking and all the children are above average.

> *Garrison Keillor (1942–   )*
> *American author*
> *(describing his mythical*
> *village, Lake Wobegon)*

On one issue at least, men and women agree: they both distrust women.

> *H. L. Mencken (1880–1956)*
> *American editor*

The trouble with life is that there are so many beautiful women and so little time.

> *John Barrymore (1882–*
> *1942)*
> *American actor*

Most men who rail against women are railing at one woman only.

> *Rémy de Gourmont (1858–*
> *1915)*
> *French writer*

A woman is only a woman, but a good cigar is a smoke.

> *Rudyard Kipling (1865–*
> *1936)*
> *English author*

I wanted to be the first woman to burn her bra, but it would have taken the fire department four days to put it out.

> *Dolly Parton (1946–   )*
> *American singer*

A woman will buy anything she thinks the store is losing money on.

> *Frank McKinney (Kin)*
> *Hubbard (1868–1930)*
> *American humorist*

The years that a woman subtracts from her age are not lost. They are added to other women's.

> *Diane de Poitiers (1499–*
> *1566)*
> *mistress of King Henry II of*
> *France*

Don't accept rides from strange men, and remember that all men are strange.

> *Robin Morgan (1941–   )*
> *American feminist and*
> *writer*

Next to the wound, what women make best is the bandage.

> *Jules-Amédée Barbey*
> *D'Aurevilly (1808–89)*
> *French writer and*
> *literary critic*

Most women are not so young as they are painted.

> *Sir Max Beerbohm (1872–*
> *1956)*
> *English critic and*
> *caricaturist*

The great question that has never been answered, and which I have not yet been able to answer despite my thirty years of research into the feminine soul, is: What does a woman want?

> *Sigmund Freud (1856–1939)*
> *Austrian psychologist*

Chapter 23

Personal Values
and Religion

RELIGION: *set of beliefs concerning the cause, nature, and purpose of the universe; frequently including a moral code for the conduct of human affairs.*

Although politicians hold no monopoly on speaking without thinking, they certainly have a knack for it. As a U.S. delegate to the United Nations from 1947 to 1953, Warren Austin was present during a debate on the Middle East question. When the meeting became disrupted by outbursts from both the Jews and the Arabs, Austin demanded that they sit down and settle their differences "like good Christians."

Most Christians believe that anything is possible with faith in God and, for Catholics, a little help from the pope is always welcome. American golfer Sam Snead, who won the PGA and Masters titles three times each, was on tour in Rome in 1961. Not having won a tournament since 1954, Snead asked one of the papal officials if the pope might bless his putter.

The monsignor nodded in sympathetic understanding. "I know, Mr. Snead. My putting is absolutely hopeless, too."

Disheartened, Snead exclaimed, "If you *live* here and can't putt, what chance is there for me?"

Heaven is an American salary, a Chinese cook, an English house, and a Japanese wife. Hell is defined as having a Chinese salary, an English cook, a Japanese house, and an American wife.

> *James H. Kabbler III*
> *chairman, Nikkal*
> *Industries, Ltd.*

If God lived on earth, people would break His windows.

> *Yiddish proverb*

A Jewish man with parents alive is a fifteen-year-old boy, and will remain a fifteen-year-boy till they die.

> *Philip Roth (1933–   )*
> *American author*

If you live in New York, even if you're Catholic, you're Jewish.

> *Lenny Bruce (1925–66)*
> *American social satirist*

I once wanted to become an atheist, but I gave up—they had no holidays.

> *Henny Youngman (1906–   )*
> *American comedian*

You can preach a better sermon with your life than with your lips.

> *Oliver Goldsmith (1728–74)*
> *British poet, novelist, and*
> *playwright*

Look at these cows and remember that the greatest scientists in the world have never discovered how to make grass into milk.

> *Michael Pupin (1858–1935)*
> *American physicist and*
> *inventor*

The devil can cite Scripture for his purpose.

> *William Shakespeare (1564–*
> *1616)*
> *English dramatist and poet*

God gave us memories so that we might have roses in December.

> *James Matthew Barrie*
> *(1860–1937)*
> *Scottish novelist and*
> *dramatist*

God will not look you over for medals, degrees, or diplomas, but for scars.

> *Elbert Hubbard (1856–*
> *1915)*
> *American writer*

You don't have to be dowdy to be a Christian.

> *Tammy Faye Bakker*
> *(1942–   )*
> *American television*
> *evangelist*

The bottom line is in heaven.

> *Edwin Herbert Land (1909–91)*
> *American inventor and founder,*
> *Polaroid Corporation*

I believe that our Heavenly Father invented man because he was disappointed in the monkey.

> *Mark Twain (1835–1910)*
> *American author*

We trust, sir, that God is on our side. It is more important to know that we are on God's side.

> *Abraham Lincoln (1809–65)*
> *16th president of the United States*

God is always on the side of the big battalions.

> *Henri de La Tour*
> *d'Auvergne (1611–75)*
> *Vicomte de Turenne*
> *marshal of France*

Man is a dog's ideal of what God should be.

> *Holbrook Jackson (1874–*
> *1948)*
> *English journalist, editor,*
> *and author*

I consider myself a Hindu, Christian, Moslem, Jew, Buddhist and Confucian.

> *Mohandas K. Gandhi*
> *(1869–1948)*
> *Indian nationalist leader*

PERSONAL PHILOSOPHIES

PERSONAL PHILOSOPHY: *general beliefs, concepts, and attitudes of an individual.*

President Lyndon Baines Johnson was well known for his use of off-color language regardless of the time or place or the audience. Having long desired to rid the Federal Bureau of Investigation of its founding director, J. Edgar Hoover, as many predecessors had unsuccessfully attempted, Johnson became thoroughly annoyed by the difficulties he encountered. Finally resigning himself to Hoover's continued presence, Johnson commented, "It's probably better to have him inside the tent pissing out, than outside pissing in.

Never play cards with a man called Doc. Never eat in a place called Mom's. Never sleep with a woman whose troubles are worse than your own.

> *Nelson Algren (1909–81)*
> *American author*

Do not say all you know, for he who says all he knows often says more than he knows.
Do not tell all you hear, for he who tells all he hears often tells more than he hears.
Do not spend all you have, for he

who spends all he has often spends more than he has.
Do not covet all you see, for he who covets all he sees often wants more than he sees.

> *Persian proverb*

I shut my eyes in order to see.

> *Paul Gauguin (1848–1903)*
> *French painter*

Some people are always grumbling because roses have thorns. I am thankful thorns have roses.

> *Alphonse Karr (1808–90)*
> *French journalist and*
> *novelist*

Rule Number 1 is don't sweat the small stuff. Rule Number 2 is it's all small stuff. And if you can't fight and you can't flee, flow.

> *Robert S. Eliot (1929–   )*
> *American cardiologist*

I can usually judge a fellow by what he laughs at.

> *Wilson Mizner (1876–1933)*
> *American author*

A gentleman never heard a story before.

> *Austin O'Malley (1858–*
> *1932)*
> *American writer*

In life, as in a football game, the principle to follow is: Hit the line hard.

> *Theodore Roosevelt (1858–*
> *1919)*
> *26th president of the United*
> *States*

The most beautiful things in the world are the most useless: peacocks and lilies, for instance.

> *John Ruskin (1819–1900)*
> *English art critic and*
> *historian*

He that scattereth thorns must not go barefoot.

> *Thomas Fuller (1654–1734)*
> *English physician and*
> *writer*

Eat with the rich, but go to the play with the poor, who are capable of joy.

> *Logan Pearsall Smith*
> *(1865–1946)*
> *American essayist*

A desk is a dangerous place from which to watch the world.

> *John le Carré (1931–   )*
> *British diplomat and*
> *novelist*

Everyone is a moon, and has a dark side which he never shows to anybody.

> *Mark Twain (1835–1910)*
> *American author*

It is easier to fight for one's principles than to live up to them.

> *Alfred Adler (1870–1937)*
> *Austrian psychiatrist*

There's a sucker born every minute.

> *Phineas Taylor (P.T.) Barnum*
> *(1810–91)*
> *American circus owner and*
> *showman*

You can fool all of the people some of the time, and some of the people all of the time, and that's good enough.

> *Laurence J. Peter (1919–90)*
> *American author*

If you pick up a starving dog and make him prosperous, he will not bite you. This is the principal difference between a dog and a man.

> *Mark Twain (1835–1910)*
> *American author*

People who don't mind their own business either have no mind or no business.

> *Leopold Fechtner (1916–   )*

In certain trying instances, urgent circumstances, desperate circumstances, profanity furnishes a relief denied even to prayer.

> *Mark Twain (1835–1910)*
> *American author*

What? You been keeping records on me? I wasn't so bad! How many times did I take the Lord's name in vain? One million and six? Jesus Ch—!

> *Steve Martin (1945–   )*
> *American actor and*
> *comedian*

Great minds discuss ideas, average minds discuss events, small minds discuss people.

> *Hyman G. Rickover*
> *(1900–86)*
> *admiral, U.S. Navy*

If a man is a minority of one, we lock him up.

> *Oliver Wendell Holmes*
> *(1809–94)*
> *American physician and*
> *author*

Do not anticipate trouble, or worry about what may never happen. Keep in the sunlight.

> *Benjamin Franklin*
> *(1706–90)*
> *American statesman and*
> *philosopher*

He who fears something gives it power over him.

> *Moorish proverb*

O wad some power the giftie gie us
To see oursel's as others see us.

> *Robert Burns (1759–96)*
> *Scottish poet*

It is not the situation that makes the man, but the man who makes the situation.

F. W. Robertson (1816–53)
English clergyman

The man who strikes first admits that his ideas have given out.

Chinese proverb

I have always believed that it's important to show a new look periodically. Predictability can lead to failure.

T. Boone Pickens (1928–   )
president, Mesa Petroleum
Company

No one is useless in this world who lightens the burdens of another.

Charles Dickens (1812–70)
English novelist

When a man has pity on all living creatures, then only is he noble.

Buddha (ca. 563–ca. 483
B.C.)
Indian philosopher and
founder of Buddhism

We have met the enemy and he is us.

Walt Kelly (1913–73)
American cartoonist

Two men were walking along a crowded sidewalk in a downtown business area. Suddenly, one exclaimed, "Listen to that lovely sound of that cricket." But the other could not hear. He asked his companion how he could detect the sound of a cricket amid the din of people and traffic. The first man, who was a zoologist, had trained himself to listen to the voice of nature. But he didn't explain. He simply took a coin out of his pocket and dropped it to the sidewalk, whereupon a dozen people began to look about them. "We hear," he said, "what we listen for."

Kermit L. Long (1915–   )
American clergyman

We are all of us richer than we think we are.

Michel de Montaigne
(1533–92)
French essayist

Nothing you can't spell will ever work.

Will Rogers (1879–1935)
American actor and
humorist

The only way to get the best of an argument is to avoid it.

Dale Carnegie (1888–1955)
American writer and
speaker

I used to be Snow White, but I drifted.

Mae West (1892–1980)
American actress

I'm as pure as the driven slush.

Tallulah Bankhead (1903–68)
American actress

Men are shits. It hit me when I real- ized that I wouldn't take myself out or go to bed with me.

> *Dustin Hoffman (1937–)*
> *American actor in Sydney*
> *Pollack's 1982 motion*
> *picture* Tootsie

Anybody who goes to see a psychia- trist ought to have his head exam- ined.

> *Samuel Goldwyn (1882–*
> *1974)*
> *American motion-picture*
> *producer*

An optimist is a fellow who believes a housefly is looking for a way to get out.

> *George Jean Nathan (1882–*
> *1958)*
> *American editor and drama*
> *critic*

Laugh and the world laughs with you, snore and you sleep alone.

> *Anthony Burgess (1917–)*
> *English author*

A celebrity is a person who works hard all his life to become well known, then wears dark glasses to avoid being recognized.

> *Fred Allen (1894–1956)*
> *American comedian*

I was probably the only revolution- ary ever referred to as "cute!"

> *Abbie Hoffman (1936–89)*
> *American author and*
> *political activist*

Animals have these advantages over man: they never hear the clock strike, they die without any idea of death, they have no theologians to in- struct them, their last moments are not disturbed by unwelcome and un- pleasant ceremonies, their funerals cost them nothing, and no one starts lawsuits over their wills.

> *Voltaire (1694–1778)*
> *French writer*

Even as a kid, I always went for the wrong women. I feel that's my prob- lem. When my mother took me to see *Snow White,* everyone fell in love with Snow White. I immediately fell for the wicked queen.

> *Woody Allen (1935–)*
> *American actor, film*
> *director, and comedian*

The trees that are slow to grow bear the best fruit.

> *Molière (1622–73)*
> *French actor and dramatist*

I don't have a lifestyle. I have a life.

> *Jane Fonda (1937–)*
> *American actress*

If you strike at a king you must kill him.

> *Ralph Waldo Emerson*
> *(1803–82)*
> *American essayist and poet*
> *(advice to Oliver Wendell*
> *Holmes, Jr.)*

I always have trouble remembering three things: faces, names, and—I can't remember what the third thing is.

Fred Allen (1894–1956)
American comedian

I have a simple philosophy. Fill what's empty. Empty what's full. Scratch where it itches.

Alice Roosevelt Longworth
(1884–1980)
daughter of President
Theodore Roosevelt

Some day each of us will be famous for fifteen minutes.

Andy Warhol (1930?–87)
American painter and
motion-picture producer

A bird in the hand is dead.

Anonymous

Courage is doing what you're afraid to do. There can be no courage unless you're scared.

Eddie Rickenbacker (1890–
1973)
American aviator

He was a bold man that first ate an oyster.

Jonathan Swift (1667–1745)
English satirist

After three days, fish and guests stink.

John Lyly (1554?–1606)
English author

So let me assert my firm belief that the only thing we have to fear is fear itself—nameless, unreasoning, unjustified terror which paralyzes needed efforts to convert retreat into advance.

Franklin D. Roosevelt
(1882–1945)
32nd president of the
United States

Home is not where you live, but where they understand you.

Christian Morgenstern
(1817–1914)
German poet

No man can think clearly when his fists are clenched.

George Jean Nathan (1882–
1958)
American editor and
drama critic

When I play with my cat, who knows but that she regards me more as a plaything than I do her?

Michel de Montaigne
(1533–92)
French essayist

The value of a principle is the number of things it will explain.

Ralph Waldo Emerson
(1803–82)
American essayist and poet

Men are much more apt to agree in what they do than in what they think.

Johann Wolfgang von Goethe
(1749–1832)
German poet and dramatist

Flattery will get you anywhere.

> *Jane Russell (1921–)*
> *American actress in Howard*
> *Hawks's 1953 motion picture*
> Gentlemen Prefer Blondes

God is really another artist. He invented the giraffe, the elephant, and the cat. He has no real style. He just goes on trying other things.

> *Pablo Picasso (1881–1973)*
> *Spanish painter and*
> *sculptor*

Bisexuality immediately doubles your chance for a date on Saturday night.

> *Woody Allen (1935–)*
> *American actor, film*
> *director, and comedian*

Never cut what you can untie.

> *Joseph Joubert (1754–1824)*
> *French essayist and moralist*

A man becomes like those whose society he loves.

> *Hindu proverb*

The great pleasure in life is doing what people say you cannot do.

> *Walter Bagehot (1826–77)*
> *English economist and*
> *journalist*

Be good and you will be lonesome.

> *Mark Twain (1835–1910)*
> *American author*

The doctor sees all the weakness of mankind, the lawyer all the wickedness, the theologian all the stupidity.

> *Arthur Schopenhauer*
> *(1788–1860)*
> *German philosopher*

The flower in the vase still smiles, but no longer laughs.

> *Malcolm de Chazal*
> *(1902–)*
> *French author*

TRUST AND TRUTH

TRUST: *confidence in or reliance on the truthfulness or accuracy of something or someone.*

TRUTH: *sincerity in action, character, and utterance; judgment, proposition, or idea that is true or accepted as true.*

When we examine ourselves as light through a prism, we become aware of the true colors that woven together make up our lives. There is an old Hebrew story about a king who heard that Moses was kind, generous, and a courageous leader. Curious about the man, the king consulted his astrologers and had his phrenologists examine a portrait of Moses. They told the king that Moses was cruel, greedy, and self-centered. The king's curiosity was stirred even more, so he went to Moses himself and found him to be a very good man, and related what his advisers had told him.

Moses listened to the king and then agreed with what the astrologers and phrenologists had said. "They saw what I was made of, but they couldn't tell you how I struggled against that so that I would become what I am."

Remember: one lie does not cost you one truth, but the truth.

Friedrich Hebbel (1813–63)
German dramatist

We are much harder on people who betray us in small ways than on people who betray others in great ones.

François Duc de La
Rochefoucauld (1613–80)
French writer and moralist

As a general rule, if you want to get at the truth—hear both sides and believe neither.

Josh Billings (1818–85)
American humorist

FAMOUS AMERICAN LIES

The check is in the mail.
I'll start my diet tomorrow.
We service what we sell.
Give me your number and the doctor will call you right back.
Money cheerfully refunded.
One size fits all.
This offer is limited to the first one hundred people who call in.
Your luggage isn't lost, it's only misplaced.
Leave your résumé and we'll keep it on file.
This hurts me more than it hurts you.

I only need five minutes of your time.
Your table will be ready in a few minutes.
Open wide, it won't hurt a bit.
Let's have lunch sometime.
It's not the money, it's the principle.

Anonymous

"Our computer's down." This is another great [business] lie. Unfortunately, it is true so often that you seldom can attack it head-on.

Charles W. Kyd
American financial
consultant and author

There are more fish taken out of a stream than were ever in it.

Oliver Herford (1863–1935)
English writer and
illustrator

Trust everybody, but cut the cards.

Finley Peter Dunne
(1867–1936)
American humorist

Men occasionally stumble over the truth, but most of them pick themselves up and hurry off as if nothing had happened.

> *Winston Churchill (1874–1965)*
> *British statesman and prime minister*

He who praises everybody praises nobody.

> *Samuel Johnson (1709–84)*
> *English lexicographer and author*

Never trust a man who speaks well of everybody.

> *John Churton Collins (1848–1908)*
> *English critic, author, and educator*

The liar's punishment is not in the least that he is not believed, but that he cannot believe anyone else.

> *George Bernard Shaw (1856–1950)*
> *British playwright and social reformer*

George Washington, as a boy, was ignorant of the commonest accomplishments of youth. He could not even lie.

> *Mark Twain (1835–1910)*
> *American author*

Love your neighbor, but don't pull down the hedge.

> *Swiss proverb*

He who speaks the truth must have one foot in the stirrup.

> *Armenian proverb*

While you're saving your face, you're losing your ass. Never trust a man whose eyes are too close to his nose. I never trust a man unless I've got his pecker in my pocket.

> *Lyndon B. Johnson (1908–73)*
> *36th president of the United States*

Keep your friends close, but keep your enemies closer.

> *Sicilian proverb*

If fifty million people say a foolish thing, it is still a foolish thing.

> *Anatole France (1844–1924)*
> *French novelist and satirist*

If you tell the truth, you don't have to remember anything.

> *Mark Twain (1835–1910)*
> *American author*

Be always sure you are right—then go ahead.

> *Davy Crockett (1786–1836)*
> *American frontiersman and soldier*

Always do right. This will gratify some people, and astonish the rest.

> *Mark Twain (1835–1910)*
> *American author*

Doing what's right isn't the problem. It's knowing what's right.

> *Lyndon B. Johnson*
> *(1908–73)*
> *36th president of the United States*

No one can be right all of the time, but it helps to be right most of the time.

> *Robert Half (1918–   )*
> *American personnel-agency executive*

Trust in Allah, but tie your camel.

> *Arab proverb*

A verbal contract isn't worth the paper it's written on.

> *Samuel Goldwyn (1882–1974)*
> *American motion-picture producer*

Chapter 24

The Graying Executive

EXECUTIVE: *a person having administrative or supervisory authority in an organization.*

The last quarter of the twentieth century has seen nations pass laws to protect the rights of older workers, attempts by companies besieged by new competition to reduce human-resource costs by offering bonuses for early retirement of older, more highly paid personnel, and—more recently—attempts by a growing number of firms to entice experienced workers out of retirement to begin new careers. A widely reprinted United Technologies Corporation advertisement sums up the question of age rather nicely:

> Ted Williams, at age 42, slammed a home run in his last official time at bat.
>
> Mickey Mantle, age 20, hit 23 home runs his first full year in the major leagues.
>
> Golda Meir was 71 when she became Prime Minister of Israel.
>
> William Pitt II was 24 when he became Prime Minister of Great Britain.
>
> George Bernard Shaw was 94 when one of his plays was first produced.

Mozart was just seven when his first composition was published.

Now, how about this? Benjamin Franklin was a newspaper columnist at 16, and a framer of the United States Constitution when he was 81.

You're never too young or too old if you've got talent. Let's recognize that age has little to do with ability.

I promise not to make my opponent's youth and inexperience an issue in this campaign.

> *Ronald Reagan (1911–   )*
> *40th president of the United States*
> *(reference by the then seventy-three-year-old president to his Democratic opponent, Walter Mondale, in a 1984 presidential campaign)*

If we could be twice young and twice old we could correct all our mistakes.

> *Euripides (ca. 484–406 B.C.)*
> *Greek dramatist*

My husband will never chase another woman. He's too fine, too decent, too old.

> *Gracie Allen (1906–64)*
> *American comedienne*

When you're too old to chase other things, you can always chase golf balls.

> *Anonymous*

I'm now at an age where I've got to prove I'm just as good as I never was.

> *Rex Harrison (1908–90)*
> *English actor*

A man is only as old as the woman he feels.

> *Groucho Marx (1890–1977)*
> *American actor and comedian*

No matter how old you get, if you can keep the desire to be creative, you're keeping the man-child alive.

> *John Cassavetes (1929–89)*
> *American actor and film director*

I'll never get old.

> *Judith A. Resnik (1949–86)*
> *American astronaut*
> *(died in Challenger space-shuttle explosion)*

The secret of staying young is to live honestly, eat slowly, and lie about your age.

> *Lucille Ball (1911–89)*
> *American actress*

I refuse to admit that I am more than fifty-two, even if that does make my sons illegitimate.

> *attributed to Lady Nancy*
> *(Witcher Langhorne)*
> *Astor (1879–1964)*
> *English political leader*

The four stages of man are infancy, childhood, adolescence, and obsolescence.

> *Art Linkletter (1912–   )*
> *American radio and TV*
> *show host*

It's not the men in my life that counts, it's the life in my men.

> *Mae West (1892–1980)*
> *American actress*

It is not the years in your life but the life in your years that counts.

> *Adlai Stevenson (1900–65)*
> *American lawyer and*
> *diplomat*

RULES FOR LONGEVITY

1. Avoid fried meats which angry up the blood.
2. If your stomach disputes you, lie down and pacify it with cool thoughts.
3. Keep the juices flowing by jangling around gently as you move.
4. Go very light on the vices, such as carrying on in society. The social ramble ain't restful.
5. Avoid running at all times.
6. Don't look back. Something might be gaining on you.

> *Leroy Robert "Satchel"*
> *Paige (1906–82)*
> *American baseball player*

Life cannot go on without much forgetting.

> *Honoré de Balzac (1799–*
> *1850)*
> *French novelist*

It is well known that the older a man grows the faster he could run as a boy.

> *Walter Wellesley (Red)*
> *Smith (1905–82)*
> *American sportswriter*

You can't turn back the clock. But you can wind it up again.

> *Bonnie Prudden (1914–   )*
> *American physical fitness*
> *proponent*

All that I know, I learned after I was thirty.

> *Georges Clemenceau (1841–*
> *1929)*
> *French statesman*

Men don't get smarter when they grow older. They just lose their hair.

> *Claudette Colbert*
> *(1905–   )*
> *American actress*
> *in Preston Sturges's 1942*
> *motion picture* The Palm
> Beach Story

The ten best years of a woman's life are between the ages of twenty-nine and thirty.

> *Peter Weiss (1916–82)*
> *Swedish author*

Age is not important unless you're a cheese.

> Helen Hayes (1900–   )
> American actress

No man is ever old enough to know better.

> Holbrook Jackson (1874–
> 1948)
> English journalist, editor,
> and author

The older they get the better they were when they were younger.

> Jim Bouton (1939–   )
> American baseball player
> and author

Life would be infinitely happier if we could only be born at the age of eighty and gradually approach eighteen.

> Mark Twain (1835–1910)
> American author

You've heard of the three ages of man: youth, middle-age, and "you are looking wonderful."

> Francis Joseph Spellman
> (1889–1967)
> American Roman Catholic
> cardinal

YOUTH

YOUTH: *time of life when one is young, especially the period between childhood and maturity.*

Like many great men, James Abbott McNeill Whistler tried his hand at several career possibilities before being recognized as an etcher and painter. He wrote brilliant critical essays and aphorisms and is considered a wit, especially abroad. Indicative of Whistler's humor is the story he tells about his short-lived military career that ended when he was discharged from West Point after failing chemistry. "If silicon had been a gas, I might have been a major general."

If you've never seen a real, fully developed look of disgust, just tell your son how you conducted yourself when you were a boy.

> Frank McKinney (Kin)
> Hubbard (1868–1930)
> American humorist

Nothing so dates a man as to decry the younger generation.

> Adlai E. Stevenson
> (1900–65)
> American lawyer and
> diplomat

Youth is a wonderful thing. What a crime to waste it on children.

> *attributed to George Bernard Shaw (1856–1950)*
> *British playwright and social reformer*

The young always have the same problem—how to rebel and conform at the same time. They have now solved this by defying their parents and copying one another.

> *Quentin Crisp (1908–   )*
> *British author and film critic*

American youth attributes much more importance to arriving at driver's license age than at voting age.

> *Marshall McLuhan (1911–80)*
> *Canadian educator and author*

A boy becomes an adult three years before his parents think he does and about two years after he thinks he does.

> *Lewis B. Hershey (1893–1977)*
> *general, U.S. Army, and director, Selective Service System*

I am not young enough to know everything.

> *James Matthew Barrie (1860–1937)*
> *Scottish novelist and dramatist*

Forty is the old age of youth. Fifty is the youth of old age.

> *Victor Hugo (1802–85)*
> *French poet, novelist, and dramatist*

The old believe everything; the middle-aged suspect everything; the young know everything.

> *Oscar Wilde (1854–1900)*
> *Irish poet, playwright, and novelist*

MIDDLE AGE

MIDDLE AGE: *period of life from about 40 to about 60.*

Hurrying through the hallowed halls of the U.S. Congress one day, American scholar and senator S. I. Hayakawa simply did not recognize the famous senior senator and chairman of the Senate Finance Committee, Russell B. Long of Louisiana. When his companion gently scolded him, Hayakawa nonchalantly remarked, "All you middle-aged white men look alike."

Middle age is when you've met so many people that every new person you meet reminds you of someone else.

> Ogden Nash (1902–71)
> American writer of
> humorous verse

Years ago we discovered the exact point, the dead center of middle age. It occurs when you are too young to take up golf and too old to rush up to the net.

> Franklin P. Adams (1881–
> 1960)
> American journalist and
> humorist

Middle age is when your age starts to show around the middle.

> Bob Hope (1903–   )
> American comedian

Middle age is the time when a man is always thinking that in a week or two he will feel as good as ever.

> Don Marquis (1878–1937)
> American humorist

Setting a good example for your children takes all the fun out of middle age.

> William Feather (1889–
> 1981)
> American author and
> publisher

I'm at the age where food has taken the place of sex in my life. In fact, I've just had a mirror put over my kitchen table.

> Rodney Dangerfield
> (1921–   )
> American actor and
> comedian

Kissing don't last. Cooking do!

> George Meredith (1828–
> 1909)
> British novelist and poet

Middle age: When you're sitting at home on Saturday night and the telephone rings and you hope it isn't for you.

> Ogden Nash (1902–71)
> American writer of
> humorous verse

The years between fifty and seventy are the hardest. You are always being asked to do things, and yet you are not decrepit enough to turn them down.

> T. S. Eliot (1888–1965)
> English poet and
> playwright

A man of sixty has spent twenty years in bed and over three years in eating.

> Arnold Bennett (1867–1931)
> English novelist

At age fifty, every man has the face he deserves.

> George Orwell (1903–50)
> English author

Middle age is when you're faced with two temptations and you choose the one that will get you home by 9 o'clock.

> Ronald Reagan (1911–)
> 40th president of the
> United States

OLD AGE

OLD AGE: *the period of human life usually considered to begin at age 65.*

A few days after his inauguration in 1933, newly elected president Franklin D. Roosevelt decided to call an old and dear friend, Justice Oliver Wendell Holmes. The ninety-two-year-old Holmes took the call in his library, where he was reading Plato. Surprised, FDR asked, "Why do you read Plato, Mr. Justice?"

Came the imperious reply: "To improve my mind, Mr. President."

Work is the basis of living. I'll never retire. A man'll rust out quicker than he'll wear out.

> Colonel Harland Sanders
> (1890–1980)
> founder, Kentucky Fried
> Chicken

It is sobering to consider that when Mozart was my age he had already been dead for a year.

> Tom Lehrer (1928–)
> American songwriter,
> entertainer, and lecturer

It is better to wear out than to rust out.

> (Bishop) Richard
> Cumberland (1631–1718)
> English philosopher

Old age is not so bad when you consider the alternatives.

> attributed to Maurice
> Chevalier (1888–1972)
> French singer and actor

To me, old age is always fifteen years older than I am.

> Bernard Baruch
> (1870–1965)
> American financier and
> statesman

A sure sign of old age is when you hear "snap, crackle, and pop" and it isn't your cereal.

> Robert Orben (1927–)
> American humorist

That is the great fallacy; the wisdom of old men. They do not grow wise, they grow careful.

> *Ernest Hemingway*
> *(1908–86)*
> *American journalist*

Youth is a blunder; manhood a struggle; old age a regret.

> *Benjamin Disraeli*
> *(1804–81)*
> *British novelist and prime minister*

Why is it that the first gray hairs stick straight out?

> *Frank McKinney (Kin)*
> *Hubbard (1868–1930)*
> *American humorist*

Whenever a man's friends begin to compliment him about looking young, he may be sure that they think he is growing old.

> *Washington Irving (1783–1859)*
> *American essayist, novelist, and historian*

The best thing about getting old is that all those things you couldn't have when you were young you no longer want.

> *Earl Wilson (1907–87)*
> *American newspaper columnist*

After the age of eighty, all contemporaries are friends.

> *Anonymous*

A man is not old till regrets take the place of dreams.

> *John Barrymore (1882–1942)*
> *American actor*

Yes, I'm 68, but when I was a boy, I was too poor to smoke, so knock off ten years. That makes me 58. And since I never developed the drinking habit, you can knock off ten more years. So I'm 48—in the prime of my life. Retire? Retire to what?

> *W. A. C. Bennett (1900–79)*
> *prime minister of British Columbia*

A person is always startled when he hears himself seriously called an old man for the first time.

> *Oliver Wendell Holmes*
> *(1809–94)*
> *American physician and author*

When I was young there was no respect for the young, and now that I am old there is no respect for the old. I missed out coming and going.

> *J. B. Priestley (1894–1984)*
> *English author*

Old age is when the liver spots show through your gloves.

> *Phyllis Diller (1917–   )*
> *American comedienne*

Most people my age are dead.

> *Casey Stengel (1891–1975)*
> *American baseball manager*

Once you get to be over 100 you have it made. You almost never hear of anyone dying who is over 100.

> *George Burns (1896–　)*
> *American actor and*
> *comedian*

I think it's wonderful you could all be here for the forty-third anniversary of my thirty-ninth birthday. We decided not to light the candles this year: we were afraid Pan Am would mistake it for a runway.

> *Bob Hope (1903–　)*
> *American actor and*
> *comedian*
> *(on his eighty-second*
> *birthday)*

A man of eighty has outlived probably three new schools of painting, two of architecture and poetry, a hundred in dress.

> *Joyce Cary (1888–1957)*
> *British novelist*

What I wouldn't give to be 70 again.

> *Oliver Wendell Holmes, Jr.*
> *(1841–1935)*
> *American jurist*

Religion often gets credit for curing rascals when old age is the real medicine.

> *Austin O'Malley (1858–*
> *1932)*
> *American writer*

Nobody grows old by living a number of years. People grow old by deserting their ideals. Years wrinkle the skin; but to give up enthusiasm wrinkles the soul. Worry, doubt, self-distrust, fear and despair—these are the long years that bow the heart and turn the greening spirit back to dust.

> *Anonymous*

You know you're getting old when the candles cost more than the cake.

> *Bob Hope (1903–　)*
> *American actor and*
> *comedian*

First you forget names, then you forget faces, then you forget to pull your zipper up, then you forget to pull your zipper down.

> *Leo Rosenburg (1896–1988)*
> *American advertising*
> *executive*

RETIREMENT

RETIREMENT: *withdrawal from one's position or occupation, or from active working life.*

Two of America's most famous golfing presidents were Dwight D. Eisenhower and Gerald Ford.

Political cartoonists of the 1950s and later in the 1970s took delight in showing the U.S. leaders on the links.

By the time Eisenhower ended his second presidential term in 1960, he was seventy. A reporter asked him how more frequent play made possible by his retirement from politics had affected his golf game. Ike replied, "A lot more people beat me now."

Sooner or later I'm going to die, but I'm not going to retire.

> *Margaret Mead (1901–78)*
> *American anthropologist*

Let me give a word of advice to you young fellows who have been looking forward to retirement: have nothing to do with it. Listen: it's like this. Have you ever been out for a late autumn walk in the closing part of the afternoon and suddenly looked up to realize that the leaves have practically all gone? And the sun has set and the day gone before you knew it —and with that a cold wind blows across the landscape? That's retirement.

> *Stephen Leacock (1869–1944)*
> *Canadian economist and humorist*

The question isn't at what age I want to retire, it's at what income.

> *George Foreman (1949–   )*
> *American boxing champion*

Retirement at sixty-five is ridiculous. When I was sixty-five I still had pimples.

> *George Burns (1896–   )*
> *American actor and comedian*

Two weeks is about the ideal length of time to retire.

> *Alex Comfort (1920–   )*
> *English author and sociologist*

Retirement is when you settle back and see which gets collected first— pensions, annuities, Social Security, or you.

> *Robert Orben (1927–   )*
> *American humorist*

To retire is the beginning of death.

> *Pablo Casals (1876–1973)*
> *Spanish conductor and composer*

Retirement is the ugliest word in the language.

> *Ernest Hemingway (1899–1961)*
> *American journalist and writer*

When a man retires and time is no longer a matter of urgent importance, his colleagues generally present him with a watch.

> *Robert C. Sherriff (1896–1975)*
> *English author and dramatist*

DEATH

DEATH: *cessation of all vital functions; the end of life.*

You win some, you lose some, and some games are rained out. Phil Rizzuto, the great New York Yankees shortstop and later broadcaster of Yankee games, was

reporting a Yankee game in 1978 when it came over the newswires that Pope Paul VI had died. Feeling a sense of loss, Rizzuto announced it on the air and solemnly added, "Well, that kind of puts the damper on even a Yankee win."

No matter how much you accomplish in life, the size of your funeral still will be determined by the weather.

Anonymous

No young man believes that he shall ever die.

William Hazlitt (1778–1830)
English essayist and critic

The fence around a cemetery is foolish, for those inside can't come out and those outside don't want to get in.

Arthur Brisbane (1864–1936)
American journalist

Let us endeavor so to live that when we come to die even the undertaker will be sorry.

Mark Twain (1835–1910)
American author

Death ... is no more than passing from one room into another. But there's a difference for me, you

know. Because in that other room I shall be able to see.

Helen Keller (1880–1968)
(blind) American essayist and lecturer

Depressions may bring people closer to the church, but so do funerals.

Clarence Darrow (1857–1938)
American lawyer and author

The fear of death is the greatest compliment we pay to life.

Anonymous

Everybody wants to go to heaven, but nobody wants to die.

Joe Louis (1914–81)
American boxing champion

There is no cure for birth and death save to enjoy the interval.

George Santayana (1863–1952)
American poet and philosopher

In peace, sons bury their fathers; in war, fathers bury their sons.

> *Herodotus (5th century B.C.)*
> *Greek "Father of History"*

All I desire for my own burial is not to be buried alive.

> *Philip Dormer Stanhope*
> *(1694–1773)*
> *Earl of Chesterfield*
> *English statesman and*
> *author*

I've never known a person to live to 110 or more, and then die, to be remarkable for anything else.

> *Josh Billings (1818–85)*
> *American humorist*

You're just walkin' around to save funeral expenses.

> *Valerie Perrine (1943–   )*
> *American actress*
> *in Sydney Pollack's 1979*
> *motion picture* The
> Electric Horseman

He that dies, pays all debts.

> *William Shakespeare (1564–*
> *1616)*
> *English dramatist and poet*

The difference between sex and death is that with death you can do it alone and no one is going to make fun of you.

> *Woody Allen (1935–   )*
> *American actor, film*
> *director, and comedian*

I detest life insurance agents; they always argue that someday I shall die, which is not so.

> *Stephen B. Leacock (1869–*
> *1944)*
> *Canadian economist and*
> *humorist*

Insurance is death on the installment plan.

> *Philip Slater (1927–   )*
> *American author*

May you get to heaven a half hour before the devil knows you're dead.

> *Irish proverb*

Death is nature's way of saying "Howdy."

> *Anonymous*

Chapter 25

The Future of Business

FORECAST: *estimate or prediction of future events or outcomes for a specified time period.*

Wayne Gretzky is, arguably, the greatest hockey player in history. Asked about his secret for continuing to lead the National Hockey League in goals year after year, Gretzky replied, "I skate to where the puck is going to be, not where it has been."

The future comes one day at a time.

Dean Acheson (1893–1971)
U.S. secretary of state

I never think of the future. It comes soon enough.

Albert Einstein (1879–1955)
American physicist

In the 1940s a survey listed the top seven discipline problems in public schools: talking, chewing gum, making noise, running in the halls, getting out of turn in line, wearing improper clothes, not putting paper in wastebaskets. A 1980s survey lists these top seven: drug abuse, alcohol abuse, pregnancy, suicide, rape, robbery, assault. (Arson, gang warfare, and venereal disease are also-rans.)

George F. Will (1941–   )
American news
commentator and author

In the space age, man will be able to go around the world in two hours—one hour for flying and the other to get to the airport.

Neil McElroy (1904–72)
chairman, Procter & Gamble;
U.S. secretary of defense

Life is just one damned thing after another.

> Elbert Hubbard (1856–1915)
> American writer

An idealist believes the short run doesn't count. A cynic believes the long run doesn't matter. A realist believes that what is done or left undone in the short run determines the long run.

> Sydney J. Harris (1917–86)
> American newspaper columnist

There are two days about which nobody should ever worry, and these are yesterday and tomorrow.

> Robert Jones Burdette (1844–1914)
> American clergyman and humorist

Life can only be understood backwards; but it must be lived forwards.

> Søren Kierkegaard (1813–55)
> Danish philosopher and theologian

To change and to improve are two different things.

> German proverb

Business more than any other occupation is a continual dealing with the future; it is a continual calculation, an instinctive exercise in foresight.

> Henry R. Luce (1898–1967)
> American editor and publisher

When you're green, you're growing. When you're ripe, you rot.

> Ray Kroc (1902–84)
> founder, McDonald's Corporation

Change is the law of life. And those who look only to the past or present are certain to miss the future.

> John F. Kennedy (1917–63)
> 35th president of the United States

Today, loving change, tumult, even chaos is a prerequisite for survival, let alone success.

> Thomas J. Peters (1942–   )
> American business writer

Things do not change; we change.

> Henry David Thoreau (1817–62)
> American naturalist and writer

A great wind is blowing, and that gives you either imagination or a headache.

> Catherine II ("The Great") (1729–96)
> empress of Russia
> (referring to the changing times)

Only the wisest and the stupidest of men never change.

> *Confucius (551–479 B.C.)*
> *Chinese philosopher and*
> *teacher*

FIFTY REASONS WHY WE/IT/THEY CAN'T CHANGE:

(1) We've never done it before. (2) Nobody else has ever done it. (3) It has never been tried before. (4) We tried it before. (5) Another company/person tried it before. (6) We've been doing it this way for 25 years. (7) It won't work in a small company. (8) It won't work in a large company. (9) It won't work in our company. (10) Why change—it's working OK. (11) The boss will never buy it. (12) It needs further investigation. (13) Our competitors are not doing it. (14) It's too much trouble to change. (15) Our company is different. (16) The ad dept. says it can't be sold. (17) Production says it's a bad idea. (18) The service dept. won't like it. (19) The janitor says it can't be done. (20) It can't be done. (21) We don't have the money. (22) We don't have the personnel. (23) We don't have the equipment. (24) The union will scream. (25) It's too visionary. (26) You can't teach an old dog new tricks. (27) It's too radical a change. (28) It's beyond my responsibility. (29) It's not my job. (30) We don't have the time. (31) It will obsolete other procedures. (32) Customers won't buy it. (33) It's contrary to policy. (34) It will increase overhead. (35) The employees will never buy it. (36) It's not our problem. (37) I don't like it. (38) You're right, but . . . (39) We're not ready for it. (40) It needs more thought. (41) Management won't accept it. (42) We can't take the chance. (43) We'd lose money on it. (44) It takes too long to pay out. (45) We're doing all right as it is. (46) It needs committee study. (47) Competition won't like it. (48) It needs sleeping on. (49) It won't work in this department. (50) It's impossible.

> *American Business Axioms*

A thousand things advance; nine hundred and ninety-nine retreat: that is progress.

> *Henri Frédéric Amiel*
> *(1821–81)*
> *Swiss philosopher and poet*

In human affairs, the best stimulus for running ahead is to have something we must run from.

> *Eric Hoffer (1902–83)*
> *American longshoreman*
> *and philosopher*

There can be no progress if people have no faith in tomorrow.

> *John F. Kennedy (1917–63)*
> *35th president of the United*
> *States*

We live together as rational human beings or die together as fools.

> *Martin Luther King, Jr.*
> *(1929–68)*
> *American clergyman and*
> *civil-rights leader*

The most distinguished hallmark of the American society is and always has been change.

> *Eric Sevareid (1912–   )*
> *American news reporter*
> *and commentator*

It's hard for me to get used to these changing times. I can remember when the air was clean and sex was dirty.

George Burns (1896–)
American actor and author

The danger of the past was that men became slaves. The danger of the future is that men may become robots.

Erich Fromm (1900–80)
American psychoanalyst

The illusion that times that were are better than those that are, has probably pervaded all ages.

Horace Greeley (1811–72)
American journalist and
politician

Just the other day I listened to a young fellow sing a very passionate song about how technology is killing us and all. But before he started, he bent down and plugged his electric guitar into the wall socket.

Paul Goodman (1911–72)
American author and poet

Ours is the age of substitutes: Instead of language we have jargon; instead of principles, slogans; and instead of genuine ideas, bright suggestions.

Eric Bentley (1916–)
American drama critic and
director

Can anybody remember when the times were not hard and money not scarce?

Ralph Waldo Emerson
(1803–82)
American essayist and poet

There is more to life than increasing its speed.

Mohandas K. Gandhi
(1869–1948)
Indian nationalist leader

This is the great folly of grown-ups—wanting what lasts, wanting to last. Only two things last: shoes too small and foolishness.

Minou Drouet (1947–)
French poet

All movements go too far.

Bertrand Russell (1872–
1970)
English mathematician and
philosopher

Once you get into this great stream of history, you can't get out.

Richard M. Nixon (1913–)
37th president of the United
States

You must be in tune with the times and prepared to break with tradition.

William M. Agee (1938–)
chairman, Bendix
Corporation

I know no way of judging the future but by the past.

> Patrick Henry (1736–99)
> American statesman and
> orator

The world hates change, yet it is the only thing that has brought progress.

> Charles F. Kettering (1876–
> 1958)
> American electrical
> engineer and inventor

A hundred years ago, Hester Prynne of *The Scarlet Letter* was given an "A" for adultery. Today, she would rate no better than a "C-plus."

> Peter DeVries (1910–   )
> American author

Just opening up the door, having this ordinary person fly, says a lot for the future. You can always equate astronauts with explorers who were subsidized. Now you are getting someone going just to observe. And then you'll have the settlers.

> Christa McAuliffe
> (1949–86)
> American educator
> (*died in* Challenger *space-
> shuttle explosion*)

Nothing endures but change.

> Heraclitus (ca. 540–
> ca. 480 B.C.)
> Greek philosopher

When a thing is done, it's done. Don't look back. Look forward to your next objective.

> George C. Marshall (1880–
> 1959)
> U.S. Army general and
> statesman

Man belongs where man wants to go.

> Wernher von Braun
> (1912–77)
> American engineer

There is nothing more difficult to take in hand, more perilous to conduct, or more uncertain in its success than to take the lead in the introduction of a new order of things.

> Jean-Jacques Rousseau
> (1712–78)
> French philosopher and
> writer

All growth is a leap in the dark, a spontaneous, unpremeditated act without benefit of experience.

> Henry Miller (1891–1980)
> American writer

My interest is in the future because I am going to spend the rest of my life there.

> Charles F. Kettering (1876–
> 1958)
> American electrical
> engineer and inventor

PREDICTIONS

PREDICTION: *a declaration in advance on the basis of observation, experience, or scientific reason.*

When incidents repeat themselves often enough, it is typically said either that fate was on a person's side or, if it is not very good, that a person was a victim of fate. The latter was the case for Robert Todd Lincoln, who was home from Harvard when his father, Abraham Lincoln, was assassinated. Seventeen years later, he was appointed secretary of war and, as fate would have it, upon his arrival at the Washington train station, he saw President Garfield shot. In 1901, Robert Lincoln, then president of the Pullman Company, and his family were invited to meet President William McKinley. Fate dealt another blow and, just before they arrived, McKinley was shot. Quite understandably, Lincoln mused, "There is a certain fatality about presidential functions when I am present."

If the automotive industry had progressed during the last two decades at the same rate as the semiconductor industry, a Rolls-Royce would today cost only three dollars and there would be no parking problem because automobiles would be one quarter of an inch on a side!

> *George H. Heilmeier*
> *(1936–   )*
> *vice president, Texas*
> *Instruments*

I don't set trends. I just find out what they are and I exploit them.

> *Dick Clark (1929–   )*
> *American disc jockey and*
> *music-industry executive*

An extrapolation of the trends of the 1880s would show today's cities buried under horse manure.

> *Norman Macrae (1923–   )*
> *English journalist*

There is a world market for about five computers.

> *Thomas J. Watson (1874–*
> *1956)*
> *founder and first president,*
> *IBM Corporation*

If they haven't heard it before, it's original.

> *Gene Fowler (1890–1960)*
> *American educator and*
> *writer*

The thing is to be able to outlast the trends.

> *Paul Anka (1941–   )*
> *American singer*

A farmer is always going to be rich next year.

> *Philemon (1st century A.D.)*
> *Christian bishop*

Never make forecasts, especially about the future.

> Samuel Goldwyn (1882–1974)
> American motion-picture producer

Who the hell wants to hear actors talk?

> Harry M. Warner (1881–1958)
> founder, Warner Bros. Studio (in 1927, considering the possibility of talking pictures)

They couldn't hit an elephant from this dist—

> last words of U.S. general John Sedgwick (1813–64) at the Battle of Spotsylvania

If rats are experimented on, they will develop cancer.

> Morton's Law

Everything is more complicated than it seems.

> Murphy's Law

Business will be better or worse.

> Calvin Coolidge (1872–1933)
> 30th president of the United States

Your chances of getting hit by lightning go up if you stand under a tree, shake your fist at the sky and say, "Storms suck!"

> Johnny Carson (1925–   )
> American TV show host

The other day a dog peed on me. A bad sign.

> H. L. Mencken (1880–1956)
> American editor

We must not be misled to our own detriment to assume that the untried machine can displace the proved and tried horse.

> John K. Herr (1878–1955)
> major general, U.S. Army

The [flying] machines will eventually be fast; they will be used in sport but they should not be thought of as commercial carriers.

> Octave Chanute (1832–1910)
> French aviation pioneer

As far as sinking a ship with a bomb is concerned, it just can't be done.

> Clark Woodward (1877–1967)
> rear admiral, U.S. Navy

That is the biggest fool thing we have ever done. . . . The [atomic] bomb will never go off, and I speak as an expert in explosives.

> William Leahy (1875–1959)
> admiral, U.S. Navy

What, sir, would you make a ship sail against the wind and currents by lighting a bonfire under her deck? I pray you excuse me. I have no time to listen to such nonsense.

> Napoleon Bonaparte (1769–1821)
> emperor of France
> (speaking to Robert Fulton)

Rail travel at high speeds is not possible because passengers, unable to breathe, would die of asphyxia.

> Dionysius Lardner (1793–1859)
> English scientist

Space travel is utter bilge.

> Sir Richard van der Riet Wooley
> The Astronomer Royal, 1956

While theoretically and technically television may be feasible, commercially and financially I consider it an impossibility, a development of which we need waste little time dreaming.

> Lee DeForest (1873–1961)
> American inventor

Radio has no future.
Heavier-than-air flying machines are impossible.
X-rays will prove to be a hoax.
I have not the smallest molecule of faith in aerial navigation other than ballooning.

> William Thomson, Lord Kelvin (1824–1907)
> English scientist; president of the Royal Society

The rule on staying alive as a forecaster is to give 'em a number or give 'em a date, but never give 'em both at once.

> Jane Bryant Quinn (1939–   )
> American business writer

The art of prophecy is very difficult, especially with respect to the future.

> Mark Twain (1835–1910)
> American author

Indexes

INDEX: *a list of specified data arranged usually in alphabetical order; a list of items such as names treated in a printed work that gives the page number where each item may be found.*

The actions of men are like the index of a book . . . they point out what is most remarkable in them.

> *Heinrich Heine (1797–1856)*
> *German poet and critic*

What's in a name? That which we call a rose
By any other name would smell as sweet.

> *William Shakespeare (1564–1616)*
> *English dramatist and poet*

I often quote myself; it adds spice to my conversation.

> *George Bernard Shaw (1856–1950)*
> *British playwright and social reformer*

It is a good thing for an uneducated man to read books of quotations.

> *Winston Churchill (1874–1965)*
> *British statesman and prime minister*

There are two types of knowledge. One is knowing a thing. The other is knowing where to find it.

> *Samuel Johnson (1709–84)*
> *English lexicographer and author*

So essential did I consider an index to be to every book that I proposed to bring a bill into Parliament to deprive an author who publishes a book without an index of the privilege of copyright and, moreover, to subject him for the offense to a pecuniary penalty.

> *John Campbell (1779–1861)*
> *English lord chancellor*

Name Index

Italics indicate pages on which persons are referred to within quotations.

Aaron, Hank, 64
Abbott, Charles F., 226
Abrams, Creighton, 19
Aburdeen, Patricia, 272
Abzug, Bella, 99
Acheson, Dean, 299
Adams, Anthony, 174
Adams, Franklin Pierce, 49, 292
Adams, Joey, 132, 167, 266
Adler, Alfred, 279
Aesop, 123
Agase, Alex, 26
Agee, William M., 302
Aitken, William Maxwell, Lord
   Beaverbrook, 271
Ajaye, Franklin, 251
Albee, Edward F., xix, 70
Alexander the Great, *14*
Algren, Nelson, 277
Ali, Muhammad, 6, 69, 137, *192*, 263
Allah, *286*
Allaire, Paul A., 113
Allen, Fred, 90, 100, 154, 223, 281, 282
Allen, George, 79, 117
Allen, Gracie, 288
Allen, Louis A., 79
Allen, Marty, 179
Allen, Steve, 72
Allen, Woody, 52, 65, 130, 157, 171,
   227, 243, 263, 266, 281, 283, 298
Ally, Carl, 10
Ameringer, Oscar, 215
Amherst, William Pitt, 163
Amiel, Henri Frédéric, 124, 301

Amory, Cleveland, 266
Anderson, Sparky, 20
Anka, Paul, 304
Anthony, Robert A., 94
Anthony, Susan B., 263
Appley, Lawrence, 235
Arbus, Diane, 5
Aristotle, 242
Armour, J. Ogden, 99
Armour, Philip D., 133
Armour, Richard, 258
Armstrong, Louis, *192*
Arnett, Ramona E. F., 13, 101
Ash, Mary Kay, 6, 42
Ashe, Arthur, 82
Asimov, Isaac, 130, 183
Asnas, Max, 162
Astaire, Fred, 49
Astor, John Jacob, 206
Astor, Lady Nancy (Witcher
   Langhorne), 262, 263, 289
Atkinson, Brooks, 4, 96
Attlee, Clement, 227
Auchincloss, Louis, 269
Auden, Wystan Hugh, 132, 233
Augustine, Norman R., 26, 65, 147,
   170, 176, 219
Augustine, Saint, 84, 250
Ausonius, 68
Austin, Warren, 275

Bacall, Lauren, 271
Bach, Richard, 139
Bacon, Francis, 12, 65, 164, 254

Todd, Mike, 209
Toffler, Alvin, 84
Toga, Deborah, 141
Tomlin, Lily, 119
Toscanini, Arturo, 273
Townsend, Marvin, 137
Townsend, Robert, 27, 38, 75, 78, 82,
    92, 93, 97, 99, 100, 101, 105, 108,
    133, 138, 181, 182
Tracy, Spencer, 209
Trowbridge, Alexander B., Jr., 214
Troy, Bertram Theodore, 105
Trudeau, Pierre, 187
Truman, Harry S, 37, 44, 82, 84, 115,
    119, 156, 176, 180, *231*, 259, 273
Trump, Donald, 143, 221, 237
Trump, Ivana, *221*
Tucker, Carol, 114
Tucker, Sophie, 165, 206
Turenne, Henri de La Tour
    d'Auvergne, Vicomte de, 61, 277
Turner, Robert Edward (Ted), III, 191
Twain, Mark (Samuel L. Clemens), 8,
    14, 35, 44, 47, 48, 53, 62, 63, 71, 102,
    120, 149, 153, 165, 170, 172, 176,
    186, 198, 206, 211, 217, 232, 235,
    236, 240, 243, 245, 248, 251, 255,
    256, 263, 277, 278, 279, 283, 285,
    290, 297, 306

Udall, Stewart, 120
Unitas, Johnny, 117

Valéry, Paul, 4, 152
Vallee, Rudy, *247*
Van Buren, Abigail, 254
Van Buren, Martin, 215
Vanderbilt, Cornelius, 3–4, 197
Vanderbilt, W. H., 202
Van Loon, Hendrik, 96
Vargo, Ed, 110
Vaughan, Bill, 93, 217
Vauvenargues, Luc de Clapiers,
    Marquis de, 176
Vickery, A. Lou, 48, 51
Vidal, Gore, 47, 64, 206
Vlasic, Robert J., 113
Volcker, Paul, 124
Voltaire (François-Marie Arouet),
    70, 99, 216, 265, 281
Vonnegut, Kurt, Jr., 253

Wada, Sadami, 104
Wagner, Richard, *251*
Waldron, Hicks, 86
Walesa, Lech, 210
Walker, James J. (Jimmy), 23

Walker, Sir Walter, 107
Wallenda, Karl, 123
Walpole, Robert, 197
Walsh, Bill, 102
Walton, Sam, 143
Wanamaker, John, 145, 151, 225, 244
Wang, An, 97
Warburg, James P., 205
Ward, Arch, 139
Ward, Artemus, 248, 258
Ward, Benjamin, 17
Warhol, Andy, 228, 256, 282
Warner, Charles Dudley, 104
Warner, Harry M., 305
Warren, Earl, 250
Washington, Booker T., 92, 202
Washington, George, 73, 74, 173, 202,
    285
Waterman, Robert H., Jr., 174
Watson, Thomas J., 25, 304
Wayne, John, 272
Wearly, William L., 214
Webb, Jack, 176
Webster, Daniel, 217
Weil, Simone, 70
Weiss, Peter, 289
Welles, Orson, 190, 252
Wells, Carolyn, 267
Wells, H. G., 12, 153
West, Jessamyn, 11
West, Mae, 82, 105, 264, 273, 280, 289
West, Roy A., 117
Westcott, E. N., 74
Westinghouse, George, 3–4
Whistler, James Abbott McNeill, 166,
    182, 290
White, E. B., 31, 103, 157
White, Jerry, 225
White, Lynn Townsend, Jr., 74
White, Stephen, 195
White, Vanna, 65
White, William Allen, 271
Whitehead, Alfred North, 131
Whitehorn, Katharine, 137
Whitney, John R., 20
Whitney, Robert A., 157
Whitton, Charlotte, 272
Wicker, Tom, 223
Wiesenfeld, Paul R., 236
Wilde, Oscar, 102, 114, 159, 163, 164,
    170, 237, 243, 253, 254, 262, 291
Wilder, Billy, 189
Will, George F., 252, 299
Williams, Edward Bennett, 79
Williams, Grace, 260
Williams, Robin, 244
Williams, Ted, 287

Subject Index

divorce, 266–67
doctors, 77, 147, 243, 244, 246, 270, 283
dogs, 183, 246, 267, 268, 269, 277, 279, 305
dollar, U.S., 190, 213
  billion, 163
down payments, 167
Dragnet, 176
dreams, 4, 5, 43, 99–100, 211, 294
dress, *see* clothes
drinking, 235, 245, 246–47, 294
  bootlegging and, 157, 204
drive-in banks, 172
driving, 246, 291
drudgery, 139
drugs, 244
drunkenness, 246–47
Duck Soup, 72
Du Pont, 97
Dutch language, 186
duty, 54, 90, 135, 198, 199, 200, 257
  see also responsibility

East of Eden, 53
eating, 180
  see also food
eccentricities, 205
economic recovery, 177
economics, 12, 85, 150, 177–80
economies (frugality), 78, 159
EDP (electronic data processing), 93, 183
Edsel, 152
education, 51, 143, 181, 203, 231–36, 240
  see also experience
efficiency, 31, 106
elections, 38, 150, 215, 216
Electric Horseman, The, 298
electricity, 149
Electronic Data Systems (EDS), 95
electronics, 234
emigration, 190
employee benefits, 46
employees, 98–111, 147, 157
  compensation of, 48–50, 90, 101, 102, 103–6, 111, 113, 131–32, 180
  conflicts among, 75
  customers and, 142
  delegating work to, 19, 42, 91, 92
  firing of, 101, 105, 107, 130, 143
  hiring of, 99, 100, 105
  human resource management and, 46, 98–101
  incompetent, 92, 106–8
  labor movement and, 110–11

  loyalty of, 18
  quitting by, 119, 139
  unemployment and, 102, 108–9, 153, 177, 180
  see also jobs; work, working
encouragement, 15, 17, 44, 52
enemies, 113, 114, 115, 116, 165, 198, 267, 268, 280, 285
energy, 132
engineers, 14
England, 107, 185, 186, 189, 192, 231, 263–64
enlightenment, 254
enthusiasm, 52, 57, 295
entrepreneurial spirit, 10–13
Equal Employment Opportunity Commission (EEOC), 213–14
equality, 8, 210, 225
errors, *see* mistakes
estate planning, 31
estates, 219
esteem:
  need for, 54–56
  self-esteem and, 253–57
ethics, 195–201
  see also principles
Europe, 185
  see also specific countries
Europeans, Americans vs., 9
events, 279
evil, 82, 161, 165, 197, 226
excellence, 133, 139
exceptions to rules, 75
excitement, 245
executives, 18, 19, 54, 60, 81, 84, 115, 287
  age of, 287–98
  career ladders of, 157, 185
  CEOs, 38, 173, 181, 196, 238
  compensation of, 104, 105
  responsibilities of, 198
  vice presidents, 90, 172
  work delegated by, 19, 42, 91, 99
  see also managers; managing, management
exercise, 243, 244, 245
expectations, 30, 78
experience, 4, 84, 104, 236–40
  age and, 288
  learning from, 37, 179, 236–40, 260
experimentation, 173, 305
  scientific, 219
experts, 26–28, 77, 99, 170, 179
explanations, 122, 268, 282
exploration, 5
extravagance, 78